Concurrences Books

Liber Amicorum

Laurence Idot – Liber Amicorum
Christophe Lemaire, Francesco Martucci (ed.), 2022

Eleanor Fox – Liber Amicorum
Nicolas Charbit, Sonia Ahmad (ed.), 2021

Herbert Hovenkamp – Liber Amicorum
Nicolas Charbit, Sonia Ahmad (ed.), 2021

Albert Foer – A Consumer Voice in the Antitrust Arena
Nicolas Charbit, Sonia Ahmad (ed.), 2020

Richard Whish – Taking Competition Law Outside the Box
Nicolas Charbit, Sonia Ahmad (ed.), 2020

Frédéric Jenny – Standing Up for Convergence and Relevance in Antitrust, Vol. I & II
Nicolas Charbit, Sonia Ahmad (ed.), 2019 & 2021

Wang Xiaoye – The Pioneer of Competition Law in China
Adrian Emch, Wendy Ng (ed.), 2019

Douglas H. Ginsburg – An Antitrust Professor on the Bench, Vol. I & II
Nicolas Charbit, et al. (eds), 2018 & 2020

Ian S. Forrester – A Scot Without Borders, Vol. I & II
Assimakis Komninos et al. (ed.), 2015

William E. Kovacic – An Antitrust Tribute, Vol. I & II
Nicolas Charbit et al. (eds), 2013 & 2014

Practical Books

Global Dictionary of Competition Law
Deborah Healey, William Kovacic, Pablo Trevisan, Richard Whish (ed.) 2021

Competition Law, Climate Change & Environmental Sustainability
Simon Holmes, Dirk Middelschulte, Martijn Snoep (ed.), 2021

Perspectives on Antitrust Compliance
Anne Riley, Andreas Stephan, Anny Tubbs (ed.), 2021

Information Exchange and Related Risks – A Practical Guide
Eric Meiring, Marcio Dias Soares (ed.), 2021

State Aid & National Enforcement
Jacques Derenne, Denis Jouve, Christophe Lemaire, Francesco Martucci (ed.), 2021

Merger Control in Latin America – A Jurisdictional Guide
Paulo Burnier da Silveira & Pamela Sittenfeld (ed.), 2020

Competition Inspections under EU Law
Nathalie Jalabert-Doury, 2020

Competition Digest – A Synthesis of EU, US and National Leading Cases, 4th ed.
Frédéric Jenny (ed.), 2020

Gun Jumping in Merger Control – A Jurisdictional Guide
Catriona Hatton, Yves Comtois, Andrea Hamilton (ed.), 2019

Choice – A New Standard for Competition Analysis?
Paul Nihoul et al., 2016

PhD Theses

Essays in Industrial Organization: Competition and Regulation in Network Industries
Jean-Marc Zogheib, 2021

The Role of Media Pluralism in the Enforcement of EU Competition Law
Konstantina Bania, 2019

Buyer Power in EU Competition Law
Ignacio Herrera Anchustegui, 2017

General Interest

Women & Antitrust – Voices from the Field, Vol. I & II
Evelina Kurgonaite & Kristina Nordlander (ed.), 2020

Conference Proceedings

Antitrust in Emerging and Developing Countries, Vol I & II
Eleanor Fox, Harry First (ed.), 2015 & 2016

Global Antitrust Law – Current Issues in Antitrust Law and Economics
Douglas Ginsburg, Joshua Wright (ed.), 2015

Competition Law on the Global Stage: David Gerber's Global Competition Law in Perspective
David Gerber, 2014

e-Book versions available for **Concurrences+** subscribers

DOUGLAS H. GINSBURG

Liber Amicorum – Volume II

106 West 32nd Street, Suite 144 New York, NY, 10001, USA
www.concurrences.com
book@concurrences.com

First Printing, January 2021
978-1-939007-68-1 (Hardcover)
Library of Congress Control Number: 2020950983

Cover Design : Yves Buliard, www.yvesbuliard.fr
Book Design and Layout implementation: Nord Compo

DOUGLAS H. GINSBURG

An Antitrust Professor on the Bench

Liber Amicorum – Volume II

Foreword by Sir Christopher Bellamy QC

Editors

Nicolas Charbit

Thomas Moretto

Foreword

Sir Christopher Bellamy QC*

It is not only a great honour but a considerable pleasure to be asked to introduce the second volume of this *Liber Amicorum* dedicated to the long career and many achievements of Judge Douglas H. Ginsburg, as professor, senior government official, and long serving federal judge in the US Court of Appeals for the district of Columbia; a true polymath (one might more accurately say "the" polymath) in the law and science of antitrust.

In this second volume the reader will find a series of essays no less brilliant than those in the first. Emphasis is, rightly, placed on Doug Ginsburg's contribution to the *structured* analysis of antitrust problems, whether in terms of the rule of reason (the "quick look" among others), the shifting burden of proof, or the assessment of potentially anticompetitive mergers. Always grounded in an unfailing belief in the market economy and the consumer welfare standard, Doug's clear sighted judicial approach has not only brought more clarity to the legal framework (an essential aspect of the rule of law) but his indefatigable work as a teacher has enlightened and assisted many students, officials and most notably other judges, not only in the US, but across the world, to come to grips with antitrust analysis, thus making a truly global contribution to the understanding of this important area of the law.

There is, moreover, in this second volume a rich feast of writings by distinguished contributors on some of the most important and topical questions in modern antitrust, for example the independence of competition authorities, competition between educational institutions, extraterritorial application, important institutional considerations, the Fair Competition Review System in China, licensing of wireless technology, the importance of due process, the use of economics in criminal enforcement, the disastrous consequences of unearthing a criminal

* Monckton Chambers; Former President of the Competition Appeal Tribunal; Former Judge on the European Court of First Instance.

conspiracy in the course of a merger investigation, and whether there better ways of compensating victims than follow-on litigation.

A number of these essays remind one of the extraordinary global evolution of antitrust that has taken place in the course of Doug Ginsburg's career. When he came down from Cornell in 1970, US antitrust law was by far the most developed – and was indeed still practically the sole such law across the world, so much so that the UK and other jurisdictions enacted blocking statutes against its extra-territorial application. In the following years EU competition law developed to a remarkable extent, becoming a "pole of enforcement" to rival the US, while more recently over 100 other countries have also adopted competition laws of one form or another. As a result, and aided by networks such the ICN, there developed a kind of global consensus of the importance of competition/antitrust law, and a common lingua franca among antitrust authorities across all five continents, reminiscent of the universal law merchant of the Middle Ages, or perhaps more exotically the ancient *ius gentium* against piracy on the high seas. So different is the world today that, for example, authorities in the UK and the EU think nothing of enforcing their laws against transactions taking place wholly outside their frontiers in ways that would have once been unthinkable.

Whether or not there are signs that this consensus is beginning to fray, with geopolitical tensions and, at least in some quarters, less faith in the ability of the market economy to deliver, is another matter. Throughout his career, Doug Ginsburg has been at the forefront, not only in the US, but globally, in the remarkable evolution that has taken place during his career, always there to explain, to encourage, to advise, and sometimes to warn. One might think, *pace* Oscar Wilde, that to have not one, but two, volumes of *Liber Amicorum* in one's honour, is a kind of carelessness. On the contrary, *Concurrences* and the contributors to both volumes rightly salute the outstanding career, over more than 50 years, of Doug Ginsburg, and in doing so add significantly to the scholarship with which his name is already synonymous.

Contributors

Jonathan B. Baker
American University Washington College of Law

Antonio Bavasso
Allen & Overy, University College London

Joseph J. Bial
Paul, Weiss, Rifkind, Wharton & Garrison

Darryl Biggar
Australian Competition and Consumer Commission

Timothy Cornell
Clifford Chance

Allan Fels AO
Universities of Melbourne, Monash & Oxford

Eleanor M. Fox
New York University School of Law

John Friel
Clifford Chance

Andrew I. Gavil
Howard University School of Law

Ting Gong
King & Wood Mallesons

Roxann E. Henry

William E. Kovacic
George Washington University Law School

Daniel Muheme
University of Liège

Susan Ning
King & Wood Mallesons

Paul O'Brien
FTC Office of International Affairs

Maureen K. Ohlhausen
Baker Botts

Jorge Padilla
Compass Lexecon

Randolph Tritell
FTC Office of International Affairs

Koren W. Wong-Ervin
Global Antitrust Institute George Mason University

Tianjie Zhang
King & Wood Mallesons

Table of Contents

Part I: Judge Douglas H. Ginsburg: Career and Legacy

Part II: Rethinking Antitrust: Institutions, Policy and Proceedings

Part III: Criminal Antitrust

Judge Douglas H. Ginsburg

Biography

Career

Senior Circuit Judge Douglas H. Ginsburg was appointed to the United States Court of Appeals for the District of Columbia in 1986; he served as Chief Judge from 2001 to 2008. After receiving his B.S. from Cornell University in 1970, and his J.D. from the University of Chicago Law School in 1973, he clerked for Judge Carl McGowan on the D.C. Circuit and Justice Thurgood Marshall on the United States Supreme Court. Thereafter, Judge Ginsburg was a professor at the Harvard Law School, the Deputy Assistant and then Assistant Attorney General for the Antitrust Division of the Department of Justice, as well as the Administrator of the Office of Information and Regulatory Affairs in the Office of Management and Budget. Concurrent with his service as a federal judge, Judge Ginsburg has taught at the University of Chicago Law School and the New York University School of Law. Judge Ginsburg is currently a Professor of Law at the Antonin Scalia Law School, George Mason University, and a visiting professor at University College London, Faculty of Laws.

Judge Ginsburg is the Chairman of the International Advisory Board of the Global Antitrust Institute at the Antonin Scalia Law School, George Mason University. He also serves on the Advisory Boards of: Competition Policy International; the Harvard Journal of Law and Public Policy; the Journal of Competition Law and Economics; the Journal of Law, Economics and Policy; the Supreme Court Economic Review; the University of Chicago Law Review; The New York University Journal of Law and Liberty; and, at University College London, both the Center for Law, Economics and Society and the Jevons Institute for Competition Law and Economics.

In 2020, Judge Ginsburg received the John Sherman Award "for his lifetime contributions to the development of antitrust law and the preservation of economic liberty. The award is the Department of Justice's highest antitrust honor."

Education

Judge Ginsburg obtained his B.S. degree from Cornell University in 1970 and his J.D. from the University of Chicago Law School in 1973.

Publications

Books and Monographs

THE GLOBAL ANTITRUST INSTITUTE REPORT ON THE DIGITAL ECONOMY (editor, with Joshua D. Wright) available at gaidigitalreport.com

GLOBAL ANTITRUST ECONOMICS – CURRENT ISSUES IN ANTITRUST AND LAW AND ECONOMICS (with Joshua D. Wright; Institute of Competition Law March 21, 2016)

REGULATION OF THE ELECTRONIC MASS MEDIA: LAW AND POLICY FOR RADIO, TELEVISION, CABLE AND THE NEW VIDEO TECHNOLOGIES, SECOND EDITION (with M. Botein and M. Director; West, 1991)

1983 SUPPLEMENT TO REGULATION OF BROADCASTING: LAW AND POLICY TOWARDS RADIO, TELEVISION AND CABLE COMMUNICATIONS (with M. Director; West, 1983)

INTERSTATE BANKING, 9 HOFSTRA LAW REV. 1133–1371 (Special Issue 1981)

REGULATION OF BROADCASTING: LAW AND POLICY TOWARDS RADIO, TELEVISION AND GOVERNMENT, TECHNOLOGY, AND THE FUTURE OF THE AUTOMOBILE (editor, with W. Abernathy; McGraw-Hill, 1980)

ANTITRUST, UNCERTAINTY, AND TECHNOLOGICAL INNOVATION (National Academy of Engineering/ National Research Council, 1980), reprinted at 24 ANTITRUST BULL. 635 (1980)

CABLE COMMUNICATIONS (West, 1979)

Articles and Book Chapters

Common Ownership: Solutions in Search of a Problem, *in* FREDERIC JENNY LIBER AMICORUM: AN ANTITRUST TRIBUTE (Nicolas Charbit ed., Vol II, forthcoming 2020) (with Keith Klovers)

A Tale of Two Systems: Mergers Reviewed in China and the U.S., 2018–2020, *in* ANTI MONOPOLY LAW – A MEMOIR OF 12 YEARS' ENFORCEMENT (Li Qing ed., 2020) (with Joanna Tsai)

Challenging Consummated Mergers Under Section 2, COMP. POL'Y INT'L, May 2020 (with Koren Wong-Ervin)

AmEx: Beyond Transaction Platforms and Section 1, COMP. POL'Y INT'L (May 14, 2020) (with Koren Wong-Ervin)

Balancing Unquantified Harms and Benefits in Antitrust Cases under the Consumer Welfare Standard, COLUM. BUS. L. REV. (2020)

The Decline in U.S. Criminal Antitrust Cases: ACPERA and Leniency in an International Context, *in* ALBERT A. FOER, LIBER AMICORUM (Nicolas Charbit ed., 2020) (with Cecilia (Yixi) Cheng)

Antitrust and Intellectual Property in the United States and the European Union, *in* THE INTERPLAY BETWEEN COMPETITION LAW AND INTELLECTUAL PROPERTY – AN INTERNATIONAL PERSPECTIVE 99 (Gabriella Muscolo and Marina Tavassi eds., 2019) (with Damien Geradin and Keith Klovers)

Posner on Antitrust Remedies: The Good, the Bad, and the Very Ugly, 18 ANTITRUST SOURCE (Oct. 2018)

Antitrust Analysis Involving Intellectual Property and Standards: Implications from Economics, 33 HARV. J. L. & TECH. 1 (forthcoming 2019) (with J. Padilla and K. Wong-Ervin)

FRAND in India, *in* COMPLICATIONS AND QUANDARIES IN THE ICT SECTOR: STANDARD ESSENTIAL PATENTS AND COMPETITION ISSUES (Ashish Bharadwaj et al. eds., 2018) (with Joshua D. Wright, Bruce H. Kobayashi, and Koren W. Wong-Ervin)

The Economic Analysis of Antitrust Consents, *in* TRIBUTE TO HENRY MANNE, 2018 EUR. J. OF L. AND ECON. (with Joshua Wright)

The Department of Justice's Long-Awaited and Much Needed Course-Correction on FRAND-Assured Standard-Essential Patents, COMP. POL'Y INT'L, N. Am. Column, Nov. 2017 (with Koren W. Wong-Ervin)

Extraterritoriality and Intra-Territoriality in U.S. Antitrust Law, 2017 Comp. Pol'y Int'l., Sept. 28., 2017 (with Josh Hazan)

A Comparative and Economic Analysis of the U.S. FTC's Complaint and the Korea FTC's Decision Against Qualcomm, 1 Antitrust Chronicle, Spring 2017 (with Koren Wong-Ervin, Anne Layne-Farrar et al.)

Extra-Jurisdictional Remedies Involving Patent Licensing, 12 Comp. Pol'y Int'l., No. 2, 41 (2016) (with Joshua D. Wright, Bruce Kobayashi, and Koren W. Wong-Ervin)

Our Illiberal Administrative Law, 10 N.Y.U. J. of L. & Liberty 475 (2016) (with Steven Menashi)

The FTC PAE Study: A Cautionary Tale About Making Unsupported Policy Recommendations, Am. Bar Ass'n Section of Antitrust l. Intell. Property Comm. Newsl. (2016) (with Joshua D. Wright)

Monetary Penalties in China and Japan, Am. Bar Ass'n Section of Antitrust L. Cartel & Criminal Practice Newsl. (2016) (with Joshua D. Wright, Bruce Kobayashi, Ariel Slonim, and Koren W. Wong-Ervin)

The Costs and Benefits of Antitrust Consents, OECD Competition Comm. DAF/COMP/WD(2016)81 (2016) (with Joshua D. Wright), available at: https://one.oecd.org/document/DAF/COMP/WD(2016)81/en/pdf

Goals of Antitrust: Welfare Trumps Choice, reprinted in Choice – A New Standard For Competition Law Analysis? (P. Hihoul, N. Charbit, & E. Ramundo, eds., 2016)

In Memoriam: Justice Scalia's Antitrust Legacy, Concurrences Review, 8 (2016)

"Excessive Royalty" Prohibitions and the Dangers of Punishing Vigorous Competition and Harming Incentives to Innovate, CPI Antitrust Chronicle, Vol. 4, No. 3, (2016) (with Joshua D. Wright, Bruce Kobayashi, and Koren W. Wong-Ervin)

Reverse Settlements in the European Union and the United States, in Competition and Patent Law in the Pharmaceutical Sector: An International Perspective 125 (Giovanni Pitruzzella & Gabriella Muscolo eds., 2016) (with Damien Geradin and Graham Safty)

Product Hopping and the Limits of Antitrust: The Danger of Micromanaging Innovation, Comp. Pol'y Int'l., Dec. (2015) (with Joshua D. Wright and Koren W. Wong-Ervin)

The Troubling Use of Antitrust to Regulate FRAND Licensing, CPI Antitrust Chronicle, Vol. 10, No.1 2–8, (2015) (with Joshua D. Wright and Koren W. Wong- Ervin)

DOJ Has the Power to Crush Price-Fixers: Column, USA Today Weekend, May 29–31, (2015) (with Albert Foer)

Actavis and Multiple ANDA Entrants: Beyond the Temporary Duopoly, 29, Antitrust 89 (2015), No. 2, Spring (2015) (with Bruce Kobayashi, Joshua D. Wright and Joanna Tsai)

Bork's "Legislative Intent" and the Courts, 79 Antitrust L. J. 3 (2015)

Rational Basis with Economic Bite, 8 N.Y.U. J. of L. & Liberty 1055 (2014) (with Steven Menashi)

Since Bork, 10 J. L. Econ. & Pol'y 599 (2014) (with Taylor M. Owings)

Enjoining Injunctions: The Case Against Antitrust Liability for Standard Essential Patent Holders Who Seek Injunctions, Antitrust Source, Oct. 2014, 1 (with Taylor M. Owings and Joshua D. Wright)

Patent Assertion Entities and Antitrust: A Competition Cure for a Litigation Disease, 79 Antitrust L. J. 501 (2014) (with Joshua D. Wright)

Resolving Conflicts between Competition and Other Values: The Roles of Courts and Other Institutions in the U.S. and the E.U., *in* European Competition Law Annual 2012: Public Policies, Regulation And Economic Distress (Philip Lowe & Mel Marquis eds., 2014) (with Daniel E. Haar)

Bork's "Legislative Intent" and the Courts, 79 Antitrust L.J. 941 (2014)

Whither Symmetry? Antitrust Analysis of Intellectual Property Rights at the FTC and DOJ, 9 COMP. POL'Y INT'L., No. 2, 41 (2013) (with Joshua D. Wright)

Antitrust Settlements: The Culture of Consent, CONCURRENCES, No. 2–2013, 56 (with Joshua D. Wright)

Antitrust Courts: Specialists Versus Generalists, 36 FORDHAM INT'L. L.J. 788 (2013) (with Joshua D. Wright)

Dynamic Economics in Antitrust Analysis, 78 ANTITRUST L.J. 1 (2012) (with Joshua D. Wright)

Behavioral Law and Economics: Its Origins, Fatal Flaws, and Implications for Liberty, 106 NW. U. L. REV. 1033 (2012) (with Joshua D. Wright); *reprinted in* LAW AND ECONOMICS: PHILOSOPHICAL ISSUES AND FUNDAMENTAL QUESTIONS (Aristides N. Hatzis & Nicholas Mercuro eds., 2015)

The Role of Economic Analysis in Competition Law, in GETTING THE BALANCE RIGHT: INTELLECTUAL PROPERTY, COMPETITION LAW, AND ECONOMICS IN ASIA (Ian McEwin ed., 2011) (with Eric M. Fraser)

Originalism and Economic Analysis: Two Case Studies of Consistency and Coherence in Supreme Court Decision Making, 33 HARV. J. OF L. & PUBLIC POL'Y 217 (2010)

Antitrust Sanctions, 6 COMP. POL'Y INT'L., No. 2, 3 (2010) (with Joshua D. Wright)

The Future of Behavioral Economics in Antitrust Jurisprudence, 6 COMP. POL'Y INT'L., No. 1, 89 (2010) (with Derek W. Moore)

The Costs and Benefits of Private and Public Antitrust Enforcement: An American Perspective, in COMPETITION LAW AND ECONOMICS: ADVANCES IN COMPETITION POLICY AND ANTITRUST ENFORCEMENT (Abel M. Mateus & Teresa Moreira, eds., 2010)

Rethinking Cartel Sanctions, 6 COMP. POL'Y INT'L., (2010) (with Joshua Wright)

The Role of Economic Analysis in Competition Law, in GETTING THE BALANCE RIGHT: INTELLECTUAL PROPERTY, COMPETITION LAW, AND ECONOMICS IN ASIA (Ian McWein ed., 2010) (with Eric M. Fraser)

Appellate Courts and Independent Experts, 60 CASE WESTERN L. REV. 303 (2010)

The Prosecutor and Post-Conviction Claims of Innocence: DNA and Beyond?, 7 OHIO STATE J. OF CRIM. L. 771 (2010) (with Hyland Hunt)

The Future of Behavioral Economics in Antitrust Jurisprudence, 6 COMP. POL'Y

INT'L 89 (2010) (with Derek W. Moore);

Originalism and Economic Analysis: Two Case Studies of Consistency and Coherence in Supreme Court Decision Making, 33 HARV. J. OF L. & PUB. POL'Y 217 (2010)

Nondelegation and the Unitary Executive, 12 U. PA. J. CONST. L. 251 (2010) (with Steven Menashi)

The Costs and Benefits of Private and Public Antitrust Enforcement – An American Perspective, in COMPETITION LAW AND ECONOMICS: ADVANCES IN COMPETITION POLICY ENFORCEMENT IN THE EU AND NORTH AMERICA (Abel M. Mateus & Teresa Moreira. eds., 2010)

Antitrust Decisions of the Supreme Court, 1967–2007, 3 COMP. POL'Y INT'L., No. 2, 3 (2007) (with Leah Brannon)

Synthetic Competition, 16 MEDIA L. & POL'Y 1 (2006)

Article I, Section 1, Legislative Vesting Clause, in THE HERITAGE GUIDE TO THE CONSTITUTION (Edwin Meese, III ed.) (2005)

Comparing Antitrust Enforcement in the United States and Europe, 1 J. COMP. L. & ECON. 427 (2005)

Determinants of Private Antitrust Enforcement in the United States, Vol. 1, No. 2 COMP. POL'Y INT'L., 29 (2005) (with L. Brannon)

On Constitutionalism, CATO SUPREME COURT REVIEW 7 (2003)

The Court En Banc: 1991–2002, 70 GEO. WASH. L. REV. 259 (2002) (with B. Boynton)

International Antitrust: 2000 and Beyond, 68 ANTITRUST L.J. 571 (2000)

Multinational Merger Review: Lessons From Our Federalism, 68 ANTITRUST L.J. 219 (2000) (with S. Angstreich)

Foreword: "An Open Letter to Vice President Gore," in ENVIRONMENTAL GORE (J.A. Baden ed., 1995)

Legal Responses to Bounded Rationality in German Administration: Comment, 150 J. OF INSTITUTIONAL & THEORETICAL ECON. 163 (1994)

Blackmail: An Economic Analysis of the Law, 141 U. PA. L. REV. 1849 (1993) (with P. Shechtman)

Nonprice Competition, 38 ANTITRUST BULL. 83 (1993)

A Property Rights Analysis of the Inefficiency of Investment Decisions by Labor- Managed Firms: Comment, 148 J. OF INSTITUTIONAL AND THEORETICAL ECON. 45 (1992)

Antitrust as Antimonopoly, REGULATION (Summer 1991)

Vertical Restraints: De Facto Legality Under the Rule of Reason, 60 ANTITRUST L.J. 67 (1991)

The Court En Banc: 1981–1990, 59 GEO. WASH. L. REV. 1008 (1991) (with D.Falk)

Rationalizing Antitrust: A Rejoinder to Professor Armentano 35 ANTITRUST BULL. (1990), *reprinted in* 2 THE ANTITRUST IMPULSE 933 (Theodore P. Kovaleff, ed., 1994)

The Appropriate Role of the Antitrust Enforcement Agencies, 9 CARDOZO L. REV. 1277 (1988)

White House Review of Agency Rulemaking, 99 HARV. L. REV. 1075 (1986) (with C. DeMuth)

The Case Against Federal Intervention in the Market for Corporate Control, 4 BROOKINGS REV. 15 (Winter/Spring 1986), *reprinted at* 32 U. OF CHICAGO L. SCHOOL RECORD 14 (1986) (with J. Robinson)

The Future of Interstate Banking, 9 J. CORP. L. 655 (1984), *reprinted at* 26 CORP. PRAC. COMMENTATOR 469 (1985)

Rights of Excess: Cable and the First Amendment, 6 COMMUNICATIONS AND THE LAW 71 (1984)

Regulating Television Violence, NAE Workshop Mimeo (1983)

Interstate Banking: A Preview of the Issues, ABA BANKING J. (1983)

The New Illinois Bank Holding Company Act, 99 BANK L. J. 598 (1982)

Making Automobile Regulation Work: Policy Options and a Proposal, in D. Ginsburg & W. Abernathy, *supra* BOOKS, *reprinted in* 2 HARV. J. L. & PUB. POL'Y 73 (1979)

Ernst Freund and the First Amendment Tradition: Afterword, 40 U. CHICAGO L. REV. 235 (1973)

Book Reviews

The Curse of Bigness, by Tim Wu, *in* LAW360: JUDGING A BOOK (2018)

The Behavior of Federal Judges: A view from the D.C. Circuit, review by Lee Epstein, William Landes & Richard Posner, *The Behavioral of Federal Judges*, 97 JUDICATURE (No. 2, 2013)

Rationalism in Regulation, review of Richard Revesz & Michael Livermore, *Retaking Rationality: How Cost Benefit Analysis Can Better Protect the Environment and Our Health*, 110 MICH. L. REV. 877 (2010) (with Christopher C. DeMuth)

Competition Rules for the 21st Century: Principles from America's Experience, by Ky P. Ewing, 103 MICH. L. REV. (2004)

Money for Nothing: Politicians, Rent Extraction, and Political Extortion, by Fred S. McChesney, 97 MICH. L. REV.6 (1999)

Power Without Responsibility: How Congress Abuses the People Through Delegation, by David Schoenbrod, REGULATION MAGAZINE No. 1 (1995)

Enterprise and American Law, by Herbert Hovenkamp, 75 PUBLIC CHOICE 396 (1993)

The Litigation Explosion, by Walter Olsen, 90 MICH. L. REV. 1609 (1992)

Regulation and Its Reform, Stephen Breyer, 20 HARV. J. LEGIS. 647 (1983)

Reluctant Regulators: The FCC and the Broadcast Audience, by Barry Cole & Mal Oettinger, 30 FED. COMMUNICATIONS L. J. 173 (1978)

Occasional Papers

Comment on the proposed "GWB Digitalization Act" before the Federal Ministry of Economic Affairs, The Global Antitrust Institute, Geo. Mason U. Sch. of L., Nov. 11, 2020

Comment on the European Commission's Notice on the Definition of Relevant Market for the Purposes of Community Competition Law, The Global Antitrust Institute, Geo. Mason U. Sch. of L., Oct. 12, 2020

Comment on the Noncompete Clauses Used in Employment Contracts, The Global Antitrust Institute, Geo. Mason U. Sch. of L. Feb. 7, 2020

Comment on the DOJ/FTC Draft 2020 Vertical Merger Guidelines, The Global Antitrust Institute, Geo. Mason U. Sch. of L., Feb. 7, 2020

Comment on the Swedish Competition Authority's Proposed Market Study of Digital Platforms, The Global Antitrust Institute, Geo. Mason U. Sch. of L., Nov. 30, 2019

Comment on the Infocommunications Media Development Authority (IMDA): Convergence of Competition Code for the Media and Telecommunications Markets, The Global Antitrust Institute, Geo. Mason U. Sch. of L., May 14, 2019

Use and Abuse of Bargaining Models in Antitrust: AT&T/TimeWarner and FTC v. Qualcomm, Truth on the Market (Mar. 14, 2019) (with Joshua Wright)

Comment on the Federal Trade Commission Hearings on Competition and Consumer Protection in the 21st Century: Deception, Materiality, and the Economics of Consumer Protection, The Global Antitrust Institute, Geo. Mason U. Sch. of L., Mar. 8, 2019

Comment on the Federal Trade Commission Hearings on Competition and Consumer Protection in the 21st Century: Consumer Privacy, The Global Antitrust Institute, Geo. Mason U. Sch. of L., Feb. 19, 2019

Comment on the Australian Competition & Consumer Commission's Digital Platforms Inquiry, Preliminary Report, The Global Antitrust Institute, Geo. Mason U. Sch. of L., Jan. 22, 2019

Comment on the U.S. FTC Hearings on Competition and Consumer Protection in the 21st Century, Reverse-Payment Settlements, The Global Antitrust Institute, Geo. Mason U. Sch. of L., Oct. 23, 2018

Comment on the U.S. FTC Hearings on Competition and Consumer Protection in the 21st Century, Innovation and Intellectual Property Policy, The Global Antitrust Institute, Geo. Mason U. Sch. of L. Oct. 23, 2018

Comment on the U.S. FTC Hearings on Competition and Consumer Protection in the 21st Century, Privacy, Big Data, and Competition, The Global Antitrust Institute, Geo. Mason U. Sch. of L., Oct. 23, 2018

Comment on the U.S. FTC Hearings on Competition and Consumer Protection in the 21st Century, Platforms, The Global Antitrust Institute, Geo. Mason U. Sch. of L., Oct. 15, 2018

Comment on the U.S. FTC Hearings on Competition and Consumer Protection in the 21st Century, Hearing on Concentration and Competitiveness in the U.S. Economy, The Global Antitrust Institute, Geo. Mason U. Sch. of L., Sept. 13, 2018

Comment on the U.S. FTC Hearings on Competition and Consumer Protection in the 21st Century, Vertical Mergers, The Global Antitrust Institute, Geo. Mason U. Sch. of L., Sept. 7, 2018

Comment on the U.S. FTC Hearings on Competition and Consumer Protection in the 21st Century, The Consumer Welfare Standard in Antitrust Law, The Global Antitrust Institute, Geo. Mason U. Sch. of L., Sept. 6, 2018

Comment on the Federative Republic of Brazil, Before the Administrative Council for Economic Defense (CADE), Draft Guidelines Concerning Antitrust Remedies, The Global Antitrust Institute, Geo. Mason U. Sch. of L., June 22, 2018

Comment on the U.S. Department of Justice Antitrust Division Public Roundtable Series on Competition and Deregulation, Third Roundtable on Anticompetitive Regulations, The Global Antitrust Institute, Geo. Mason U. Sch. of L., May 30, 2018

Comment on the U.S. Department of Justice Antitrust Division Public Roundtable Series on the Relationship Between Competition and Regulation, Second Roundtable – On Consent Decrees, The Global Antitrust Institute, Geo. Mason U. Sch. of L., Apr. 25, 2018

Comment on the Japan Patent Office (JPO) Guide to Licensing Negotiations Involving Standard Essential Patents, The Global Antitrust Institute, Geo. Mason U. Sch. of L., Apr. 9, 2018

Comment on the U.S. Department of Justice Antitrust Division Public Roundtable Series on Competition and Deregulation, First Roundtable on State Action, Statutory Exemptions and Implied Immunities, The Global Antitrust Institute, Geo. Mason U. Sch. of L., Mar. 13, 2018

Comment on the Dominican Republic's Resolution on Cartel Leniency, The Global Antitrust Institute, Geo. Mason U. Sch. of L., Feb. 28, 2018

Comment on the Procompetencia's Regulations for the Processing of Commitment Proposals by Economic Agents, The Global Antitrust Institute, Geo. Mason U. Sch. of L., Feb. 28, 2018

Comment on the Canadian Competition Bureau's White Paper, "Big Data and Innovation: Implications for Competition Policy in Canada", The Global Antitrust Institute, Geo. Mason U. Sch. of L., Nov. 29, 2017

Comment on the Japan Patent Office's Tentative Guidelines on Licensing Negotiations Involving SEPs, The Global Antitrust Institute, Geo. Mason U. Sch. of L., Nov. 10, 2017

Comment on the Proposed Revisions to the People's Republic of China Anti-Unfair Competition Law, The Global Antitrust Institute, Geo. Mason U. Sch. of L., Mar. 19, 2017

Comment on the U.S. Antitrust Agencies' Proposed Update of the Antitrust Guide- lines for the Licensing of Intellectual Property, The Global Antitrust Institute, Geo. Mason U. Sch. of L., Sept. 20, 2016

Comment on the Proposed Revisions to the Guidelines of the Anti-Monopoly Commission of the State Council on Determining the Illegal Gains Generated from Monopoly Conduct and on Setting Fines, The Global Antitrust Institute, Geo. Mason U. Sch. of L., July 9, 2016

Comment on the Japan Fair Trade Commission's Consultation on the Administrative Surcharge System, The Global Antitrust Institute, Geo. Mason U. Sch. of L., Aug. 6, 2016

Comment on the India Department of Industrial Policy and Promotion's Discussion Paper on Standard Essential Patents, The Global Antitrust Institute, Geo. Mason U. Sch. of L., Mar. 31, 2016

Comment on the Proposed Revisions to the People's Republic of China Anti-Unfair Competition Law, The Global Antitrust Institute, Geo. Mason U. Sch. of L., Mar. 24, 2016

Comment on National Development and Reform Commission's Draft Anti-Monopoly Guideline on Intellectual Property Abuse, The Global Antitrust Institute, Geo. Mason U. Sch. of L., Jan. 13, 2016

Comment on the State Administration for Industry and Commerce Anti-Monopoly Guidelines on the Abuse of Intellectual Property Rights, The Global Antitrust Institute, Geo. Mason U. Sch. of L., Jan. 11, 2016

Comment on the Korea Fair Trade Commission's Amendment to its Review Guidelines on Unfair Exercise of Intellectual Property Rights, The Global Antitrust Institute, Geo. Mason U. Sch. of L., Jan. 3, 2016

Comment on the European Commission's Public Consultation on the Regulatory Environment for Platforms, The Global Antitrust Institute, Geo. Mason U. Sch. of L., Dec. 29, 2015

Comment on the Questionnaire for the Revision of China's Anti-Monopoly Law, The Global Antitrust Institute, Geo. Mason U. Sch. of L., Dec. 10, 2015

Comment to China's National Development and Reform Commission's (NDRC's) Anti- Monopoly Guide on Abuse Intellectual Property Rights, The Global Antitrust Institute, Geo. Mason U. Sch. of L., Nov. 12, 2015

Comment on the Korea Fair Trade Commission's Revised Review Guidelines On Unfair Exercise of Intellectual Property Rights, The Global Antitrust Institute, Geo. Mason U. Sch. of L., Oct. 5, 2015

Comment on China's NDRC's Questionnaire on Intellectual Property Rights Misuse Antitrust Guidelines, The Global Antitrust Institute, Geo. Mason U. Sch. of L., Sept. 30, 2015

Comment on the Japan Fair Trade Commission's Draft Partial Amendment to the Guidelines for the Use of Intellectual Property Under the Antimonopoly Act, (Geo. Mason Legal Studies, Research Paper No. LS 15-13, 2015) (with Joshua D. Wright)

Comment on the Canadian Competition Bureau's Draft Updated Intellectual Property Enforcement Guidelines (Geo. Mason Legal Studies, Research Paper No. LS 15-14, 2015) (with Joshua D. Wright)

Introduction to R.H. Bork, Legislative Intent and the Policy of the Sherman Act, 2 COMP. POL'Y INT'L 225 (2006), *excerpted at Judge Bork, Consumer Welfare, and Antitrust Law*, 31 HARV. J. L. & PUB. POL'Y 449 (2008)

Reflections of the Twenty-Fifth Anniversary of the Harvard Journal of Law & Public Policy, 25 HARV. J. L. & PUB. POL'Y 835 (2002)

Preface, FIRST AMENDMENT LAW HANDBOOK, 1997–98 Ed. (1997)

Introduction: COMPETITIVE ENTERPRISE INSTITUTE, ANTITRUST READER (1997)

The Goals of Antitrust Revisited: Comment, 147 J. OF INSTITUTIONAL & THEORETICAL ECON. 24 (1991)

Introduction, Federal Spending and the Deficit: Is a Constitutional Remedy Necessary?, 11 GEO. MASON L. REV. 115 (1989)

In Memoriam: Judge Carl McGowan, 56 GEO. WASH. L. REV. (1988)

The Reagan Administration's Legislative Initiative in Antitrust, 31 ANTITRUST BULL. 851 (1986)

Selected Presentations

Challenging Consummated Mergers Under Section 2, Concurrences Seminar (Sept. 8, 2020)

Common Minority Interests: Major or Minor Problem? ABA Section of Antitrust Law Virtual Spring Meeting (May 1, 2020)

Does Competition Law and Enforcement Need a Radical Overhaul? Time to reconsider the error cost framework in competition enforcement?; and Remedies: past experiences, effectiveness, and new tools, Jevon's Institute Colloquium (London, June 18, 2019)

General Court of The European Union: Standards of Review in Competition Cases in the U.S. and Europe (Luxembourg, June 14, 2019)

Effects-Based Analysis: Where Do We Stand on Both Sides of the Atlantic? LeadershIP Conference (Brussels, Nov. 13, 2018)

6th Bill Kovacic Antitrust Salon: Where is Antitrust Policy Going?, George Washington University (Washington, DC, Sept. 24, 2018)

Judge Richard Posner on Antitrust Remedies, ABA Section of Antitrust Law (Washington, DC, Apr. 12, 2018)

International Antitrust Policy in the Trump Administration, Heritage Foundation (Washington, DC, Jan. 23, 2018)

Extraterritorial Reach of Remedies, OECD Competition Committee (Paris, Dec. 5, 2017)

Antitrust and the Economics of Vertical Restraints, Ministry of Industry and Informational Technology (Beijing, Nov. 29, 2017)

The Legacy of Goldfarb v. Virginia, ABA Section of Antitrust Law (Washington, DC, Mar. 29, 2017)

China Competition Policy Forum – Implementation of Competition Policy in Supply-side Structural Reform (Beijing, Oct. 27–28, 2016)

Is Territoriality Still Meaningful?, New Frontiers of Antitrust, 7th International Concurrences Review Conference (Paris, June 13, 2016) (with Joshua Hazan)

Antitrust Policy to Benefit Companies and Consumers Alike, Forum for EU – US Legal Economic Affairs (Brussels, Apr. 12, 2016)

Antitrust in High-Tech Markets, Second Advanced Conference on Contemporary Competition Law Issues (Istanbul, Mar. 11, 2016)

FTC v. NC Dental Board, Where Administrative Law Meets Antitrust, ABA Section of Administrative Law and Regulatory Practice, Administrative Law Conference (Washington, DC, Oct. 29, 2015)

Non-practicing Entities, Patent Assertion Entities, and Antitrust, 2015 Innovation and Competition Forum at the University of International Business and Economics (Beijing, Oct. 12, 2015)

Extraterritoriality of Antitrust Law in the US and Abroad: A Hot Issue, George Washington University Law School (Washington, DC, Sept. 28, 2015)

The Global Antitrust Economics Conference, George Mason University School of Law (Washington, DC, May 29, 2015)

Hot Topics in Antitrust Law Competition and Global Economy, University of Chicago Alumni Law Society (Chicago, Apr. 13, 2015)

Discovery and Creation in the Common Law, Mont Pelerin Society (Lima, Mar. 24, 2015)

The United States Department of Justice (DOJ), Obama Administration Antitrust Policies: A Report Card, Heritage Foundation (Washington, DC, Jan. 29, 2015)

Regulating Competition in High Tech Industries, Federalist Society, Silicon Valley Chapter (Silicon Valley, Nov. 8, 2014)

Judicial Ethics & Election Law in the United States, (Mexico City, Aug. 26, 2014)

Competition and the Administrative State, Transatlantic Legal Forum, Annual Conference (Hamburg, June 10, 2014)

Un autre regard, Cour de Cassation, 130 ème anniversaire du Conseil supérieur de la magistrature, «la contribution des Conseils de Justice à la séparation des pouvoirs» (Paris, Oct. 25, 2013)

Problems of Adjudication in Competition Law Cases, International League of Competition Law, Oxford Congress (Oxford, U.K., Sept. 22, 2011)

DNA & Post-Conviction Exonerations, Federalist Society, Florida International University Student Chapter (Miami, Apr. 19, 2011)

Federal Antimonopoly Service of Russia, Competition Development in Russia (Moscow, July 8–9, 2010)

Cartel Sanctions and the Balance of Optimal Enforcement, Jevons Institute Advanced Training for Judges in Competition Law and Economics (University College London, Feb. 2010)

Presentations on *Private Enforcement* and *Market Dominance*; panels on *Conwood v. U.S. Tobacco* and *3M v. LaPage's*, China Intellectual Property Training Centre, Private Enforcement of Antimonopoly Law in China and the US (Beijing, Oct. 26–30, 2009)

PART I

Judge Douglas H. Ginsburg: Career and Legacy

Judge Douglas H. Ginsburg: An Influential Professor, Scholar, and Jurist

MAUREEN K. OHLHAUSEN*
Baker Botts

Abstract

This chapter pays tribute to Judge Douglas H. Ginsburg, with a focus on his advocacy for the consumer welfare standard as the guiding light of antitrust enforcement. The article explores two areas of recent antitrust enforcement by the Federal Trade Commission (FTC), Standard Essential Patents and exclusionary practices, to assess if and to what extent Judge Ginsburg's approach to the principles underlying antitrust law is reflected within them. The chapter benefits from the author's extensive experience at the FTC.

---

* Partner and Chair Antitrust and Competition Law Practice, Baker Botts LLP; former Acting Chairman of the United States Federal Trade Commission (2017-2018). The views expressed in these remarks are my own.

I. Introduction

It is truly an honor to contribute to this volume, which pays tribute to my professor, mentor, and friend, Judge Douglas Ginsburg. Judge Ginsburg is not only a renowned antitrust scholar and professor, but also a leader for change in how we view and apply antitrust laws in the United States. Over the course of his long and distinguished career, he has been a staunch advocate for the consumer welfare standard as the lodestar for antitrust enforcement. The defense of this principle is perhaps the most critical single policy choice in all of antitrust.

Antitrust enforcement has a critical role to play in the protection of competition and the maintenance of the free and open markets that do so much to improve our living standards through greater productivity, innovation, and capital formation. Free markets are the engine of our economic life, and thoughtful antitrust enforcement keeps that engine running smoothly.

That said, antitrust is not a panacea: it has an important, but limited, role to play. Focusing antitrust on the protection of consumer welfare ensures that regulators direct their attention to conduct that harms the competitive process, without sweeping in otherwise efficient conduct that may simply harm competitors.[1] The pursuit of consumer welfare provides the master template against which all competition matters must be judged.

One way to measure Judge Ginsburg's impact is to examine how the principles that underlie his approach to antitrust law have played out in antitrust enforcement. Thus, in this article, I will explore two areas of recent antitrust enforcement by the Federal Trade Commission (FTC) and how these actions either met those principles or missed the mark. But first, a little history.

I believe strongly in the importance of a free-market economy,[2] and that belief influenced my decision to attend the George Mason University School of Law. I attended night school at George Mason, which in the late 1980s was a lesser-known but growing law-and-economics law school housed in a converted department store in Arlington, Virginia. It was a far cry from the well-polished Antonin Scalia Law School it is today, which not only graduates outstanding future lawyers but also serves as a research institution producing important legal scholarship and empirical work on a variety of subjects. In the 1980s, when George Mason was the new kid on the law school block, it became a center for law and economic teaching. What I learned as soon as I enrolled was that George

---

1 *See, e.g.* Douglas H. Ginsburg, *Bork's "Legislative Intent" and the Courts*, 79 ANTITRUST L. J., No. 3 (Nov. 2014); *see also* Joshua D. Wright & Douglas H. Ginsburg, *The Goals of Antitrust: Welfare Trumps Choice* (Geo. Mason Law & Economics Research Paper No. 13–22, Mar. 2013).

2 *See, e.g.* Maureen K. Ohlhausen, *The Procrustean Problem with Prescriptive Regulation*, 23 CommLaw Conspectus: J. of Comm. Law and Tech Pol'y, 2014, at 1, https://www.ftc.gov/public-statements/2014/12/procrustean-problem-prescriptive-regulation-commlaw-conspectus-journal.

Mason had many top antitrust scholars, including future FTC Chairman William Kovacic, Henry Manne, and many others. Also teaching antitrust in that renovated department store was Judge Douglas Ginsburg of the US Court of Appeals for the DC Circuit, former head of the Antitrust Division, and one of the world's leading scholars in antitrust. With the law school as a platform, Judge Ginsburg also became the backbone of seminars that taught other federal judges about law and economics and ways to use these concepts in all legal disciplines. His efforts helped change how America's judges look at the law, and his influence is seen today throughout the judiciary and the halls of government.

As with my choice of law school, I dedicated my career as a public servant to promoting and protecting competition, the cornerstone of our free-market economy.[3] When I was an FTC Commissioner and Acting Chairman, I encouraged and guided antitrust enforcement toward this goal[4] and voiced opposition to enforcement that I believed deviated from it.[5] Through enforcement and competition advocacy, I particularly focused on challenging restraints that reduce competition by hampering market entry and innovation.[6]

During my tenure at the FTC, I saw firsthand the significant challenges that make antitrust enforcement a highly complex undertaking. Investigations are often generated by a combination of consumers complaining about higher prices or lower output, competitors frustrated by hard bargaining with other companies or exclusions from the marketplace, and combinations of these and other observed behavior resulting in disfavored market conditions. Presented with these problems, the enforcer's natural tendency is to try to do something to help solve the perceived problem. Sometimes this has led to a willingness to intervene in markets based on speculative harms to competition, not grounded in either testable empirical facts or sound economic theory. However, the observations

---

3 *See, e.g.* Maureen K. Ohlhausen, Competition and Liberty, Remarks before the 44th Ann. Conf. on Int'l Antitrust L. and Pol'y at Fordham Competition Law Inst. (Sept. 15, 2017), https://www.ftc.gov/public-statements/2017/09/competition-liberty.

4 *See, e.g.*, Maureen K. Ohlhausen, What Are We Talking About When We Talk About Antitrust?, Remarks at the Concurrences Review Dinner (Sept. 2016), https://www.ftc.gov/public-statements/2016/09/what-are-we-talking-about-when-we-talk-about-antitrust (Concurrences Review Dinner).

5 *See, e.g.*, Maureen K. Ohlhausen, Competition Policy at the FTC in the New Administration, Remarks before the 5th Joint Conf. by Concurrences Rev. and the Geo. Wash. U. L. Sch. (Sept. 11, 2017), https://www.ftc.gov/public-statements/2017/09/competition-policy-ftc-new-administration (Concurrences 5th Conference); *see also, e.g.*, Dissenting Statement of Commissioner Maureen Ohlhausen – In the Matter of Robert Bosch GmbH, FTC File No. 121-0081, at 3-4 (Nov. 26, 2012), https://www.ftc.gov/public-statements/2012/11/dissenting-statement-commissioner-maureen-ohlhausen-matter-robert-bosch (*Robert Bosch GmbH);* Dissenting Statement of Commissioner Maureen Ohlhausen – In the Matter of Motorola Mobility LLC and Google Inc., FTC File No. 121-0120, at 1–3 (Jan. 3, 2013), https://www.ftc.gov/public-statements/2013/01/statement-commissioner-maureen-ohlhausen-0 (*Google/Motorola Mobility*).

6 Maureen K. Ohlhausen & Gregory P. Luib, *Brother, May I?: The Challenge of Competitor Control over Market Entry*, 4 J. ANTITRUST ENFORCEMENT 111 (2015), https://www.ftc.gov/system/files/documents/public_statements/801861/150917brothermayi.pdf; *see also, e.g.*, Concurrences 5th Conference, *supra* note 5.

giving rise to complaints may not be indicative of competition problems that require antitrust intervention. They may simply be indicators consistent with and reflecting the dynamic and sometimes abrupt impacts of competitive market behavior. Investigating these types of issues requires a rigorous inquiry to determine whether the conduct in question warrants correction under the antitrust laws, as opposed to changes in regulations, private contract suits, or no remedy whatsoever. This careful approach respects the foundational belief that a market economy, free of private restraints and unnecessarily burdensome regulations, produces superior outcomes over time.[7]

II. Recent FTC Enforcement

1. Standard Essential Patents

Competitive markets often reinvent themselves, as entrepreneurs identify and exploit inefficiencies to improve productivity or innovate in ways that restructure entire markets. The need to zero in on harm to competition, rather than simply disruption to competitors, is especially important in markets that are in transition or subject to rapid innovation. I have therefore argued that in markets with fast-changing technologies, the agency should apply its enforcement tools in a manner that is nimble, transparent, and incremental.[8]

One area of keen interest for the FTC in recent years has been Standard Essential Patents (SEPs). Standards play a critical role in the modern economy. They foster interoperability, avoid costly wars between rival systems, and facilitate competition in product markets. It is thus not surprising that competition enforcers want to ensure that the standard-setting process benefits from, and promotes, competition. Alleged holdup by holders of SEPs who have made commitments to license on fair, reasonable, and non-discriminatory (FRAND) terms, has attracted the most attention. The conventional narrative is that when firms commit to a standard, they can no longer look to alternative technologies that were previously available. SEP holders' bargaining power may therefore "surge" after industry adopts an infringing standard, potentially allowing them to demand outsize royalties.[9] Armed with an injunction – the thinking goes – a SEP owner can threaten all revenue flowing from the standard and extract more than the competitive price.

The issue of SEPs and injunctions emerged early in my tenure as a Commissioner in two FTC decisions, *Robert Bosch GmbH* and *Google/Motorola Mobility*. In both

---

7 *See* Concurrences Review Dinner, *supra* note 4.

8 *Id.*, *see also* Maureen K. Ohlhausen, *Antitrust Enforcement in the Digital Age*, Remarks before the Global Antitrust Enforcement Symposium (Sept. 12, 2017), https://www.ftc.gov/public-statements/2017/09/antitrust-enforcement-digital-age.

9 Apple, Inc. v. Motorola, Inc., 869 F. Supp. 2d. 901, 913 (N.D. Ill. 2012), rev'd in part, 757 f.3d 1286 (Fed. Cir. 2014).

matters, I dissented from the Commission's actions.[10] In investigating the acquisition of SPX Service Solutions (SPX) by Robert Bosch GmbH, for example, the FTC learned that SPX had previously used patents to try to enjoin willing licensees.[11] As part of its review of the merger, the Commission set forth its view that patent-holders that seek injunctive relief against willing licensees of their FRAND-encumbered SEPs are engaged in an unfair method of competition under section 5 of the FTC Act (though not a violation of the Sherman Act).[12] The Commission proceeded on a similar theory shortly thereafter in *Google/Motorola Mobility*[13]

Among the concerns I raised in my dissents was that the Commission majority failed to explain how the conduct it targeted (a breach of an allegedly implied contract term with no allegation of deception to the standard-setting body) harmed competition any more than would any garden variety breach-of-contract or other business dispute between private parties. My point was that even if a requested injunction violates a RAND-licensing guarantee (which was not even clear in these two matters), it is not always an antitrust problem. Rather, such issues typically sound in contract law, as litigants and courts have recognized.[14] I have thus repeatedly argued that, instead of intervening broadly in this space, antitrust agencies should focus on conduct that actually harms the competitive process, such as when a patentee's deception before the standard-setting organization causes the adoption of proprietary technology over a substitute technology, followed by holdup.[15]

The points I raised in *Robert Bosch GmbH* and *Google/Motorola Mobility* resonated in the broader antitrust community. Writing with other scholars in the years after the FTC actions, Judge Ginsburg noted the lack of legal and economic support for the majority's position.[16] The authors also emphasized that

> [w]ith respect to reneging on a FRAND commitment, as the Supreme Court explained in *NYNEX Corp. v. Discon, Inc.*, while

10 *Robert Bosch GmbH* and *Google/Motorola Mobility, supra* note 5.

11 *Robert Bosch GmbH, supra* note 5.

12 *Id.*

13 *Google/Motorola Mobility, supra* note 5.

14 See, e.g., Microsoft Corp. v. Motorola, Inc., No. 14-35393, 2015 WL 4568613 (9th Cir. July 30, 2015); In re Innovatio IP Ventures, LLC Patent Litig., No. 11 C 9308, 2013 WL 5593609 (N.D. Ill. Oct. 3, 2013), Michael A. Carrier, *The US District Court for the Northern District of Illinois issues second ruling determining RAND rate for standard essential patent (Innovatio)*, 3 October 2013, *e-Competitions* October 2013, Art. N° 58558; Realtek Semiconductor Corp. v. LSI Corp., 946 F. Supp. 2d 998 (N.D. Cal. 2013).

15 *See, e.g*, Maureen K. Ohlhausen, *The Elusive Role of Competition in the Standard-Setting Antitrust Debate*, 20 Stan. Tech. L. Rev. 93 (2017), https://www.ftc.gov/system/files/documents/public_statements/1229923/20-1-3-ohlhausen-antitrust-debate.pdf.

16 Douglas H. Ginsburg et al., *The Troubling Use of Antitrust to Regulate FRAND Licensing*, CPI Antitrust Chronicle, Oct. 2015, at 6–7; *see also* Douglas H. Ginsburg et al., *Enjoining Injunctions: The Case Against Antitrust Liability for Standard Essential Patent Holders Who Seek Injunctions*, The Antitrust Source, Oct. 2014.

the evasion of a pricing constraint may hurt consumers, it does not harm the competitive process. The Court distinguished the mere breach of a pricing commitment from the unlawful exercise of monopoly power by pointing out that, with the breach, the "consumer injury naturally flowed not so much from a less competitive market as… from the exercise of market power lawfully in the hands of a monopolist."[17]

2. Exclusionary Practices

Another difficult area of antitrust enforcement involves exclusionary conduct by a monopolist. This was at issue in the FTC's enforcement action in *McWane.*[18] In that case, the Commission issued a seven-count administrative complaint against McWane in January 2012[19] – prior to my arrival as a Commissioner. Ultimately, the Commission dismissed six of the seven counts, finding liability solely on the Sherman Act section 2 exclusive-dealing count.[20] In particular, the Commission found that McWane had used an exclusive-dealing policy to prevent its sole rival, Star Pipe Products, Ltd. (Star), from meaningfully competing and thus maintained the monopoly that McWane enjoyed in the market for domestically-manufactured ductile iron pipe fittings.

The thrust of the case was that McWane, with over 90% market share, had imposed a policy on distributors that required them to purchase all of their domestic fittings from McWane; otherwise, they would lose their rebates and lose access to all of McWane's products. There were two exceptions to this so-called Full Support Program permitting the purchase of competing domestic fittings: where McWane products were not readily available, and where the customer bought domestic fittings and accessories along with another manufacturer's ductile iron pipe. The Commission found that, to the extent that Star was able to gain sales, it did so primarily under these limited exceptions, and those sales were insufficient to have a competitive impact.

In finding liability on the exclusive-dealing count, the Commission determined that McWane had monopoly power in the domestic fittings market, that the Full Support Program constituted an exclusive-dealing arrangement that substantially

---

17 Douglas H. Ginsburg et al., *The Troubling Use of Antitrust to Regulate FRAND Licensing*, CPI Antitrust Chronicle, Oct. 2015, at 6–7, citing *NYNEX v. Discon, Inc.* 525 U.S. 128, 129, 135–37 (1998).

18 In re McWane, Inc., No. 9351, Opinion of the Commission (Jan. 30, 2014) (*McWane Commission Opinion*), https://www.ftc.gov/system/files/documents/cases/140206mcwaneopinion_0.pdf. Commissioner Wright dissented in this matter.

19 Administrative Complaint, In re McWane, Inc., No. 9351 (Jan. 4, 2012), https://www.ftc.gov/sites/default/files/documents/cases/2012/01/120104ccwanestaradmincmpt.pdf (alleging conspiracy, information exchange, invitation to collude, restraint of trade based on distribution agreement, conspiracy to monopolize, monopolization, and attempted monopolization).

20 *McWane Commission Opinion*, *supra* note 18, at 2 & n.1.

foreclosed its rivals' access to the most efficient sales channel, and that this resulted in harm to competition and consumers in the domestic fittings market. As the Commission opinion concluded, "the evidence that McWane's exclusive-dealing policy significantly impaired the access of McWane's only rival, Star, to the main channel of distribution, thereby increasing its costs and keeping it below the critical level necessary to pose a real competitive threat, is plainly sufficient to meet the standard of harm to competition set forth in the prevailing case law."[21]

One of the key cases on which the Commission relied for this conclusion was the DC Circuit's *Microsoft* opinion,[22] in which Judge Ginsburg participated as part of the en banc panel. The *Microsoft* decision highlighted the difficult but necessary task for antitrust enforcers of focusing on harm to competition, stating,

> [w]hether any particular act of a monopolist is exclusionary, rather than merely a form of vigorous competition, can be difficult to discern: the means of illicit exclusion, like the means of legitimate competition, are myriad. The challenge for an antitrust court lies in stating a general rule for distinguishing between exclusionary acts, which reduce social welfare, and competitive acts, which increase it.[23]

The decision established an influential framework for this analysis and emphasized that harm to the competitive process and thus consumer welfare is the touchstone for an antitrust violation, rather than merely harm to individual competitors. Ultimately, the court in *Microsoft* found that the company's exclusionary behavior harmed the competitive process and thereby harmed consumers.[24]

The 11th Circuit eventually upheld the Commission's *McWane* decision, affirming our determinations regarding market definition, McWane's monopoly power, and harm to competition.[25] The court followed the approach taken by the DC Circuit in determining whether a monopolist's conduct has harmed competition, noting, among other things, that substantial foreclosure is just one of several factors in the analysis and that harm to competitors is insufficient for purposes of section 2 of the Sherman Act.

---

21 *Id.* at 26.

22 United States v. Microsoft Corp., 253 F.3d 34 (D.C. Cir. 2001).

23 *Id.* at 58.

24 *Id.*

25 McWane, Inc. v. FTC, No. 14–11363, 2015 WL 1652200, at *9–12, *19–21 (11th Cir. Apr. 15, 2015); Helen Cho Eckert, David R. Garcia, *The US Court of Appeals for the 11th Circuit holds that a rebate program requiring exclusivity from distributors was an unlawful maintenance of monopoly power (McWane)*, 15 April 2015, *e-Competitions* April 2015, Art. N° 72658.

Now, to be clear, economic literature clearly supports the proposition that exclusive dealing is likely to be procompetitive in many instances, a fact that the Commission acknowledged in *McWane*.[26] However, as shown by *Microsoft* and *McWane*, in cases where courts or the Commission are able to identify substantial harm to competition that is not outweighed by cognizable efficiencies that benefit consumers, antitrust should act to protect the competitive process. It is antithetical to free-market principles for private parties to use their significant market power simply to cordon off large portions of the market from would-be competitors that may provide lower-priced, higher-quality, or more innovative products and services, through behavior that does not benefit consumers. It is decidedly the role of antitrust to address such market restrictions and facilitate entry by new and innovative competitors.

III. Conclusion

This brief discussion of the FTC enforcement during my tenure on the Commission has barely scratched the surface of Judge Ginsburg's impact on antitrust law in the courts and in competition enforcement agencies around the world. I am sure other contributors to this volume will expound on his legacy in many other areas of legal scholarship and enforcement. I will simply conclude by saying it has been an honor to have been both his student and his colleague in the antitrust endeavor.

26 *See McWane Commission Opinion*, *supra* note 18, at 18.

Judge Douglas H. Ginsburg and Antitrust Law's Rule(s) of Reason

JONATHAN B. BAKER AND ANDREW I. GAVIL*

American University Washington School of Law

Howard University School of Law

Abstract

This chapter explores Judge Ginsburg's influence on the evolution of the rule of reason and its development into a common, structured, burden-shifting approach that emphasizes the primacy of competitive effects analysis. That approach now informs judicial decision-making in the United States under Sections 1 (unreasonable restraints of trade) and 2 (monopolization) of the Sherman Act and under Section 7 of the Clayton Act (mergers and acquisitions). It highlights the influential role that Judge Ginsburg and the Court of Appeals for the D.C. Circuit, on which he served, played in that evolution, as well as the common conceptual core of contemporary competition law.

---

* Jonathan B. Baker is Research Professor of Law, American University Washington College of Law, and Andrew I. Gavil is Professor of Law, Howard University School of Law. The authors are grateful to Judge Douglas H. Ginsburg for helpful exchanges about some of the issues addressed in this paper.

I. Introduction

For more than a century, the interpretation and application of the Sherman Act has been guided by the "rule of reason." Its history is well known. The US Supreme Court famously declared in its 1911 *Standard Oil* decision that Section 1 of the Sherman Act was to be guided by "the standard of reason which had been applied at common law."[1] Seven years later, the Supreme Court elaborated on the content of the rule of reason in *Chicago Board of Trade*, directing courts to evaluate a competitive restraint's nature, purpose, and effect, and providing a laundry list of factors that might be considered in doing so.[2]

For the next sixty years, the Supreme Court largely turned away from further exploration of the kind of comprehensive rule-of-reason analysis it envisioned in *Chicago Board of Trade*, focusing instead on what became known as the "per se rule." By 1978, this would lead the Court to describe the "rule of reason" and the "per se rule" as if they were two distinct "rules."[3] In truth, however, they were but two ways of applying the same standard, the "standard of reason" that the Court had endorsed in *Standard Oil* and that, as elaborated in *Chicago Board of Trade*, called for something akin to a totality-of-the-circumstances assessment of a restraint's nature, purpose, and effects.

But by the late 1970s, with changes in the makeup of the Court and the political climate, new life was breathed into the content of the rule of reason in cases like *Sylvania*[4] and *Broadcast Music, Inc.*,[5] igniting a generational wave of reform that continues to this day. These reforms – efforts to operationalize the rule of reason and adapt it to the decisional needs of various kinds of cases – have spawned something of a "meta" rule of reason[6] that now guides antitrust decision-making under both the Sherman and Clayton Acts, applying in analogous fashion to challenges of concerted conduct under Section 1, unilateral exclusionary conduct under Section 2, and mergers under Section 7 of the Clayton Act.[7]

---

1 Standard Oil Co. v. United States, 221 U.S. 1, 61 (1911).

2 Bd. of Trade of Chicago v. United States, 246 U.S. 231, 238 (1918).

3 Nat'l Soc'y Prof'l Eng'rs v. United States, 435 U.S. 679, 692 (1978).

4 Cont'l T.V., Inc. v. GTE Sylvania Inc., 433 U.S. 36 (1977).

5 Broad. Music, Inc. v. Columbia Broad. Sys., Inc., 441 U.S. 1 (1979).

6 Mark S. Popofsky, *Defining Exclusionary Conduct: Section 2, the Rule of Reason, and the Unifying Principle Underlying Antitrust Rules*, 73 ANTITRUST L.J. 435, 456 (2006) (describing common use of "reasonableness" test under §§ 1 and 2 of the Sherman Act and labelling it a "'meta' rule of reason").

7 *Cf.* Jonathan B. Baker, *Exclusion as a Core Competition Concern*, 78 ANTITRUST L.J. 528, 544–51 (2013) (describing a common approach to truncated condemnation of collusive conduct and convergence toward a common approach to truncated condemnation of exclusionary conduct under the Sherman Act and Clayton Act across doctrinal categories).

Judge Ginsburg played an instrumental role in this period of reform for antitrust law. It coincided with his ascent to positions of authority at the Antitrust Division of the US DOJ, where he served first as Deputy Assistant Attorney General for Regulatory Affairs (1983–84) and then as Assistant Attorney General (1985–86), and later when he was appointed to the US Court of Appeals for the DC Circuit, which he joined in 1986.[8] When he was a Deputy Assistant Attorney General at the Antitrust Division he was a signatory to the government's influential amicus brief in the Supreme Court in the *NCAA* case,[9] which is often cited as the source of the modern "quick look" approach to the rule of reason. And as a judge of the US Court of Appeals for the DC Circuit, he participated in the en banc decision in *United States v. Microsoft Corp.*,[10] a monopolization case that elaborated a reasonableness approach to evaluating conduct under Section 2 of the Sherman Act, and authored the court's opinion in *Polygram Holding, Inc. v. FTC*,[11] further contributing to the development of structured and abbreviated application of the rule of reason in cases involving anticompetitive collaborative conduct by rival firms. Viewed together, these two decisions advanced the cause of a structured, pan-antitrust rule of reason, drawing attention to the similarities of approach between Sections 1 and 2 and bringing the "rule of reason" full circle to its origins in *Standard Oil*, where the Supreme Court had recognized that it lies at the heart of both Section 1 and Section 2.

Finally, the paper will explore his influence on the analysis of mergers. It highlights the role played by the Justice Department's legislative proposal for revising Clayton Act §7, presented to Congress when Ginsburg served as Assistant Attorney General for Antitrust, in moving the courts away from employing a strict, near – per se rule approach to merger review. It also explores the parallels between the DC Circuit's influential approach to horizontal merger analysis, adopted in 1990 and reaffirmed in 2001, and the reasonableness analysis employed by the same circuit in Sherman Act agreement and monopolization decisions.

II. Origins and Development of the Rule of Reason "Continuum"

The late 1970s ushered in a period of unprecedented and rapid evolution of antitrust law in the United States, facilitated by accumulating criticisms of the doctrine that had developed in the preceding decades, changes in the makeup of the Supreme Court, and a significant shift in the political climate that brought

8 In 1984 and 1985, between his positions at the Antitrust Division, Ginsburg served as the Administrator of the Office of Information and Regulatory Affairs (OIRA) at the Office of Management and Budget (OMB).

9 Nat'l Collegiate Athletic Ass'n v. Bd. of Regents of the Univ. of Okla., 468 U.S. 85 (1984).

10 253 F.3d 34 (D.C. Cir. 2001). Although en banc decisions are by their nature attributed to the full court, it is widely believed that Judge Ginsburg played a significant role in the drafting of the opinion.

11 416 F.3d 29 (D.C. Cir. 2005).

new and reform-minded leadership to federal antitrust enforcement agencies. The Court's move away from extensive reliance on per se prohibitions for a wide range of conduct and its return to the rule of reason as the presumptive, default standard for analysis of conduct challenged under Section 1 of the Sherman Act[12] invited renewed interest in judicial methods for structuring what seemed to be the open-ended and unguided approach of *Chicago Board of Trade*.[13]

One of the more influential commentaries of the time was Phillip Areeda's *The "Rule of Reason" in Antitrust Analysis: General Issues*, a short monograph prepared for the Federal Judicial Center as a study aid for federal judges.[14] Areeda questioned the Supreme Court's "impulse to categorize"[15] as displayed in *National Society of Professional Engineers* (*NSPE*), which described Section 1 analysis as falling into two complementary, but seemingly distinct, categories – "per se" and "rule of reason."[16] In his view, the "dichotomy between the per se and rule of reason categories is far less sharp than first appears."[17] He observed that "so-called per se rules are nothing more mysterious or special than presumptions of varying strength and breadth" and that similarly "the so-called rule of reason also contains within itself numerous presumptions of varying strength and breadth." He concluded that "we might clarify our thinking and enhance the understanding of bar and business by dropping per se and rule of reason terminology altogether."[18]

The Antitrust Division and the Federal Trade Commission (FTC) received this invitation and took up the cause in *NCAA*.

1. NCAA

In *National Collegiate Athletic Association v. Board of Regents of the University of Oklahoma*,[19] the University of Oklahoma and the University of Georgia

---

12 Cont'l T.V., Inc. v. GTE Sylvania Inc., 433 U.S. 36, 58–59 (1977) ("we do make clear that departure from the rule-of-reason standard must be based upon demonstrable economic effect rather than… upon formalistic line-drawing").

13 For a more complete account of the evolution of the rule of reason, see Andrew I. Gavil, *Moving Beyond Caricature and Characterization: The Modern Rule of Reason in Practice*, 85 S. Cal. L. Rev. 733 (2012).

14 Phillip Areeda, The "Rule of Reason" in Antitrust Analysis: General Issues (1981).

15 *Id.* at 42.

16 Nat'l Soc'y Prof'l Eng'rs v. United States, 435 U.S. 679, 692 (1978).

17 Areeda, *supra* note 14, at 25.

18 *Id.* at 36. *See also* Timothy J. Muris, *The New Rule of Reason*, 57 Antitrust L.J. 859 (1989). Muris observes that since the mid-1970s the Supreme Court "has consistently applied one rule of reason" and that "[p]er se rules do not represent a separate form of analysis, but instead result from applying the one rule." *Id.* Frank Easterbrook, who argued the *NCAA* case for the government, wrote an influential article recommending use of presumptions (or filters) to structure the rule of reason inquiry that was published in the same year *NCAA* was decided. Frank H. Easterbrook, *Limits of Antitrust*, 63 Tex. L. Rev. 1 (1984).

19 468 U.S. 85 (1984).

contended that certain features of the NCAA's contracts with broadcasters for the rights to televise NCAA-sanctioned college football games unreasonably restrained trade in violation of Section 1 of the Sherman Act. The district court and the court of appeals had both agreed that the television contracts violated Section 1, but whereas the district court had conducted a lengthy trial that took into account the NCAA's proffered defenses, the court of appeals affirmed invoking the "per se rule," in part. As presented to the Supreme Court, therefore, the standard for judging conduct under Section 1 was the seemingly binary choice offered by *NSPE*: per se or rule of reason, as if each represented a distinct standard and carried with it a highly differentiated burden of proof. The contrast was between "facial" condemnation and "full-blown" rule-of-reason analysis, which, the NCAA argued, demanded proof of a relevant market, market power, and competitive harm.

The Justice Department had taken an early interest in the case, filing an amicus brief in support of the plaintiff universities in the 10th Circuit. It again supported them before the Supreme Court, this time joined by the FTC, but with something of a twist.[20] Although the parties before the court did not advocate any less characterization-dependent approach, the brief filed by the United States did, arguing that even though the court of appeals may have erred in condemning the NCAA's conduct as per se unlawful, the characterization line between "per se" and "rule of reason" was far less defined than the court's previous decisions had suggested.

The government's brief, which Judge Ginsburg signed in his capacity as a Deputy Assistant Attorney General, directed the Court's attention to Areeda's monograph, prompting the Court to quote one of his most memorable observations: "[t]he essential point is that the rule of reason can sometimes be applied in the twinkling of an eye."[21] In a lengthy footnote, the Court also embraced the views expressed by the government more broadly, specifically as it related to the role of market power in the analysis of competitive effects. The Court quoted the government's brief at length, stating that the Solicitor General "correctly observes":

> There was no need for the respondents [plaintiffs below] to establish monopoly power in any precisely defined market for television programming in order to prove the restraint unreasonable. Both lower courts found not only that NCAA has power over the market

---

20 *See* Brief for the United States as Amicus Curiae in Support of Affirmance, *NCAA*, 468 U.S. 85 (1984).

21 *NCAA*, 468 U.S. at 109 n.39 (*quoting* Areeda, *supra* note 14, at 38). For further insights into the development of the Justice Department's position in *NCAA*, see Timothy J. Muris, *The Federal Trade Commission and the Rule of Reason: In Defense of Massachusetts Board*, 66 Antitrust L.J. 773, 774 n. 4 (1998) (discussing the connection between the FTC's later 1988 decision in *In re Massachusetts Bd. of Registration of Optometry*, 110 F.T.C. 549 (1988), and the Justice Department's amicus brief in *NCAA*). *See also* Muris, *supra* note 18.

> for intercollegiate sports, but also that in the market for television programming – no matter how broadly or narrowly the market is defined – the NCAA television restrictions have reduced output, subverted viewer choice, and distorted pricing. Consequently, unless the controls have some countervailing procompetitive justification, they should be deemed unlawful regardless of whether petitioner has substantial market power over advertising dollars. While the "reasonableness" of a particular alleged restraint often depends on the market power of the parties involved, because a judgment about market power is the means by which the effects of the conduct on the market place can be assessed, market power is only one test of "reasonableness." And where the anticompetitive effects of conduct can be ascertained through means short of extensive market analysis, and where no countervailing competitive virtues are evident, a lengthy analysis of market power is not necessary.[22]

The Supreme Court agreed, holding that "[a]s a matter of law, the absence of proof of market power does not justify a naked restriction on price or output. To the contrary, when there is an agreement not to compete in terms of price or output, 'no elaborate industry analysis is required to demonstrate the anticompetitive character of such an agreement.'"[23] The case came to be associated with the labels "quick look" or "abbreviated" rule-of-reason analysis, a seemingly middle ground between per se condemnation and "full" rule of reason treatment.

The implications of the decision, however, were more far-reaching. In large part due to the government's brief, the Court had turned away from a simple, binary conception of the rule of reason, opening the door to a more flexible approach – one not inconsistent with *NSPE*, notwithstanding that decision's description of a bifurcated analysis, because it was informed by the decision's overarching direction that the relevant analysis must focus on an assessment of competitive effects.[24] As was implicit in the government's brief, the Court also took an important step towards acknowledging that the "per se rule" was actually an application of the rule of reason, and that applying the rule of reason should not proceed haphazardly, but in a step-by-step approach that starts with anticompetitive effect and then moves on to consider procompetitive justifications.

---

22 *NCAA*, 468 U.S. at 110, n. 42.

23 *Id.* at 109 (*quoting NSPE*, 435 U.S. at 692). *See also FTC v. Indiana Fed'n of Dentists*, 476 U.S. 447, 460–61 (1986) (noting that "proof of actual detrimental effects" can "obviate the need for an inquiry into market power").

24 *NSPE*, 435 U.S. at 690 (footnotes omitted) (emphasis added):
The test prescribed in *Standard Oil* is whether the challenged contracts or acts "were unreasonably restrictive of competitive conditions." Unreasonableness under that test could be based either (1) on the nature or character of the contracts, or (2) on surrounding circumstances giving rise to the inference or presumption that they were intended to restrain trade and enhance prices. *Under either branch of the test, the inquiry is confined to a consideration of impact on competitive conditions.*

2. Polygram[25]

In one of his most substantial antitrust opinions, Judge Ginsburg built on the earlier work to which he had contributed at the Justice Department in *NCAA* with the benefit of almost two additional decades of developments. By the time *Polygram* came before the DC Circuit, the Supreme Court also had decided *California Dental Association v. FTC*,[26] in which it had further elaborated on the role of abbreviated or "quick look" rule-of-reason analysis and its relationship to per se condemnation, holding that "[t]he truth is that our categories of analysis of anticompetitive effect are less fixed than terms like 'per se,' 'quick look,' and 'rule of reason' tend to make them appear... What is required, rather, is an enquiry meet for the case, looking to the circumstances, details, and logic of a restraint."[27] The DC Circuit had also decided *Microsoft*, discussed below, which refined the approach to evaluating the reasonableness of conduct under Sherman Act §2.[28]

In *Polygram*, the FTC challenged an agreement between two joint venture partners, Polygram and Warner Communications, to suspend the promotion of two previously and independently released recordings of the "Three Tenors" during the introductory period of a third album, which they had co-produced. The FTC had concluded that the agreement was anticompetitive, but the defendants sought review of that decision in the DC Circuit.

The DC Circuit's unanimous decision, authored by Judge Ginsburg, provided the court with an opportunity to review the history and development of the rule of reason, with particular attention to the use of non-per se, yet still "abbreviated," rule-of-reason analysis. As the court explained, that analysis "has gone through a transition over the last 25 years, from a dichotomous categorical approach to a more nuanced and case-specific inquiry."[29] Citing *California Dental*,

---

25 Polygram Holding, Inc. v. FTC, 416 F.3d 29 (D.C. Cir. 2005); Jr. Don T. Hibner, *The US Court of Appeals for the District of Columbia Circuit upholds the finding of the FTC that the prohibition of discounts and advertising was inherently suspect as they would tend to raise prices and reduce output (PolyGram)*, 22 July 2005, *e-Competitions* July 2005, Art. N° 67413.

26 526 U.S. 756 (1999).

27 *Id.* at 780–81. In dissent, Justice Breyer proposed a structured approach to the rule of reason inquiry. *Id.* at 782 (Breyer, J., dissenting).

28 In another important antitrust opinion by Judge Ginsburg, the DC Circuit had also decided Superior Court Trial Lawyers Ass'n v. FTC, 856 F.2d 226 (D.C. Cir. 1988). Although the Supreme Court reversed the decision in part, *see* FTC v. Superior Court Trial Lawyers Ass'n, 493 U.S. 411 (1990), the DC Circuit opinion analyzed the Supreme Court's previous decisions in *NSPE* and *NCAA*, and can be understood in retrospect as foreshadowing the structured, burden-shifting analysis later adopted by the DC Circuit in *Polygram*. *See, e.g.*, *Superior Court Trial Lawyers Ass'n*, 856 F.2d at 249 ("Nor did the Commission look for market power when it analyzed the SCTLA boycott under the Rule of Reason; under that approach it was not necessary for it to proceed any further once it determined that there were no countervailing procompetitive justifications for the facially anticompetitive boycott.")

29 416 F.3d at 33–34.

the court concluded its review of that history by noting that "[i]t would be somewhat misleading... to say... the Court has moved from a dichotomy to a trichotomy, when in fact it has backed away from any reliance upon fixed categories and toward a continuum."[30] What remained to be sorted out was how a court can apply this rule of reason "continuum" in a specific case.

For that, the FTC had "revived the analytic framework" it had earlier developed in its 1988 decision in *Mass. Board* – a post-*NCAA* effort to structure the rule-of-reason inquiry through distinct, burden-shifting steps that were oriented towards the litigation process, and which allowed for abbreviated condemnation of conduct having relatively obvious anticompetitive effects and no procompetitive justifications. As explained by the court, the FTC's approach proceeded in several steps:

> First, the Commission must determine whether it is obvious from the nature of the challenged conduct that it will likely harm consumers. If so, then the restraint is deemed "inherently suspect" and, unless the defendant comes forward with some plausible (and legally cognizable) competitive justification for the restraint, summarily condemned. "Such justifications," the Commission explained, "may consist of plausible reasons why practices that are competitively suspect as a general matter may not be expected to have adverse consequences in the context of the particular market in question, or they may consist of reasons why the practices are likely to have beneficial effects for consumers." ...
>
> If the defendant does offer such an explanation, then the Commission "must address the justification" in one of two ways. First, the Commission may explain why it can confidently conclude, without adducing evidence, that the restraint very likely harmed consumers... Alternatively, the Commission may provide the tribunal with sufficient evidence to show that anticompetitive effects are in fact likely... If the Commission succeeds in either way, then the evidentiary burden shifts to the defendant to show the restraint in fact does not harm consumers or has "procompetitive virtues" that outweigh its burden upon consumers.[31]

---

30 *Id.* at 35.

31 *Id.* at 35–36. Although the FTC associated its framework with *Mass. Board*, decided in 1988 (*In re Massachusetts Bd. of Registration of Optometry*, 110 F.T.C. 549 (1988)), Areeda's 1981 monograph for the Federal Judicial Center had also proposed a structured rule of reason inquiry as "three pronged":

> (1) What harm to competition results or may result from the collaborators' activities? (2) What is the object they are trying to achieve and is it a legitimate and significant one? That is, what are the nature and magnitude of the "redeeming virtues" of the challenged collaboration? (3) Are there other and better ways by which the collaborators can achieve their legitimate objectives with fewer harms to competition? That is, are there "less restrictive alternatives" to the challenged restraint?

The defendants objected to the FTC's framework on the ground that it conflicted with the Supreme Court's previous decisions, especially *California Dental*. Specifically, they argued that it improperly allowed a restraint that is not per se illegal to be condemned "without the Commission having to prove the restraint actually harms competition."[32] In the defendants' view, *California Dental* had limited use of abbreviated rule-of-reason analysis to cases involving proof of "actual" competitive harm.[33]

Although the DC Circuit did not endorse the Commission's analytical framework in all of its particulars, it rejected the defendants' cramped interpretation of *California Dental* as inconsistent with the Supreme Court's "continuum" concept.[34] Instead, the court concluded that, at least as applied by the FTC in *Polygram*, the *Mass. Board* framework was an acceptable way "to ascertain whether the challenged restraint hinders competition" and so satisfied the requirements of the Sherman Act.[35] Reviewing the record assembled by the FTC, it thereafter had no difficulty in affirming the FTC's conclusion with respect to the challenged agreement to suspend promotional efforts.

Polygram thus made two important contributions to the evolution of the contemporary rule of reason. First, it provided a comprehensive and coherent explanation of the evolution of the Supreme Court's rule-of-reason jurisprudence from a dichotomous approach to the more flexible rule of reason continuum of *California Dental*. In doing so, it explained how "per se" and "rule of reason" are best understood as two ways to apply the same standard – the standard of reason – and not as two distinct "rules." It also advanced the cause of structured rule-of-reason analysis as an alternative to the mythologized "full-blown" and unguided rule of reason that was a manifestation of the dichotomous approach.[36] That approach has now been more fully endorsed by the Supreme Court.[37]

> As difficult as they are, those inquiries are much easier than the final judgment which depends upon some kind of weighing and balancing of pluses and minuses.

AREEDA, *supra* note 14, at 2. Foreshadowing the concept of abbreviated rule-of-reason analysis, Areeda went on to observe that "[f]ortunately, a satisfying resolution is possible in a good number of cases where one of the three elements is significant and the others are not." *Id.*

32 416 F.3d at 36.

33 For a further examination of *California Dental's* implications for quick look analysis, specifically the relative importance of evidence of "actual" as opposed to relatively obvious "theoretical" harm, see Gavil, *supra* note 13, at 757–59.

34 416 F.3d at 36 ("we reject PolyGram's attempt to locate the appropriate analysis, and the concomitant burden of proof, by reference to the vestigial line separating per se analysis from the rule of reason.").

35 *Id.* at 36–37.

36 For a more complete analysis of the current state of the rule of reason, see ANDREW I. GAVIL, WILLIAM E. KOVACIC, JONATHAN B. BAKER & JOSHUA D. WRIGHT, ANTITRUST LAW IN PERSPECTIVE: CASES, CONCEPTS AND PROBLEMS IN COMPETITION POLICY 246–58 (3d ed. 2017).

37 Ohio v. American Express Co., 138 S. Ct. 2274, 2284 (2018) (noting the parties' agreement that "[t]o determine whether a restraint violates the rule of reason… a three-step, burden-shifting framework

III. The Reintegration of Sections 1 and 2 of the Sherman Act: *Microsoft*

As noted at the outset of this paper, the Supreme Court's 1911 decision in *Standard Oil* still stands as the acknowledged origin of the "rule of reason." But the rule of reason is most often associated solely with Section 1 of the Sherman Act. In *United States v. Microsoft Corp.*,[38] the DC Circuit reestablished the close tie between Sections 1 and 2 of the Sherman Act in two important ways. First, as in *Polygram*, which followed it four years later, the court spelled out a step-by-step, burden-shifting framework for evaluating allegedly exclusionary conduct by single firms. In addition, it revived the long-dormant notion that Section 2, like Section 1, ought to be guided by a "rule of reason."

As Judge Ginsburg would later do in *Polygram*, the en banc court in *Microsoft* commenced its discussion of the relevant legal standard for judging exclusionary conduct by reviewing the Supreme Court's previous decisions interpreting Section 2 of the Sherman Act, concluding that "[f]rom a century of case law on monopolization under § 2" a four-step framework had developed.[39] Much like the structured, burden-shifting approach later articulated in *Polygram*, Section 2's framework as interpreted in *Microsoft* begins with "anticompetitive effect... That is, [the challenged conduct]... must harm the competitive *process* and thereby harm consumers... [And] the plaintiff, on whom the burden of proof of course rests,... must demonstrate that the monopolist's conduct indeed has the requisite anticompetitive effect."[40] If the plaintiff can do so, "then the monopolist may proffer a 'procompetitive justification' for its conduct... a nonpretextual claim that its conduct is indeed a form of competition on the merits because it involves, for example, greater efficiency or enhanced consumer appeal – then the burden shifts back to the plaintiff to rebut that claim."[41] The court continued: "if the monopolist's procompetitive justification stands unrebutted, then the plaintiff must demonstrate that the anticompetitive harm of the conduct outweighs the procompetitive benefit."[42] It concluded by

---

applies"); Mark Giuseppini, *The US Supreme Court dismisses an appeal brought by the US Government and a number of US States regarding a two-sided platform (Ohio / AMEX)*, 25 June 2018, *e-Competitions* June 2018, Art. N° 88608.

38 253 F.3d 34 (D.C. Cir. 2001).

39 *Id.* at 58.

40 *Id.* at 58–59.

41 *Id.* at 59.

42 *Id.* The framework articulated in *Microsoft* has been followed by other courts of appeals, as well. *See, e.g.*, Viamedia, Inc. v. Comcast Corp., 951 F.3d 429, 463-64 (7th Cir. 2020); Suture Express, Inc. v. Owens & Minor Distrib., Inc., 851 F.3d 1029, 1038 (10th Cir. 2017); New York, *ex rel.* Schneiderman v. Actavis PLC, 787 F.3d 638, 652 (2d Cir. 2015); McWane, Inc. v. FTC, 783 F.3d 814, 833 (11th Cir. 2015); Helen Cho Eckert, David R. Garcia, *The US Court of Appeals for the*

connecting this approach to Section 1's rule of reason: "[i]n cases arising under § 1 of the Sherman Act, the courts routinely apply a similar balancing approach under the rubric of the 'rule of reason.'"[43]

Although the court's mere mention of the "rule of reason" in connection with Section 2 prompted criticism from commentators concerned about the purportedly "unstructured" nature of Section 1's rule of reason, the DC Circuit stood on sound historical ground. As it noted,[44] *Standard Oil*, itself, had linked Sections 1 and 2 together, asserting that the concept of reasonableness was at the core of both provisions of the Sherman Act:

> ... having, by the first section [of the Sherman Act] forbidden all means of monopolizing trade, that is, unduly restraining it by means of every contract, combination, etc., the second section seeks, if possible, to make the prohibitions of the act all the more complete and perfect by embracing all attempts to reach the end prohibited by the first section, that is, restraints of trade, by any attempt to monopolize, or monopolization thereof, even although the acts by which such results are attempted to be brought about or are brought about be not embraced within the general enumeration of the first section. *And, of course, when the second section is thus harmonized with and made as it was intended to be the complement of the first, it becomes obvious that the criteria to be resorted to in any given case for the purpose of ascertaining whether violations of the section have been committed is the rule of reason, guided by the established law and by the plain duty to enforce the prohibitions of the act, and thus the public policy which its restrictions were obviously enacted to subserve.*[45]

Viewed together, therefore, *Microsoft* and *Polygram* paved the way to a more operational rule of reason for all Sherman Act offenses that was better equipped for use in the context of litigation and more focused on the centrality of competitive effects.

11th Circuit holds that a rebate program requiring exclusivity from distributors was an unlawful maintenance of monopoly power (McWane), 15 April 2015, *e-Competitions* April 2015, Art. N° 72658. It is structurally similar to the burden-shifting framework that had been endorsed by the Supreme Court for employment discrimination claims in McDonnell Douglas Corp. v. Green, 411 U.S. 792, 802–03 (1973).

43 253 F.3d at 59. *See also* Aspen Skiing Co. v. Aspen Highlands Skiing Corp., 472 U.S. 585, 602–03; 605–09 (1985) (defining "exclusionary" and implicitly embracing a burden-shifting approach that takes into account anticompetitive and procompetitive effects).

44 253 F.3d at 59 ("The source of the rule of reason is *Standard Oil*... in which the Supreme Court used the term to describe the proper inquiry under both sections of the Act.").

45 *Standard Oil Co.*, 221 U.S. at 61–62 (emphasis added).

IV. Structured Analysis of Horizontal Mergers

The DC Circuit, on which Judge Ginsburg serves, took the lead in developing the modern approach to the review of horizontal mergers under Section 7 of the Clayton Act, which combines burden-shifting with application of a sliding scale.[46] The circuit court did so in parallel with its efforts to structure rule-of-reason review under the Sherman Act. The Clayton Act and Sherman Act decisions evolved analogously and, most likely, influenced each other.

Before the first of the key DC Circuit decisions was handed down in 1990, horizontal merger analysis was governed primarily by Supreme Court precedents from the 1960s and early 1970s. In those cases, the Court employed an approach analogous to the bifurcated rule of reason it applied contemporaneously to resolve horizontal agreements reviewed under Sherman Act §1. In *Philadelphia National Bank* (*PNB*),[47] decided in 1963, the Court established that horizontal mergers would be presumed to harm competition when the merged firm would control an "undue" share of the market and the merger would result in a "significant" increase in market concentration.

As applied by the courts, the structural presumption established in *PNB* operated much like a per se rule against horizontal mergers. First, the presumption was easily triggered: it kicked in at very low levels of market concentration. In two cases decided three years later, *Von's Grocery*[48] and *Pabst*,[49] the Court applied the presumption to block mergers when the merged firm had, by today's standards, small shares in unconcentrated markets. In addition, although the *PNB* presumption was formally rebuttable through evidence "clearly showing" that a merger was not likely to lessen competition substantially, the 1960s Supreme Court consistently expressed hostility towards any reliance on merger efficiencies to do so.[50] In practice, therefore, as Justice Stewart observed in his *Von's Grocery* dissent, it seemed that "the Government always wins."[51] In the

---

46 Judge Ginsburg did not sit on the panels that wrote the influential merger opinions. He pushed toward less structured merger review while serving as Assistant Attorney General for Antitrust, and, in recent writing, endorsed the way the DC Circuit relaxed the evidentiary burden on defendants in one of its key merger decisions. *See* Douglas H. Ginsburg & Joshua D. Wright, Philadelphia National Bank: *Bad Economics, Bad Law, Good Riddance,* 80 Antitrust L.J. 377, 392–93 (2015). He did the latter without commenting on the court's burden-shifting approach and sliding-scale analysis, except insofar as his hostility to the *PNB* presumption suggested that he would prefer that plaintiffs not be permitted to rely on market concentration alone to establish a prima facie case.

47 United States v. Philadelphia Nat'l Bank, 374 U.S. 321 (1963).

48 United States v. Von's Grocery Co., 384 U.S. 270 (1966).

49 United States v. Pabst Brewing Co., 384 U.S. 546 (1966).

50 *PNB*, 374 U.S. at 370–71; FTC v. Procter & Gamble Co., 386 U.S. 568, 580 (1967). *See also* Brown Shoe Co. v. United States 370 U.S. 294, 344 (1962).

51 *Von's Grocery*, 384 U.S. at 301 (Stewart, J, dissenting).

wake of these cases, the Justice Department promulgated merger guidelines expressing its intention to challenge all but the smallest mergers when the four leading firms accounted for at least three-fourths of market sales, outside of unusual circumstances.[52]

General Dynamics,[53] the last major Supreme Court decision governing mergers,[54] handed down in 1974, showed that the merging firms could actually prevail. But the successful rebuttal was on narrow grounds: the government did not successfully establish the factual predicate for applying the structural presumption because it relied on market shares measured in units that did not reflect the merged firm's future competitive significance.[55] Only later, as discussed below, did the lower courts recognize that *General Dynamics* could be read more broadly to permit a wide-ranging rebuttal based on an analysis of whether market shares provided a basis for an accurate prediction of the merger's competitive effects.

During the Reagan administration, the Justice Department questioned the near – per se approach established in the 1960s. Perhaps taking its cue from non-merger decisions like *GTE Sylvania*[56] and *BMI*,[57] which narrowed the application of per se prohibitions under Sherman Act §1, the Department advocated for a wider reasonableness review of horizontal mergers. When it revised the merger guidelines in 1982, the Justice Department indicated that unless market shares and concentration were low, it would examine "a variety of other factors," including entry conditions and factors related to the ease and profitability of collusion, in determining whether to challenge a proposed acquisition.[58]

---

52 US Dep't of Justice, Merger Guidelines (1968), *reprinted in* 4 Trade Reg. Rep (CCH) ¶ 13,101.

53 United States v. General Dynamics, 415 U.S. 486 (1974).

54 *See also* United States v. Citizens & S. Nat'l Bank, 422 U.S. 86, 120 (1975) ("the Government plainly made out a prima facie case of a violation of [§] 7 under several decisions of this Court. It was thus incumbent upon C & S to show that the market-share statistics gave an inaccurate account of the acquisitions' probable effects on competition"). *General Dynamics* is generally regarded as the last major Supreme Court decision interpreting the Clayton Act § 7, although the Supreme Court issued substantive decisions in three bank merger cases, including *Citizens & Southern*, shortly after *General Dynamics* was handed down. The enactment of the Hart-Scott-Rodino Antitrust Improvements Act in 1976, which created a system of premerger notification, contributed to the absence of Supreme Court merger decisions by drastically reducing post-consummation challenges, which are more likely than pre-consummation challenges to be litigated and appealed. In addition, 1974 amendments to the antitrust expediting act eliminated direct appeals by the Justice Department to the Supreme Court. Antitrust Procedures and Penalties Act – Expediting Act, Pub. L. 93-528, § 4, 88 Stat. 1708 (1974).

55 *See* Hospital Corp. of Am. v. FTC, 807 F.2d 1381, 1385–86 (7th Cir. 1986) (Posner, J.) (describing *General Dynamics* as a case with "highly unusual facts" that "carve[d] only [a] limited exception[] to the broad holdings of some of the merger decisions of the 1960s.").

56 Cont'l T.V., Inc. v. GTE Sylvania Inc., 433 U.S. 36 (1977).

57 Broad. Music, Inc. v. Columbia Broad. Sys., Inc., 441 U.S. 1 (1979).

58 US Dep't of Justice, Merger Guidelines (1982), *reprinted in* 4 Trade Reg. Rep (CCH) ¶ 13,102.

The guidelines' shift toward an unstructured reasonableness review was dramatic but not quite complete. The "other factors" were described as most relevant when market concentration and its increase from merger were in a middle range, above safe harbor levels and below levels where a challenge was termed likely. In addition, the guidelines suggested how litigation burdens should be allocated by terming efficiencies a "defense" and requiring that the merging firms establish them "by clear and convincing evidence."[59]

In 1986, as Assistant Attorney General for Antitrust, Douglas Ginsburg asked Congress to revise Clayton Act §7 to codify a much less structured merger review.[60] The Merger Modernization Act he advocated would have directed courts to consider six economic factors – market shares, ease of entry, the ability of small rivals to expand, the nature of the product and terms of sale, past conduct of market participants, and efficiencies – as well as any other evidence indicating whether the acquisition would substantially increase the likelihood of a greater exercise of market power.[61] Ginsburg described the proposed merger legislation as an effort to simply codify the Justice Department's enforcement policy under the revised merger guidelines,[62] though it seemed somewhat less skeptical about efficiencies than the then-current guidelines.[63]

Major appellate merger precedents handed down during the early to mid-1980s followed the Justice Department's lead by adopting what amounted to a comprehensive reasonableness review of mergers. In *United States v. Waste Management, Inc.*, the Second Circuit framed that review with *General Dynamics* in mind as an inquiry as to whether market shares accurately predict future market power.[64] The appeals court held that a defendant could rebut the government's prima facie case based on market concentration – the basis for the structural presumption in *PNB* – by showing that entry is easy. Two years later, in an opinion for the

---

59 Although the guidelines are formally a statement of government enforcement policy, they are often viewed as persuasive authority by courts interpreting the merger statute.

60 The proposed legislation also sought to remove the incipiency language in § 7 and to focus merger analysis on market power rather than social and political goals. These aspects of the Clayton Act had supported the hostility to mergers reflected in 1960s Supreme Court merger decisions. *See* Douglas H. Ginsburg, *The Reagan Administration's Legislative Initiative in Antitrust*, 31 ANTITRUST BULL. 851 (1986).

61 *Id.*

62 *Interview with Douglas H. Ginsburg*, 55 ANTITRUST L.J. 255, 270–71 (1986).

63 The 1984 revisions to the merger guidelines, US DEP'T OF JUSTICE, MERGER GUIDELINES (1984), *reprinted in* 4 Trade Reg. Rep (CCH) ¶ 13,103, described the Department's approach to efficiencies in more detail than the 1982 guidelines, but both required the merging firms to establish efficiencies "by clear and convincing evidence." The proposed merger statute contemplated that the merging firms would be required to demonstrate efficiencies, but not by clear and convincing evidence. *See* Andrew G. Berg, *Cost Efficiencies in the Section 7 Calculus: A Review of the Doctrine*, 37 CASE W. RES. L. REV. 218, 230 (1986).

64 United States v. Waste Management, Inc., 743 F.2d 976 (2d Cir. 1984).

Seventh Circuit in *Hospital Corp. of America* upholding an FTC decision finding two acquisitions in violation of the Clayton Act, Judge Posner undertook a wide-ranging analysis of the competitive consequences of the transactions.[65] Posner emphasized that it was prudent for the FTC "to inquire into the probability of harm to consumers" rather than to rely solely on "the very strict merger decisions of the 1960s."

By the end of the 1980s, accordingly, horizontal merger law was shifting away from the near – per se illegality approach of the 1960s Supreme Court, and toward a wide-ranging reasonableness analysis of the economic effects of the transaction. The alternatives were presented implicitly as a bifurcated choice reminiscent of the way the rule of reason was described in *NSPE*: between the near – per se approach employed by the Supreme Court in the wake of *PNB* and a largely unstructured analysis of the merger's economic effects suggested by the merger guidelines and the mid-1980s appellate decisions.

Following the analytical structure laid out in *PNB,* the alternatives were described in burden-shifting terms. But in the 1980s, burden-shifting was a vehicle for determining whether to classify the case in a category where it would likely be found to violate the statute, or in a category in which an unstructured economic review would be undertaken. The contested terrain in that period was largely concerned with the concentration level above which the near – per se approach would apply.[66]

Against this background, the DC Circuit made two critical analytical moves toward adopting a hybrid analysis – one located between the traditional poles – in its 1990 *Baker Hughes* decision,[67] though that implication was not fully evident until 2001, when the same court decided *Heinz*.[68] Judge Ginsburg was on the circuit court at the time but did not serve on either panel.[69] The analytical innovations were to make the burden-shifting structure more explicit and to emphasize the use of a sliding scale to determine the magnitude of the defendant's rebuttal burden. Neither decision referred to key Sherman Act decisions like *BMI* and *NCAA* that opened the door to structured analyses under that statute, but they had a similar effect in authorizing a structured reasonableness analysis akin to that which was developing in the contemporary cases under Sections 1 and 2.

---

65 Hospital Corp. of Am. v. FTC, 807 F.2d 1381 (7th Cir. 1986) (Posner, J.).

66 *Cf.* William E. Kovacic, *Assessing the Quality of Competition Policy: The Case of Horizontal Merger Enforcement*, 5 Competition Pol'y Int'l 129, 143 (2009) (describing a reduction in the threshold number of significant rivals above which the enforcement agencies would begin to scrutinize mergers strictly, based in part on changing judicial interpretations of merger law, "in the following manner: 1960s (12 to 11), 1970s (9 to 8), 1980s (6 to 5), 1990s (4 to 3), 2000s (4 to 3)").

67 United States v. Baker Hughes, Inc., 908 F.2d 981 (D.C. Cir. 1990).

68 FTC v. H.J. Heinz Co., 246 F.3d 708 (D.C. Cir. 2001). *Heinz* extended the *Baker Hughes* framework from the merits stage of merger litigation to preliminary injunction review.

69 We do not know the extent to which either panel drew informally on Judge Ginsburg's antitrust expertise.

Baker Hughes cast a long shadow because the federal enforcement agencies are the plaintiffs in almost all merger challenges, and those agencies typically prefer to file suit in the District of Columbia. It was also influential because it was written by Clarence Thomas and joined by Ruth Bader Ginsburg, both of whom were elevated from the DC Circuit to the Supreme Court within the next three years.

The *Baker Hughes* decision brought to the foreground the burden-shifting structure of the analytical approach set forth in *PNB*. The decision described the factual predicate for invoking the structural presumption – a showing that the proposed merger will lead to undue concentration – as establishing a prima facie case. When a plaintiff does so, the burden of production shifts to the merging firms to produce rebuttal evidence sufficient to undermine the prediction of anticompetitive effects suggested by *PNB*. If the merging firms successfully satisfy their burden, the government bears the burden of undermining that evidence and/or producing additional evidence of anticompetitive effect and retains the ultimate burden of persuasion. In addition, the decision announced that evidence would be weighed on a sliding scale: "The more compelling the prima facie case, the more evidence the defendant must present to rebut it successfully." The sliding scale recognized that evidence satisfying the plaintiff's initial burden can vary in strength, and it calibrated the merging parties' burden to reflect that strength.

In applying its interpretation of *PNB* to the facts before it, though, the *Baker Hughes* panel used language that encouraged an unstructured reasonableness analysis. It characterized the Supreme Court's decisions as having "adopted a totality-of-the-circumstances approach to the statute, weighing a variety of factors." The decision went on to explain that "Evidence of market concentration simply provides a convenient starting point for a broader inquiry into future competitiveness."[70] On the facts, moreover, the Court concluded that the district court properly found that "the prima facie case inaccurately depicted the probable anticompetitive effect" of the merger. It credited evidence that market shares were volatile and shifting, that sophisticated buyers would promote competition, and that entry barriers were low. In practice, therefore, the court's totality-of-the-circumstances analysis operated similarly to the unstructured review characteristic of mid-1980s appellate decisions.

The possibility for a structured review that would fall between the per se and comprehensive reasonableness approaches, created by the combination of

70 The court also indicated that it would be "anomalous" to impose a heavy burden of production on a defendant when it is easy to establish a prima facie case "simply by presenting market concentration statistics." *Baker Hughes,* 908 F.2d at 992. In a recent article Judge Ginsburg argued, consistent with a possible implication of this language, that courts should not rely on high post-merger concentration as a basis for presuming that horizontal mergers are illegal. Douglas H. Ginsburg & Joshua D. Wright, Philadelphia National Bank*: Bad Economics, Bad Law, Good Riddance,* 80 ANTITRUST L.J. 377, 384–86 (2015).

burden-shifting and a sliding scale, became evident 11 years later, when a different DC Circuit panel decided *Heinz*.[71] In applying the framework for merger analysis set forth in *Baker Hughes*, the *Heinz* panel indicated that courts should, in practice as well as in theory, give more weight to a strong prima facie case based on concentration.

The district court had declined to enjoin the merger. It found that coordination was unlikely after the merger of the two smaller firms in a three-firm market, for two main reasons: the remaining two firms would have difficulty deterring cheating, and the substantial efficiencies that the merger would generate would give the merged firm a greater ability and incentive to compete more aggressively with the industry leader than either merging firm had before.

The circuit court reversed and remanded for entry of a preliminary injunction. It observed that the lower court had found that the market was highly concentrated: the merger would have created a duopoly. The district court also found that the merger would result in the loss of substantial direct competition, and that barriers to market entry were high. These facts added up to a strong prima facie case.

To rebut that case, the appellate panel held, the district court would have needed to specify reasons unique to the industry to support the conclusion that post-merger coordination would be especially difficult, sufficient to overcome the ordinary presumption of coordination in a merger to duopoly. In its view, the rebuttal facts in the record were insufficient to overcome this elevated bar, so, the panel concluded, the government plaintiff should prevail.[72]

As the *Heinz* decision implicitly recognized, the combination of burden-shifting and a sliding scale can order merger analysis to permit a type of structured inquiry. As with the analogous rules developed for evaluating reasonableness under the Sherman Act, this has the practical consequence of creating a hybrid form of analysis between a bright line per se rule and a comprehensive and unstructured reasonableness review. On the facts credited by the circuit court in *Heinz*, the government met its initial burden of demonstrating probable anticompetitive effects owing to a very high degree of post-merger concentration, but the defendants failed to satisfy their burden of production to rebut it. The court

---

71 One of the authors of this paper, Jonathan Baker, testified for *Heinz* in the district court as an economic expert. He describes the economic evidence presented in litigation in Jonathan B. Baker, *Efficiencies and High Concentration: Heinz Proposes to Acquire Beech-Nut (2001)*, *in* The Antitrust Revolution 157 (John E. Kwoka, Jr. & Lawrence J. White eds., 5th ed. 2008).

72 Post-merger concentration levels in *Baker Hughes* were nearly as high as in *Heinz*. But when *Baker Hughes* was decided, proof of ease of entry, the main defense in that case, was well established as a route for rebutting the government's prima facie case. By contrast, proof that competition would not be harmed because of the beneficial effects of merger-related efficiencies, the main defense in *Heinz*, was less well established when that case was decided (and remains so today). This difference provides an alternative explanation for the differing outcomes of the two cases.

decided the case for the government based importantly on the heavy probative weight it gave to the evidence of market concentration introduced by the government to satisfy its prima facie case.

Lower court decisions reviewing horizontal mergers since, even outside the DC Circuit, routinely apply the burden-shifting framework articulated in *Baker Hughes* and *Heinz*.[73] In some cases, courts have used the combination of burden-shifting and the sliding scale to condemn proposed mergers on an abbreviated review, without undertaking a comprehensive balancing of the evidence of predicted pro- and anticompetitive effects. That happens when the government wins because the defendant does not successfully rebut the prima facie case,[74] and when the court relies on the observation that the merging firms' rebuttal burden is heightened by very high concentration.[75] On the other hand, the merging parties have benefited from the sliding scale, and prevailed on a review that falls short of comprehensive reasonableness analysis, when the court determines that the government's prima facie case, while satisfied, is relatively weak.[76] The merging firms have also prevailed when the court concluded that the government failed to establish a prima facie case.[77] The burden-shifting

---

73 The DC Circuit's influence has been both direct and indirect. Looking to appellate decisions from outside the DC Circuit, Chicago Bridge & Iron Co. v. FTC, 534 F.3d 410, 423–24 (5th Cir 2008), relied heavily on *Baker Hughes*. In Saint Alphonsus Med. Ctr. v. St. Luke's Health Sys., 778 F.3d 775, 783 (9th Cir 2015), the Ninth Circuit looked primarily to *Chicago Bridge* in setting forth its analytical framework. See, Jonathan L. Lewis, *A U.S. Court of Appeals upholds that the theory of harm articulated by the FTC in hospital merger cases is fully applicable to physician acquisition cases and that the positive impact on competition of the claimed efficiencies must be clearly demonstrated (St. Luke's Health System / Saltzer Medical Group)*, 10 February 2015, *e-Competitions* February 2015, Art. N° 71656. In FTC v. Penn State Hershey Med. Ctr., 838 F.3d 327, 337 (3d Cir. 2016), the Third Circuit relied mainly on *Saint Alphonsus*. See, Ashley M. Fischer, Jeffrey Brennan, *The US Court of Appeals for the Seventh Circuit overturns a district court decision which denies a motion by the FTC to enjoin the proposed merger in a hospital merger case (FTC / Advocate Health Network)*, 31 October 2016, *e-Competitions* October 2016, Art. N° 93137.

74 *See, e.g.*, ProMedica Health Sys., Inc. v. FTC, 749 F.3d 559, 572 (6th Cir. 2014), Steven C. Sunshine, Clifford H. Aronson, Sharis A. Pozen, *The US Court of Appeals for the Sixth Circuit confirms the decision of the FTC regarding a merger in the healthcare sector (ProMedica)*, 22 April 2014, *e-Competitions* April 2014, Art. N° 66909; United States v. Bazaarvoice, Inc., 2014 WL 203966, at *70 (N.D. Cal. 2014), Gregory E. Heltzer, Andrea L. Hamilton, Christian Krohs, Daniel Powers, David Henry, *The US Court of the Northern District of California rules against an acquisition of a competitor on the basis that it would lead to anticompetitive effects in the high-tech market (Bazaarvoice / PowerReviews)*, 8 January 2014, *e-Competitions* January 2014, Art. N° 93319; Olin Corp. v. FTC, 986 F.2d 1295, 1305 (9th Cir 1993); United States v. United Tote, Inc., 768 F. Supp. 1064, 1087 (D. Del. 1991); United States v. Energy Solutions, Inc., 265 F. Supp.3d 415 (D. Del 2017); United States v. Tribune Pub. Co., 2016 WL 2989488, at *4–5 (C.D. Cal. 2016).

75 United States v. Anthem, Inc., 855 F.3d 345, 364 (D.C. Cir. 2017); *Bazaarvoice,* 2014 WL 203966, at *70; FTC v. OSF Healthcare Sys., 852 F. Supp.2d 1069, 1082 (N.D. Ill. 2012).

76 FTC v. Foster, 2007 WL 1793441, at *56 (D. N.M, 2007); FTC v. Arch Coal, Inc., 329 F. Supp.2d 109, 129-30 (D.D.C. 2004).

77 United States v. Sungard Data Sys., Inc., 172 F. Supp.2d 172 (D.D.C. 2001); United States v. Oracle Corp., 331 F. Supp.2d 1098, 1155, 1175 (N.D. Cal. 2004); FTC v. Lab. Corp., 2011 WL 3100372, at *21 (C.D. Cal. 2011).

structure does not invariably mandate the result: even if the merging firms successfully rebut the government's prima facie case, the government may still satisfy its burden of persuasion by bringing additional evidence to bear beyond the concentration statistics it relied on to meet its initial burden of production.[78] Under such circumstances, a strong prima facie case may count in the government's favor,[79] or the government may simply prevail on what amounts to totality-of-the-circumstances reasonableness review.[80]

As this brief survey suggests, courts now routinely seek to structure horizontal merger reviews using the analytical framework established by the DC Circuit in *Baker Hughes* and *Heinz* and influenced more broadly by developments under Sections 1 and 2 of the Sherman Act. That approach may shape horizontal merger analysis going forward in two ways. First, the courts may adopt the views of commentators who call for strengthening the sliding scale by heightening the practical burden of production on merging firms when the plaintiff has made a strong prima facie case.[81] Second, the courts can be expected to allow the government to meet its prima facie case, and shift the burden with evidence other than concentration: particularly evidence that one merging firm's products are the second choice for a substantial fraction of the customers of its merger partner's products, which suggests unilateral competitive effects, or that one of the merging firms is a maverick constraining coordination from becoming more likely or more effective, which suggests coordinated effects.[82] These possibilities would probably not have been evident to Judge Ginsburg in 1986, to then-judges Clarence Thomas and Ruth Bader Ginsburg in 1990, or to the DC Circuit panel that decided *Heinz* in 2001, but they are reasonable forecasts about the way *Baker Hughes* and *Heinz* will evolve in the current environment.[83]

---

78 FTC v. Cardinal Health, Inc., 12 F. Supp.2d 34, 63 (D.D.C.1998); FTC v. Staples, Inc., 190 F. Supp.3d 100 (D.D.C. 2016).

79 FTC v. CCC Holdings Inc., 605 F. Supp. 2d 26, 75 (D.D.C. 2009), Steven C. Sunshine, James A. Keyte, Benjamin C., Jr. Crisman, *The US District Court of Columbia grants FTC request for preliminary injunction to block a 3-2 transaction in the market for electronic systems used to estimate the cost of collision repairs (CCC Holdings / Aurora Equity Partners)*, 18 March 2009, *e-Competitions* March 2009, Art. N° 45551; FTC v. Sysco Corp., 113 F. Supp.3d 1, 72 (D.D.C. 2015); FTC v. Wilh. Wilhelmsen Holding ASA, 341 F. Supp.3d 27, 66 (D.D.C. 2018). That is, the presumption of anticompetitive effect continues to have probative weight after the merging firms successfully meet their burden of production.

80 United States v. H&R Block, Inc., 833 F. Supp. 2d 36, 81, 92 (D.D.C. 2011), James A. Keyte, *The US District Court for the District of Columbia blocks a merger in the digital do-it-yourself tax preparation software industry providing insights on evidence to use on S. 7 challenge (H&R Block / TaxAct)*, 10 November 2011, *e-Competitions* November 2011, Art. N° 45926; United States v. Aetna Inc., 240 F. Supp.3d 1 (2017); FTC v. Tronox Ltd., 332 F. Supp.3d 187 (D.D.C. 2018).

81 Jonathan B. Baker, The Antitrust Paradigm: Restoring a Competitive Economy 79 (2019); John Kwoka, *The Structural Presumption and the Safe Harbor in Merger Review: False Positives or Unwarranted Concerns*, 81 Antitrust L.J. 837, 872 (2017).

82 *See generally* Baker, *supra* note 81, at 79–80.

83 Truly "truncated" analysis in the sense of *NCAA* (i.e., "evidence of actual harm") is more likely to occur in the evaluation of consummated mergers than in the evaluation of proposed acquisitions.

V. Conclusion

Today's rule of reason is moored by the analysis of competitive effects, and the structured framework for assessing those effects can be observed across all areas of antitrust law. In this paper, we have sketched the formative period in which this framework emerged and evolved, often not as a means of filtering "weak" cases, although it served that function, too, but instead as a way to assist courts in identifying and more readily condemning unreasonably anticompetitive conduct, be it collusion between rivals, exclusionary conduct by a single firm, or mergers. In multiple ways across his impressive career, Judge Ginsburg played an important role in promoting these kinds of improvements to the administrability of the antitrust laws, and to our understanding of the common role of structured analysis across all of these types of conduct.

PART II

Rethinking Antitrust: Institutions, Policy and Proceedings

Independence in Competition Policy and Enforcement

Antonio Bavasso*
Allen and Overy LLP, University College London

Abstract

Independence has been a mainstay of competition policy and enforcement in Europe and other jurisdictions. However, this principle has been called into question in recent years. This paper looks at the principle of independence, focusing on the EU and the UK, along two axes: (1) appointment and institutional design; (2) case selection and prioritisation. It argues that independence remains fundamental to effective competition law enforcement. The paper describes how the EU and UK institutions are designed to foster independence and argues that accountability is necessary to maintain it, with competition authorities subject to both "hard" accountability (thought judicial review) and "soft" accountability vis à vis the political system. Ultimately, independence does not mean competition authorities should be oblivious to the political context in which they operate; but rather, must maintain a dialogue with the executive to ensure the relevance of their actions.

---

* Partner, Allen & Overy LLP; Visiting Professor at University College London, Co-founder and Executive Director of the Jevons Institute for Competition Law and Economics at University College London. I am grateful to Chris Best for his excellent research and input and to Mark Friend, John Fingleton, Philip Marsden and Louise Tolley for their comments on earlier drafts.

I. Introduction

Independence has been a mainstay of competition policy and enforcement in Europe and in many jurisdictions that have followed the same model. However, the perception of regulatory failure that led to the financial crisis, the rhetoric of political supremacy over technical expertise, the renewed attention on the application of "public interest" tests in some jurisdictions, and the quest for new tools of enforcement to meet the challenges of the so-called "new economy" in light of the alleged inadequacies of the current antitrust paradigm, all call this principle into question.

The principle of political independence of competition authorities is widely accepted internationally. However, in practice it takes a multiplicity of forms from jurisdiction to jurisdiction and it has an impact on a number of dimensions of competition law and policy. This paper looks in greater detail at the experience of the EU and that of the UK with comparative references to other jurisdictions within the EU and elsewhere. The experience in the EU and the UK jurisdictions is interesting for a number of reasons.

First, the origin and rationale for independence in competition law enforcement have some peculiarities which derive from the nature of competition law and practice within the institutional framework of the EU. However, as is the case with many aspects of the EU legal order, the principle has evolved beyond its original rationale over the initial decades of application. In light of the inter-relation between the EU and national jurisdictions, the principle of independence in competition law enforcement has had an impact on the institutional design of Member States' competition authorities, which have proliferated over the last 20 years and aligned to the EU system with some important distinctions. Moreover the general principles that have emerged within this system have often been looked at and considered elsewhere as a result of international organisations such the OECD and the ICN.

The comparison with the UK regime is particularly interesting for two reasons. First, because, notwithstanding its substantive alignment with the EU, the UK regime has maintained a number of interesting distinctive features, such as the ability to intervene on public interest grounds in relation to mergers and more widely in relation to markets (with the potentially far-reaching ability to impose remedies in case of a negative finding, even in the absence of unlawful conduct and competition law infringement). Second, because Brexit provides at least an opportunity to consider certain aspects of the institutional design and remit of UK competition enforcement, and the strength of the independence of the UK Competition & Markets Authority (CMA) can be an important consideration.

This paper looks at the principle of independence along two axes: (1) appointment and institutional design, (2) case selection and prioritisation. It then offers some conclusions and reflections on outcome and accountability. It concludes that now more than ever independence in competition law enforcement is required. Independence does not mean that a competition authority should be oblivious of the general political context within which it operates. To the contrary, a competition authority must maintain a dialogue with both the executive branch and elected representatives to ensure the relevance of its actions as well as to maintain a credible advocacy role in assisting other areas of policy and even legislation when it is afforded those powers. This form of "soft accountability" is desirable, if coupled with strong measures to protect an authority from pressure points. As a law enforcement agency, a competition authority should also be subject to hard accountability through the judicial process. This is important and, far from creating tension, this dimension is a guarantor of independence because judicial oversight of the application of the law has the effect of pushing a competition authority to adopt procedures that would withstand judicial scrutiny and indirectly preserve the integrity of the system.

I hope that this paper will be a fitting tribute to Judge Douglas Ginsburg, whose distinguished career has traversed at the highest level federal government positions (including as head of the antitrust division at the US Department of Justice (DoJ) and as administrator of the Office of Information and Regulatory Affairs), the bench and academia. Judge Ginsburg has made a gigantic contribution to the field of antitrust internationally with intellectual rigour, independence and integrity of the highest calibre.

II. Independence: Why and From What?

The benefits of political independence are generally widely accepted within the "community" of regulatory experts and enforcers, but it is worth looking at a commonly held assumption to understand its rationale. John Vickers, in comparing the rationale for independence in competition and monetary policy independence, put forward a convincing reason along two strands: "comparative advantage" and "commitment".[1] First, if competition policy is comparatively better at achieving the goal of preserving competition to the exclusion of other objectives (for instance employment) that task can be safely entrusted to technocrats, independent from political interference. Second, in Vickers' view, independent competition authorities are more committed to "resistance of certain kinds of anticompetitive policy at national level".

These strands focus on specific dimensions of competition policy: the direct relationship with the executive political power and the relationship between national policy and the international order. There is also a rationale in ensuring that competition policy is insulated from partisan interests (either business or

1 J Vickers, "Central Banks and Competition Authorities: Institutional Comparisons and New Concerns" (November 2020) BIS Working Paper N 331, 16.

consumer groups) that can infiltrate more readily the political sphere or indeed "capture" policymaking and enforcement,[2] a concern more frequently raised in relation to sectoral regulators who have repeated contacts with their stakeholders.

Crucially, a large part of competition policy is made through decision-making. The remit of a competition authority typically has a strong component of law enforcement (and through repeated application of the law to the same question, e.g. abuse of dominant position) forming a body of precedents which is necessarily subject to judicial review. Therefore the guarantees that we expect from the judiciary – including independence and absence of bias – necessarily need to apply to competition authorities providing a further rationale in a way that does not apply to other policy areas, including monetary policy. Such a judicial accountability of law enforcement (and the policymaking that comes with it) is therefore ultimately a guarantor of independence.

Of course, independence remains subject to the sovereign powers of the democratically elected legislator which retains supremacy to set the substantive test to be applied with the ordinary checks and balances of primary legislation and the relevant constitutional framework. In this respect, independence of competition law at EU level is particularly resilient because the substantive competition law provisions (and indeed many of the rules underpinning its enforcement) are based on the treaties (from the original Treaty of Rome to the current Treaty on the Functioning of the European Union (TFEU)). Within the EU these safeguards of "constitutional ranking" have indirectly spread at national level as a result of the 2004 reform decentralising EU competition law enforcement. Under Regulation 1/2003, national competition authorities ensure effective compliance with treaty provisions relating to competition law.[3] Notwithstanding the acknowledgement of a "wide variation… in the public enforcement systems of Member States",[4] the interdependence that is inherent in the decentralised application of EU competition law brings about a certain degree of "commitment" (in the sense used by Vickers above) to shared principles and soft oversight within the European Competition Network.[5] A similar dynamic would apply in the context of merger control, given the potential for referrals to and from the European Commission to Member States.

---

2 F Jenny, "Competition Authorities: Independence and Advocacy", in I Lianos and DD Sokol (eds), *The Global Limits of Competition Law* (Stanford University Press 2012), 160.

3 See Council Regulation 1/2003 on the implementation of the rules on competition laid down in Articles 81 and 82 of the Treaty [2003] OJ L1/1, Art 35 (Regulation 1/2003).

4 ibid, recital 35.

5 See Commission Staff Working Document, "Enhancing competition enforcement by the Member States' competition authorities: institutional and procedural issues" (SWD(2014) 231) in which the European Commission reviewed the independence and adequacy of financial resources of national competition authorities. See generally G Monti, "Independence, Interdependence and Legitimacy: The EU Commission, National Competition Authorities, and the European Competition Network" (2014) Working Paper, EUI Law 2014/01.

Moreover, the requirement to ensure effective application of the competition law provisions of the Treaty has given the Court of Justice an opportunity to interpret EU law so as to prompt reform of national rules.[6] Notwithstanding the principle of national procedural autonomy, it is not hard to see a similar approach being extended to other areas of the institutional design. In other areas that are regulated at European level, the principle of independence has an explicit legislative backing. For instance, Directive 95/46/EC on the processing of personal data required national regulatory authorities to act with complete independence in the exercise of their duties.[7] In that context, the Court of Justice has had an opportunity to clarify that independence involves remaining free from any external influence, including the direct or indirect influence of the state.[8] Maintaining such independence precludes any directions or influence that may "have an effect on the supervisory authority's decision".[9] Although functional or operational independence is instrumental in providing for the kind of independence required of a national supervisory authority, "such functional independence is not sufficient by itself to protect that supervisory authority from all external influence".[10] The mere risk that state scrutiny could result in political influence is enough to hinder the independence of a supervisory authority's tasks.[11] This is due to the fact that:

> First, there could be "prior compliance" on the part of those authorities in the light of the scrutinising authority's decision-making practice. Secondly, in view of the role adopted by those authorities as guardians of the right to private life, the second subparagraph of Article 28(1) of Directive 95/46 requires that their decisions – and, therefore, the authorities themselves – remain above all suspicion of partiality.[12]

Additionally, the Court found that the exercise of independence necessitates a Member State allowing a regulatory authority to serve its full term of office.[13]

---

6 In case C-439/08 *VEBIC* [2010] ECR I-2471, para 58, in a reference for preliminary ruling under Article 234 TFEU, the Court of Justice concluded that national rules that prevent a competition authority from appearing in judicial proceedings jeopardise the effectiveness of Articles 101 TFEU and 102 TFEU. This subsequently prompted a reform of the Belgian national rules. See, Martin Favart, *The European Court of Justice rules on the right of national competition authorities to participate in appeals against their own decisions (VEBIC)*, 7 December 2010, *e-Competitions* December 2010, Art. N° 41270.

7 Directive 95/46/EC of the European Parliament and of the Council on the protection of individuals with regard to the processing of personal data and on the free movement of such data, art 28(1). In the energy sector similar regulatory provisions apply: article 35(4) of Directive 2009/72/EC (electricity) and article 39(4) of Directive 2009/73/EC (gas) both require Member States to guarantee the independence of the regulatory authority and to ensure that it exercises its powers impartially and transparently.

8 Case C-518/07 *Commission v Germany* [2010] ECR I-1885, para 30.

9 Case C-614/10 *Commission v Austria* EU:C:2012:631, para 43.

10 ibid, para 42.

11 Case C-288/12 *Commission v Hungary* EU:C:2014:237, para 53.

12 ibid, para 53.

13 ibid, para 62.

The independence requirement "must necessarily be construed as covering the obligation to allow supervisory authorities to serve their full term of office and to have them vacate office before expiry of the full term only in accordance with the rules and safeguards established by the applicable legislation".[14]

So independence is justified – and indeed required – to support a number of fundamental features of a well-designed competition law enforcement system. It enables competition authorities to focus on their task to the exclusion of other areas of enforcement which are, and should remain, the domain of the executive branch of government with political responsibility; it recognises the important nature of authorities as decision-makers and law enforcers, subject to judicial accountability, absence of bias and avoidance of capture. The element of policy-making that derives from the decision-making function needs to provide the legal certainty and predictability to ensure the level playing field that is a fundamental prerequisite for investment.[15]

Crucially, however, independence does not mean that a competition authority itself should be oblivious of the general political context within which it operates. To the contrary, a competition authority must maintain a dialogue with both the executive branch and elected representatives to ensure the relevance of its action as well as to maintain a credible advocacy role in assisting in other areas of policy and even legislation when it is afforded those powers.[16]

A competition authority is subject to a number of potential "universal pressure points" for political control and influence. These include the appointment process, the funding mechanism, routine oversight, the nature of judicial review and ultimately a change of its remit and powers. As put by Kovacic, "no agency can prosper unless it takes into account [pressure points from executive and legislative bodies] and considers how to manoeuvre through the external political environment" and "complete forms of insulation from the political process deny the agency the ability to be an effective advocate for competition".[17] Kovacic goes as far as saying that "the more insulated the competition agency is from the political process, the narrower will be the powers a legislature is likely to entrust the agency".[18]

There are many shades and degrees of independence and to cover them all is outside the scope of this paper. Various aspects of institutional design have a

---

14 ibid, para 55.

15 Jenny (n 2) 160.

16 In the UK, the CMA has the power, under section 7 of the Enterprise Act 2002, to make and publish written recommendations to ministers on the impact of proposals for legislation on competition within any UK market(s) for goods or services.

17 W Kovacic, "Competition Agencies, Independence, and the Political Process" in J Drexl, W Kerber and R Podszun (eds), *Competition Policy and the Economic Approach* (Edward Elgar 2011).

18 ibid.

bearing on it. These range from the appointment procedure, the degree of operational independence and the relationship with the judiciary.

In the remainder of this paper I will selectively concentrate on two axes of independence, comparing the EU and the UK: appointment and prioritisation.

III. Appointment Mechanisms and Independence

1. European Commission and the Competition Commissioner

EU competition enforcement is entrusted to the European Commission, an institution which is essentially the European Union's executive, with a hybrid political and administrative dimension. However, the role of competition enforcement within the EU legal framework is designed to achieve the establishment of the internal market; therefore, the primary aim of independence at EU level is independence from Member States and, indirectly, the political influence that may come from the national level. Moreover, the European Commission is also in charge of State aid control against Member States. Independence is therefore in the "institutional DNA" of the Commission; it is an essential feature of its *raison d'etre*. This is reflected in the procedure for the appointment of the institution and extends into its modus operandi.

The President of the Commission is appointed through a procedure that originates from a political decision. The European Council, acting by a qualified majority, having (i) taken into account the elections to the European Parliament and (ii) held the appropriate consultations, proposes a candidate to the European Parliament (Article 17(7) of the Treaty on European Union (TEU)). Once that is completed, the standing President of the Commission requests the candidate to make a statement and present his or her political guidelines to the European Parliament (Rule 117(1) of the Rules of Procedure of the European Parliament (RPEP)). Parliament debates the statement, and the Council is invited to participate in the debate (Rule 117(1) RPEP). Parliament then elects the candidate by a majority of its component members (Article 17(7) TEU). The vote is taken by secret ballot (Rule 117(2) RPEP). Additionally, the Commission (including its President) is subject as a body to a vote of consent by the European Parliament. Following the grant of such consent, the Council appoints the Commission, acting by a qualified majority (Article 17(7) TEU).

Under Article 17(3) TEU, members of the Commission, including, of course, the Competition Commissioner, "shall be chosen on the ground of their general competence and European commitment from persons whose independence is beyond doubt". The President of the Commission conducts individual interviews with each nominated member of the Commission prior to their appointment in order to determine their independence.

The Competition Commissioner has the power to adopt various decisions in relation to the enforcement of EU competition law, through a number of different measures.[19] These powers are delegated to the Competition Commissioner under a comprehensive set of empowerments adopted by the Commission.[20] The Competition Commissioner may, unless prohibited under an empowerment decision and with the exception of the power to determine and issue a statement of objections (as discussed below), further sub-delegate her powers to a Director General and Head of Service.[21]

All empowerments must be exercised in accordance with the general rules relating to the empowerment procedure. In particular, before taking a decision, the Competition Commissioner must determine whether, on grounds of political sensitivity or because of its importance, the matter should be brought to the attention of the full Commission. Should there be any doubt as to this, the President of the Commission must be consulted.[22]

The decisions the Competition Commissioner is empowered to make in relation to enforcement of Regulation 1/2003 include the decision requesting information from undertakings; ordering inspections of undertakings; determination and issuance of a statement of objections to undertakings; preliminary assessments and decisions to reopen proceedings after a commitment decision; opinions for national courts; and refusal to supply confidential information.[23]

The determination and issuance of a statement of objections must be by agreement with the President of the Commission. The explanatory memorandum to the Regulation 1/2003 empowerments states that the involvement of the President of the Commission in this process is designed to ensure that he "intervenes as guarantor both of the principle of collegiality and of the credibility of the Commission as an impartial and objective enforcer of the law".[24] Moreover, in the event another Commissioner involved expresses "serious concern about any aspect of the case", they may seek a meeting with the President and/or the Competition Commissioner.[25]

---

19 DG Competition, "Antitrust Manual of Procedures" (2012) Internal working documents on procedures for the application of articles 101 and 102 TFEU, paras 22 and 24.

20 ibid, para. 23.

21 ibid, para 27.

22 ibid, para 30.

23 ibid, paras 25 and 26. The Competition Commissioner is empowered to make these decisions pursuant to Commission decisions PV(2004) 1655, SEC(2204) 520/2 as extended by PV(2006) 1763, SEC(2006) 1368, for the application of Regulation 1/2003 and implementing Regulation 773/2004.

24 Explanatory Memorandum to PV(2004) 1655, SEC(2204) 520/2, para 44.

25 ibid, para 45.

All final decisions on substance (including interim measures) and/or decisions of principle implying a wide margin of appreciation are reserved to the College. The normal procedure for the adoption of such decisions is the written procedure. However, for any matters that, in view of their economic or political sensitivity, the Competition Commissioner (having consulted the President of the Commission) considers should be debated, the oral procedure is used.[26] Independence from political influence from member states is regularly tested and often very visibly so. The most recent example related to the Commission's decision to prohibit the proposed merger between Alstom and Siemens in February 2019.[27] The Parties had argued that the merger was necessary to enable them to compete with global rivals, including China's CRRC. The Commission's prohibition provoked strong objections from the French and German governments, which had endorsed the transaction. French finance minister, Bruno Le Maire, described the decision as "a political mistake: the role of the commission is to defend the economic interests of Europe…The rejection of the Alstom-Siemens merger will serve China's economic and industrial interests."[28] Following the decision, France and Germany put forward joint proposals for reform, including to give representatives of Member States (through the Council) the power to override the Commission's merger decisions.[29] This particular reform proposal has seen little meaningful engagement from the Commission and, in fact, in later Franco-German proposals (including those made jointly with Poland[30], and more recently with both Poland and Italy[31]) this recommendation was not reiterated, although both subsequent proposals called for broader competition policy and decision-making input from Member States. Another (less radical) proposal, which formed part of the proposal by France, Germany, Poland and Italy, has, however, gained traction with the Commission: the review and update of the Commission's 1997 guidance on market definition.[32]

---

26 ibid, paras 19–21.

27 European Commission, "Mergers: Commission prohibits Siemens' proposed acquisition of Alstom" (6 February 2019) <https://ec.europa.eu/commission/presscorner/detail/en/IP_19_881>.

28 Financial Times, "EU blocks planned Siemens-Alstom rail deal in landmark decision" (6 February 2019) < https://www.ft.com/content/6e344f6a-29fd-11e9-88a4-c32129756dd8>.

29 "A Franco-German Manifesto for a European industrial policy fit for the 21st Century" (19 February 2019), available at <https://www.gouvernement.fr/sites/default/files/locale/piece-jointe/2019/02/1043_-_a_franco-german_manifesto_for_a_european_industrial_policy_fit_for_the_21st_century.pdf>. Also see Financial Times, "France calls for biggest shake-up of EU merger rules in 30 years" (12 February 2019) (<https://www.ft.com/content/ad7a02f4-2ebd-11e9-8744-e7016697f225>).

30 "Modernising EU Competition Policy" (4 July 2019), available at <https://www.bmwi.de/Redaktion/DE/Downloads/M-O/modernising-eu-competition-policy.pdf?__blob=publicationFile&v=4>.

31 Letter to Margrethe Vestager (4 February 2020) <https://g8fip1kplyr33r3krz5b97d1-wpengine.netdna-ssl.com/wp-content/uploads/2020/02/Letter-to-Vestager.pdf>.

32 Commission Notice on the definition of relevant market for the purposes of [EU] competition law [1997] OJ C372/5. In June 2020 the Commission launched a public consultation on whether and how this guidance can be revised in light of increasing globalisation and digitisation Available at <https://ec.europa.eu/

It is interesting to compare the EU rules to those for the appointment of the Chair and Chief Executive of the CMA. The basic rules governing the appointment of the Chair of the CMA are set out in Schedule 4 to the Enterprise and Regulatory Reform Act 2013 (ERRA).[33]

2. The Chair and Chief Executive of the UK CMA

The CMA Chair is appointed by the Secretary of State for a term of not more than five years. It is for the Secretary of State to determine the terms and conditions of appointments of the CMA, including remuneration.

In addition, the appointment of the Chair of the CMA is regulated by the Commissioner for Public Appointments (the Commissioner), under the Public Appointments Order in Council 2016 (the Order).[34] The Commissioner's primary role is to provide independent assurance that public appointments are made in accordance with the Governance Code (the Code) published by the Minister for the Cabinet Office under Article 3(1) of the Order. The Code sets out eight principles that apply to public appointments, as well as detailed guidance on how competitions should be run.

Under the Code, Ministers are to be assisted in their decision-making by Advisory Assessment Panels (Panels), including a departmental official and an independent member. Further, since the appointment of the Chair of the CMA is a "significant appointment" under paragraph 6.1 of the Code,[35] the Panel must also include a Senior Independent Panel Member: an individual familiar with senior recruitment and the Code, who is independent of the department and the body concerned, and not currently politically active. This member has specific responsibility for highlighting any material breaches of the Code in the appointments process.

The role of the Panel is to decide objectively which candidates meet the published selection criteria for the role – i.e., who is "appointable" – and to put forward all "appointable" candidates to the Secretary of State. However, the Secretary of State is to be involved at every stage of the process. Notably, this includes not just matters such as the job description, the design of the advertising and selection process and the composition of the Panel, but also the opportunity to provide their views on candidates at every stage, and to meet with candidates before and/or

info/law/better-regulation/have-your-say/initiatives/12325-Evaluation-of-the-Commission-Notice-on-market-definition-in-EU-competition-law>.

33 D Currie, A Chisholm and T Jarvis, "Institutional Design and Decision-Making in the Competition and Markets Authority" (2014) 10(1) Competition Policy International.

34 Available at <https://publicappointmentscommissioner.independent.gov.uk/wp-content/uploads/2017/04/OIC-2016-1.pdf>.

35 See the list of "significant appointments" agreed between ministers and the Commissioner, available at <https://publicappointmentscommissioner.independent.gov.uk/wp-content/uploads/2017/04/20170403-HMG-List-of-significant-appointments-1.pdf>.

after interview. Before a competition opens, the Secretary of State and other stakeholders are to be asked for names of individuals who should be approached for the role.

The Secretary of State makes the final decision, and may choose not to appoint any of the candidates and rerun the competition. The Secretary of State may also choose to appoint someone whom the Panel does not deem "appointable" (but in that case must consult the Commissioner before public announcement, and must justify their decision publicly). Exceptionally, the Secretary of State may decide to appoint a candidate without a competition, but must then make their decision public, alongside their reasons for doing so, and consult the Commissioner in good time beforehand.

The appointment of the Chairman is also subject to pre-appointment scrutiny by the House of Commissions Business, Energy and Industrial Strategy Select Committee.[36] The Committee holds a public pre-appointment hearing with the candidate and then publishes a report of the hearing, setting out its views on the candidate's suitability. The report will be provided to the Secretary of State and the candidate at least 24 hours before publication. In some instances, the Committee may initially raise concerns privately, with a view to the Secretary of State reconsidering whether to press ahead with the appointment. However, the Committee does not have the power to veto the appointment of the Chair of the CMA.

The Chief Executive of the CMA is appointed by the Secretary of State, for a term of not more than five years and otherwise on such terms and conditions as the Secretary of State considers fit.[37] The Chief Executive must not be the Chair of the CMA, a member of the CMA Panel or a member of the Competition Appeal Tribunal. The appointment of the Chief Executive of the CMA does not fall within the remit of the Commissioner or the Code.[38] Nor is the appointment subject to pre-appointment scrutiny in Parliament.

The above demonstrates that the appointment system for key individuals in both the Commission and the CMA is rigorous, and designed to foster independence of the authorities. In addition, in the UK, there is an additional layer of independent scrutiny in the form of review of second phase merger and markets investigations.

36 Guidelines for this process have been published by the House of Commons Liaison Committee (<http://www.parliament.uk/business/committees/committees-a-z/commons-select/liaison-committee/role/pre-appointment-guidelines/>) and the Cabinet Office (<https://www.gov.uk/government/uploads/system/uploads/attachment_data/file/259686/Guidance_publication.pdf>). Annex A to the Cabinet Office guidance provides that the appointment of the Chair of the CMA is subject to a pre-appointment hearing.

37 schedule 4, para 4.

38 The schedule to the Order specifically excludes the appointment of the Chief Executive of the CMA.

Importantly in the UK, market investigations and in-depth merger investigation are decided by an inquiry group comprising inquiry chairs and CMA Panel members. CMA Panel members are appointed by the Secretary of State, following consultation with the Chair of the CMA.[39] CMA Panel members may not be members of the Competition Appeal Tribunal, and may only be reappointed for the purpose of continuing to act as a member of an inquiry group constituted before the expiry of their term of office. The relevant legislation does not prescribe detailed eligibility criteria for CMA Panel membership; however, in a recent appointment process, the requisite characteristics were described in the following broad terms.

> The CMA is seeking candidates who have had senior level experience (for example Board level or equivalent) in competition policy and law, consumer law and policy, economics, accountancy, business, public policy and/or regulation… Panel Members are not required to be competition experts but should have recent expertise relevant to competition and have a broad perspective on consumer, business, and economic matters… Members must be independent and not represent particular interest groups.[40]

CMA Panel members are appointed for a term of not more than eight years (the most recent appointment process specified a term of six years). Terms and conditions of appointment are otherwise determined by the Secretary of State.[41] The appointment of CMA Panel members is regulated by the Commissioner for Public Appointments; however, unlike the appointment of the Chair of the CMA, such appointments are not "significant appointments" requiring a Senior Independent Panel Member, and are not subject to pre-appointment scrutiny by Parliament.

The default position under ERRA is that members of a CMA inquiry group, including its chair, are selected by the Chair of the CMA.[42] However this function may, with the consent of the CMA Board, be exercised on behalf of the Chair by a person who is a member of both the CMA Panel and the CMA Board, or by a member of the CMA Panel designated by the Secretary of State. In practice, the Chair of the CMA delegates these responsibilities to the CMA Panel Chair or one of the Deputy Panel Chairs.[43]

Each inquiry group must consist of at least three members. ERRA also requires that groups constituted for certain specialist inquiries include certain specialist

39 ERRA schedule 4, part 1, paras 1(1)(b) and 1(2).

40 <https://publicappointments.cabinetoffice.gov.uk/appointment/cma-panel-members-2017/>

41 ERRA schedule 4, part 1, paras 2 and 3.

42 Schedule 4, part 3, paragraphs 37 and 38(8).

43 CMA, *Mergers: Guidance on the CMA's jurisdiction and procedure* (2014) CMA2, para. 10.5.

panel members.[44] In making appointments to an inquiry group, the Chair (or their delegate) must have regard to any guidance published by the CMA on handling conflicts of interest,[45] and take into account any other factors which, in their opinion, might prejudice the independence and impartiality of the group. In addition, a panel member is ineligible for appointment to an inquiry group if they participated in the CMA Board's consideration of whether to refer the matter.[46]

The CMA Panel system is significant in the UK regime because it is designed to add a further layer of independence as well as reducing the risk of confirmation bias within the institution for matters that are subject to a two-phase review (both mergers and market investigations).

IV. Prioritisation

Given the hybrid political and administrative nature of the European Commission, it is not surprising that its President would give a Commissioner some indication of the broad level of priorities to be pursued during their mandate. Presidents of the European Commission have followed the practice of addressing individual "mission letters" to each of the Commissioners, detailing the President's expectations of the Commissioners and stipulating their roles and objectives.

For instance, the mission letter addressed to the current Commissioner for Competition states:

Your task over the next five years will be to ensure our competition policy and rules are fit for the modern economy, vigorously enforced and contribute to a strong European industry at home and in the world.

> – Competition rules are only as effective as their implementation. I want you to focus on strengthening competition enforcement in all sectors. You should focus on improving case detection, speeding up investigations and facilitating cooperation with and between national competition authorities. You should also actively contribute to stronger global cooperation among competition authorities.

---

44 Specifically, under paragraph 38, a newspaper merger reference group must include at least one newspaper panel member; a specialist communications reference group must include at least one, but not more than three, specialist communications panel members; a specialist utility group must include at least one specialist utility panel member; and a specialist payment systems group must include at least one payment systems member. A newspaper panel member can only be appointed to a newspaper merger reference group.

45 The CMA's policy on conflicts of interest is set out as Annexe D to the CMA's Board Rules of Procedure (2013). Further guidance for Panel members on conflicts of interest is set out in the Code of Conduct for CMA Panel Members.

46 CMA, *CMA rules of procedure for merger, market and special reference groups* (2014) CMA17, para. 6.2.

> – You will evaluate and review Europe's competition rules. This will cover the antitrust regulations that will expire in the course of the mandate, the ongoing evaluation of merger control and the review of State aid rules and guidance.
>
> – In the first part of your mandate, you should consider using the tool of sector inquiries into new and emerging markets that are shaping our economy and society.
>
> – Competition will have an important role in our industrial strategy. The competitiveness of our industry depends on a level playing field that provides business with the incentive to invest, innovate and grow. EU State aid rules should support this where there are market failures and the need to strengthen value chains. As part of this, you should continue to work with the Member States to make the most of Important Projects of Common European Interest.
>
> – As part of the industrial strategy, you should develop tools and policies to better tackle the distortive effects of foreign state ownership and subsidies in the internal market.
>
> – While fully preserving the confidentiality of competition procedure, you will be expected to pro-actively share any relevant general market knowledge within the Commission, notably in the digital sector. This will help ensure new legislative proposals continue to fair and open competition in the single market and support evidence-based policymaking.[47]

The mission is couched in very general terms but some marginal differences in emphasis, such as specific references to sectors or areas of activity (in this case digital), may appear from different Commissions.

Legally, the Commission enjoys a wide margin of discretion as to how it will direct its enforcement. Under Article 105(1) TFEU, the Commission is tasked with ensuring the application of the principles laid down in Articles 101 and 102, and investigating cases of suspected infringement of these principles. However, the case law of the EU courts confirms that the Commission is entitled to apply different degrees of priority to the competition cases before it. The classic statement of this principle is found in the *Automec II* case:

> … it should be observed that, in the case of an authority entrusted with a public service task, the power to take all the organisational measures necessary for the performance of that task, including setting priorities within the limits prescribed by the law – where

47 See letter from Ursula von der Leyen to Margrethe Vestager (10 September 2019) <https://ec.europa.eu/commission/sites/beta-political/files/mission-letter-margrethe-vestager_2019_en.pdf>.

> those priorities have not been determined by the legislature – is an inherent feature of administrative activity. This must be the case in particular where an authority has been entrusted with a supervisory and regulatory task as extensive and general as that which has been assigned to the Commission in the field of competition. Consequently, the fact that the Commission applies different degrees of priority to the cases submitted to it in the field of competition is compatible with the obligations imposed on it by Community law.[48]

Before setting out specific points regarding the Commission's approach to handling of complaints of anticompetitive behaviour (as to which, see below), the Commission's Complaints Notice states some general principles regarding the Commission's enforcement priorities:[49]

1. The Commission will enforce the competition rules in cases for which it is "well placed" to act (i.e. rather than one or more of the national competition authorities, which, under the system of concurrent public enforcement of competition rules that operates within the EU, are also competent to apply Articles 101 and 102).
2. The Commission will concentrate its resources on the most serious infringements.
3. The Commission will handle cases in relation to which it should act with a view to defining Union competition policy and/or to ensure coherent application of Articles 101 and 102 (this overlaps with the "well placed" criterion mentioned above).[50]

Guidance on where the Commission will consider itself "well placed" to act, rather than one or more national competition authorities, is set out in the notice published by the Commission on cooperation within the network of national competition authorities (Cooperation Notice).[51] The Commission considers itself particularly well placed to deal with a case involving agreements or practices having effects on competition in more than three Member States (either because they involve cross-border markets or because they involve several national markets); or, if a case is closely linked to other EU law provisions which may be exclusively or more effectively applied by the Commission, if EU interest requires the adoption of a Commission decision to develop EU competition policy when a new competition issue arises or to ensure effective enforcement.[52]

---

48 Case T-24/90 *Automec v Commission* [1992] ECR II-2223 (*Automec II*), para 77.

49 Commission Notice on the handling of complaints by the Commission under Articles [101] and [102] of the [TFEU] [2004] OJ C101/65.

50 ibid, point 11.

51 Commission Notice on cooperation within the Network of Competition Authorities [2004] C 101/43.

52 ibid, paras 14–15.

The case law on the Commission's ability to prioritise cases has largely developed in the context of the handling of complaints submitted to it regarding alleged anticompetitive activity. In this context, the principles and procedures to be followed are set out in case law, regulations and the Complaints Notice.

Where the Commission receives a complaint, it is under no obligation to carry out an investigation to establish the existence or non-existence of an infringement, or to render a final decision. However, the Commission must examine carefully the factual and legal particulars brought to its notice by the complainant in order to decide whether they disclose conduct of such a kind as to distort competition in the internal market and affect trade between Member States.[53]

Where a complaint appears to disclose a breach or potential breach of Article 101 or 102, the Commission may nevertheless reject it on the basis of a lack of EU interest.[54] The courts have indicated certain factors that the Commission must consider in assessing whether a complaint has an EU interest, including the seriousness and duration of the infringement and the persistence of its effects,[55] and the existence of other similar complaints. The Complaints Notice provides guidance as to matters that have been taken into account in determining whether EU interest exists.[56]

Given the assessment of EU interest depends upon the specific factual and legal circumstances of each case, this is not a closed list – the Commission is entitled to apply novel criteria. In addition, where appropriate, the Commission may give priority to a particular criterion.[57]

---

53 See e.g. *Automec II*, paras. 74–76; Case T-204/03 *Haladjian Frères v Commission* [2006] ECR II-3779, paras 27–28; Case T-432/05 *EMC Development v Commission* [2010] ECR II-1629, paras 54–60 (Richard Burton, *The EU General Court affirms Commission's rejection of complaint on cement standard (EMC Development)*, 12 May 2010, *e-Competitions* May 2010, Art. N° 41526). See also points 41–42 of the Complaints Notice and further case law cited therein.

54 See e.g. *Automec II*, paras 84–96 (upholding the Commission's decision not to investigate the compatibility with article [101] of a distribution system operated by BMW Italia, on the basis that a dispute relating to this was already before the national courts, and Automec could submit the question of the system's compatibility with article [101] to the courts). An exception is where the complaint involves a matter within the Commission's sole jurisdiction, such as the withdrawal of a block exemption, in which case the complainant is entitled to a decision on the merits.

55 Case C-119/97 P *Ufex v Commission* [1999] ECR I-1341.

56 This includes: the possibility of the complainant asserting its rights through an action before national courts; the seriousness of the alleged infringements and the persistence of their consequences (including the duration and extent of the infringements and their effect on competition); the significance of the alleged infringement for the functioning of the internal market; the probability of establishing the existence of an infringement; the scope of investigation required; the stage of the Commission's investigation of a case; whether the practices in question have ceased (however, the Commission cannot regard past infringements as excluded in principle from investigation; it must consider whether anticompetitive effects persist, and whether the seriousness of the infringements or the persistence of their effects nevertheless gives rise to a EU interest in pursuing the case); and whether the undertakings concerned agree to change their conduct in such a way that the Commission can consider there is no longer a EU interest in intervening. See point 44 of the Complaints Notice.

57 Point 43 of the Complaints Notice, citing *Ufex v Commission* (n 49), paras 79–80 and C-450/98 P *IECC v Commission* [2001] I-3875, paras 57–59.

The Commission may also have regard to measures taken by national authorities, reflecting the system of concurrent competence in antitrust matters under Regulation 1/2003.[58] In addition, and as a prior matter, under Article 13 of Regulation 1/2003, the Commission can reject a complaint on the basis that a national competition authority of a Member State is dealing with the case, without considering whether there would be an EU interest in the Commission pursuing it.[59]

The Commission is not obliged to refrain from pursuing a case due to lack of EU interest.[60] Before rejecting a complaint, the Commission must comply with the procedural requirements set out in Regulation 773/2004.[61] This requires it to inform the complainant of its reasons, set a period of not less than four weeks for the complainant to make written representations and, if requested, provide access to the documents on which the Commission bases its provisional assessment. If no representations are made, the complaint is deemed withdrawn. If representations are made, but do not change the Commission's view, it must reject the complaint by decision (which may then be challenged before the courts).

The Commission has published specific guidance regarding its enforcement priorities in investigating possible abuses of dominance. The guidance applies only to exclusionary abuses (but notes in relation to exploitative abuses that the Commission may intervene in relation to such conduct "in particular" where the protection of consumers and the proper functioning of the internal market cannot otherwise be adequately ensured).[62]

The guidance states that the Commission will normally intervene under Article 102 where, "on the basis of cogent and convincing evidence, the allegedly abusive conduct is likely to lead to anticompetitive foreclosure".

In contrast to antitrust cases, the Commission has little scope to "prioritise" merger cases (except perhaps with regard to the pace of pre-notification discussions). Undertakings are obliged to notify transactions meeting the relevant jurisdictional thresholds under the EU Merger Regulation (EUMR),[63] and the

---

58 Case T-432/10 *Vivendi v Commission (France Télécom)*, judgment of 16 October 2013, paras 26 and 42–47.

59 Case T-201/11 *Si.mobil v Commission* EU:T:2014:1096, paras 33-41; Pablo Figueroa, Catherine Derenne, *The EU General Court extends the EU Commission discretion when rejecting complaints (Si.mobil)*, 17 December 2014, *e-Competitions* December 2014, Art. N° 76168.

60 T-77/92 *Parker Pen v Commission* [1994] ECR II-549, paras 60–66.

61 [2004] OJ L123/18.

62 Communication from the Commission – Guidance on the Commission's enforcement priorities in applying Article [102] of the [TFEU] to abusive exclusionary conduct by dominant undertakings [2009] OJ C45/7, para 7.

63 Council Regulation (EC) 139/2004 on the control of concentrations between undertakings [2004] OJ L24/1.

Commission is then obliged to review and render a decision on each notified concentration, within the strict timetable prescribed by the EUMR.

In certain respects, the system for referral of merger cases between the Commission and the national competition authorities of Member States achieves similar ends to the "EU interest" criterion applied in antitrust cases, in that it provides a mechanism to allow cases that are particularly suitable to be dealt with by the Commission to be brought within its remit, and for cases that are particularly suitable for consideration by national authorities to be referred down to them. However, the initiative lies with the parties (Article 4) and the Member States (Articles 9 and 22), not the Commission.[64] Having said this, in cases that threaten to significantly affect competition in a market, the Commission has broad discretion to retain jurisdiction and deal with the case (see Article 9(3)) and it has done so in a number of cases affecting national competition when it considers it important to maintain consistency in the decisional practice for issues affecting a number of markets within the EU.[65]

Prioritisation by the CMA

The UK has a somewhat more structured approach to prioritisation. Although the CMA is an independent non-ministerial department and is free to prioritise its work, the Government publishes a "strategic steer", setting out its view of the priorities for the CMA's work. The first strategic steer was published in October 2013 by the Department for Business, Innovation and Skills (BIS, now the Department for Business, Enterprise and Industrial Strategy), following a process of consultation. BIS published an updated strategic steer (again following consultation) in December 2015.[66] The Government has since committed to consult on and publish a strategic steer in each Parliament, with the most recent steer published in July 2019.[67]

---

64 Although the Commission may invite a Member State to make a referral request under article 9 or 22, it cannot require one.

65 See for instance in relation to European mobile telephony consolidation cases in the UK (*T-Mobile/ Orange* (Case COMP/M.5650) Commission Decision of 1 March 2010), Jocelyn Guitton, Boryana Hristova, Vera Pozzato, *The EU Commission conditionally approves joint venture between two UK mobile network operators (T-Mobile / Orange)*, 1 March 2010, *e-Competitions* March 2010, Art. N° 34854; Austria (*Hutchison 3G Austria/Orange Austria* (Case COMP/M.6497) Commission Decision of 12 December 2012), Cristina Caffarra, *The EU Commission clears a merger between two Austrian mobile networks operators subject to remedies (Hutchison 3G / Orange Austria)*, 28 June 2012, *e-Competitions* June 2012, Art. N° 51817; Germany (*Telefónica Deutschland/E-Plus* (Case COMP/M.7018) Commission Decision of 2 July 2014); and Italy (*Hutchison 3G Italy/Wind/JV* (Case COMP/M.7758) Commission Decision of 1 September 2016).

66 Department for Business Innovation & Skills, "Government's Response to the Consultation on the Strategic Steer to the Competition and Markets Authority" (December 2015) <https://www.gov.uk/government/uploads/system/uploads/attachment_data/file/481040/BIS-15-659-government-response-governments-strategic-steer-to-the-competition-and-markets-authority.pdf>.

67 Department for Business, Energy & Industrial Strategy, "The Government's strategic steer to the Competition and Markets Authority" (July 2019) <https://assets.publishing.service.gov.uk/government/uploads/system/uploads/attachment_data/file/818214/cma-strategic-steer.pdf>.

The 2019 strategic steer is framed in rather broad, non-specific terms. Overall, it indicates that the government wishes the CMA, in undertaking its activities, to focus on five main elements. It is interesting to note that one of these elements pertains to the CMA's independence, recognising that it is "an independent decision-making body, separate from ministers".

1. Supporting the Government's industrial strategy, which includes taking timely action in sectors that impact productivity, minimising barriers to new businesses successfully entering markets, and reporting publicly on issues affecting productivity;
2. Championing consumers by focusing on businesses and markets with clear potential for harm, protecting consumers from illegal and anti-competitive practices and making markets work well for vulnerable consumers;
3. Making the most of the challenges and opportunities of the digital economy;
4. Being ambitious in taking action against anti-competitive behaviour; and
5. Remaining a strong and independent voice and fulfilling its functions of providing information to the public and recommendations and advice to the Government.

The strategic steer is not binding on the CMA. The Government asks the CMA to have regard to it in carrying out its work, and appears to view it as complementing the formal accountability framework set out in statute.[68] This requires the CMA to report annually to the Secretary of State on its activities and performance during the year, and to arrange for the report to be laid before Parliament and published. The CMA is also required to prepare, lay before Parliament and publish an annual plan, after consulting publicly on its proposals and laying them before Parliament.[69]

The CMA's approach to prioritisation is set out in published "prioritisation principles".[70] In general, the CMA prioritises its work by considering four factors: impact, strategic significance, risks and resources.

1. Impact: the direct and indirect effect of intervention on consumer welfare, and the expected additional economic impact on efficiency, productivity and the wider economy. Indirect effects on consumer

68 "Government's Response to the Consultation on the Strategic Steer", para 4: "The Steer aligns fully with the CMA's formal accountability framework. It does not affect the scope of the CMA's powers or the legal tests it applies when making decisions."

69 ERRA, schedule 4, paras 12–14.

70 CMA, *Prioritisation principles for the CMA* (April 2014) CMA16.

welfare may result, for example, from the deterrent effect of action, from clarification of the law in ways that enable procompetitive practices, from action that informs and empowers consumers or from action that demonstrates to government the benefits from removing unjustified restrictions of competition.

2. Strategic significance: the fit of the work with the CMA's strategy and other objectives (including whether there are elements of strategic significance additional to impact); whether the CMA is best placed to act (as opposed to public enforcement by other bodies – sectoral competition regulators, other UK regulators or law enforcement bodies, or the Commission; private enforcement; market developments; self-regulation; or legislation); and the impact on the balance of the CMA's current portfolio of work.

3. Risks: the likelihood of a successful outcome (however, the CMA may take on cases with only a relatively small likelihood of success where justified by the likely scale of the detriment and the value of providing clarity on the law).

4. Resources: the resource implications of the work, including whether the resource requirements are proportionate to the benefits of the work, the period over which the resources will be needed, and any savings created for the CMA by enabling it to meet its objectives more efficiently. The CMA will take into account the resource availability of other enforcement authorities.

These principles are not confined to particular areas of the CMA's work; however, as the CMA notes in the same document, there are instances in which the CMA comes under a legal duty to act once certain circumstances have arisen. These are discussed in relation to particular areas of the CMA's work below.

Section 25 of the Competition Act 1998 sets out circumstances in which the CMA *may* conduct an investigation into anticompetitive behaviour – i.e., it does not require the CMA to act in such circumstances. The CMA will apply its prioritisation principles, as set out above. However, (i) where the Commission requests the CMA's assistance in carrying out an inspection, it is under a duty to assist, and (ii) where the CMA applies the national Chapter I and II prohibitions, it must apply articles 101 and 102 as appropriate and applicable.

Certain UK sectoral regulators have concurrent power with the CMA to enforce antitrust rules, providing scope for a form of prioritisation between regulators somewhat similar to concurrent competences of the Commission and national competition authorities in applying EU antitrust rules. As noted above, the possibility of action by a sectoral regulator is one of the considerations taken into account by the CMA in prioritising cases, allowing it to focus resources elsewhere where appropriate; just as the Commission will consider the possibility of action by national authorities in determining whether to act (under the Cooperation Notice and case law relating to EU interest discussed above).

The UK Competition Network provides a forum for the regulators to coordinate on enforcement activity, with a view to encouraging consistency of approach and ensuring that sector regulators consider the use of their competition powers before using sector-specific powers. The Concurrency Regulations[71] also set out formal consultation and information-sharing requirements between the competent regulators. The Regulations permit the CMA to direct sectoral regulators to transfer competition cases to it, where it is satisfied that this would further the promotion of competition.

The scope for prioritisation in merger cases for the CMA is more nuanced than for the Commission, as a result of the voluntary nature of the UK merger control regime. Whereas the Commission's role is essentially reactive – having a duty to scrutinise notified concentrations – the CMA not only reviews transactions that are voluntarily notified to it by the parties, but also gathers intelligence on market activity to identify transactions that may merit investigation of its own initiative. This is done by the CMA's mergers intelligence staff, who monitor sources of information on mergers and present potential candidates for investigation to weekly meetings of the mergers intelligence committee. Where the CMA believes there is a reasonable chance that the test for a Phase 2 investigation is met, the CMA will take a decision to investigate.[72]

The CMA's own-initiative role in merger control is not a matter of complete discretion. The CMA's mergers intelligence activity reflects the CMA's statutory function to obtain, compile and keep under review information about matters relating to the carrying out of its functions – including information relating to merger situations.[73] Where it believes that it is or may be the case that a relevant merger situation has or will be created, and that the merger situation has resulted or may be expected to result in a substantial lessening of competition (SLC) in any market in the UK, the CMA is under a duty to refer the matter for an in-depth Phase 2 investigation by an inquiry group of CMA Panel members (as described earlier). The inquiry group, in turn, must decide whether the transaction will result in an SLC and, if so, take remedial action. The Secretary of State can also serve intervention notices, requiring the CMA to investigate cases raising certain specified public interest issues.[74] Also, where the duty to refer would

71 Competition Act 1998 (Concurrency) Regulations 2014, SI 2014/536.

72 CMA, *Guidance on the CMA's mergers intelligence function* (17 June 2016) CMA56, para. 2.

73 Enterprise Act 2002 (EA 2002), s 5.

74 EA 2002, s 42–68. The currently specified public interest considerations on which intervention may be based are national security, the stability of the UK financial system and various media-related considerations (including media plurality) (EA 2002, s 58).

otherwise apply, the CMA nevertheless has some limited scope for prioritisation, as a result of the "de minimis" exception. Under the EA 2002, the CMA may decide not to make a reference where the market or markets concerned are not of "sufficient importance" to justify the making of a reference.[75] The CMA has recently published updated guidance on how it applies this exception.[76]

One of the distinctive features of the UK regime is that the CMA has the power to conduct wide-ranging "market investigations" into entire sectors of the economy, in order to determine whether there are features of the relevant markets that prevent, restrict or distort competition and therefore give rise to an "adverse effect on competition" (AEC), and to take action to remedy those AECs. Unlike the Commission's power to conduct a sector inquiry, the CMA can take remedial action directly, regardless of whether the AECs involve behaviour punishable under antitrust laws.

In order to commence a market investigation, the CMA must have reasonable grounds for suspecting that any feature, or combination of features, of a market in the UK prevents, restricts or distorts competition. In general, the CMA is free to decide which markets to examine with a view to determining whether a market investigation is warranted. Even where the CMA concludes the test for referring a market for a market investigation is met, it is not under a duty to make a reference (in contrast to the position in merger cases). Again, the CMA will apply the prioritisation principles described above.

In addition, the CMA has published specific guidance regarding the circumstances in which it will make a market investigation reference. In addition to the test for reference being met, the CMA will make a reference only where:

– It would not be more appropriate to deal with the competition issues identified by applying antitrust enforcement powers or using other powers available to the CMA or, where appropriate, to sectoral regulators;

---

75 EA 2002, s (22)(2)(a) and 33(2)(a). The CMA may also decide not to make a reference where the arrangements are not sufficiently far advanced, or likely to proceed, to justify the making of a reference, or where "relevant customer benefits" outweigh the substantial lessening of competition concerned and its adverse effects. The CMA considers these exceptions *before* accepting undertakings in lieu of reference (but the potential availability of undertakings may be relevant to the exercise of its discretion).

76 CMA, *Mergers: Exception to the duty to refer in markets of insufficient importance* (16 June 2017) CMA64; The guidance sets out a three-tier approach, based on the annual value in the UK of the market(s) concerned: (1) where the annual value is below £5m, the CMA will generally not consider a reference justified, unless a clear-cut undertaking in lieu of reference is in principle available; (2) where the annual value exceeds £15m, the CMA considers that the market(s) will generally be of sufficient importance to justify a reference; and (3) where the annual value is between £5m and £15m, the CMA will conduct a balancing exercise, assessing whether the expected customer harm resulting from the merger is materially greater than the average public cost of a Phase II reference (currently around £400,000); taking into account the size of the market, the likelihood that an SLC will occur, the magnitude of any competition that would be lost, and the expected duration of the SLC. The CMA will also take into account the wider implications of its de minimis decisions.

- It would not be more appropriate to address the problem identified by means of undertakings in lieu of a reference;
- The scale of the suspected problem, in terms of its AEC, is such that a reference would be an appropriate response to it; and
- There is a reasonable chance that appropriate remedies will be available.

It seems reasonable to suppose that prioritisation in market investigation cases raises particularly difficult questions, given the substantial resource implications of an 18 – or 24-month long inquiry into an entire market or markets on the one hand, and the potential scale of consumer detriment on the other.[77]

In certain circumstances, however, the CMA is under a duty to conduct a market investigation:

- In regulated sectors, the relevant sectoral regulator has the power to make a market investigation reference to the CMA (concurrent with the CMA's power to do so). For example, the CMA's energy market investigation followed a market investigation reference by the Gas and Electricity Markets Authority (Ofgem), while the CMA's predecessor, the Competition Commission, investigated the supply of movies for premium pay-television following a reference by the communications regulator Ofcom, and leasing of rolling stock following a reference from the Office of Rail Regulation.
- The Secretary of State may make a market investigation reference to the CMA either where they are dissatisfied with a decision of the CMA not to make a reference, or where they have brought to the attention of the CMA information which they consider to be relevant to the CMA's decision to make a reference but they are not satisfied that the CMA will decide within a reasonable period whether to make such a reference.[78]
- The Secretary of State may intervene in cases that involve public interest issues (in contrast to the position in merger cases, only national security is currently specified as a public interest consideration).[79]

Finally the EA 2002, section 11, permits the Secretary of State to designate consumer representative bodies as "super-complainants". This gives them a role

---

77 While not initiated by the CMA (see further below), the CMA's energy market investigation provides an interesting example. It was reported to have involved 30 full-time staff working on the investigation for two years, with a total cost of around £5m (including £440,000 paid to lawyers and external advisers), and industry figures suggested the total cost of the process to the industry could be in excess of £80m ("Investigation into energy market 'may top £80m'" *The Times* (London, 23 June 2016)). On the other hand, the CMA's final report claimed to have identified an annual overcharge to customers of £1.4B, and suggested that one of the more than 30 remedial measures proposed in the report, a price cap for customers on prepayment meters, would reduce bills by around £300m per year.

78 EA 2002, s 132.

79 EA 2002, s 139–153.

in shaping the CMA's activities in relation to antitrust and markets work (as well as its consumer law responsibilities), by submitting "super-complaints".[80]

Therefore both the European Commission and the CMA enjoy a high degree of discretion in prioritisation and case selection and this is a core element of their independence. How can this be reconciled with the appropriate level of accountability?

V. Independence and Accountability

According to Kovacic there is "an inherent tension between the preservation of an acceptable level of independence and the attainment of necessary level of accountability."[81] While there may be a short-term trade-off, accountability is necessary to maintain independence in the long term.[82] A competition authority typically has a composite function. It clearly has both a policymaking function in competition matters and a law enforcement function including, in the EU and UK regimes, an adjudication role. In relation to the former (which is exercised through case selection in the first instance) a competition authority is performing an executive function. Moreover, often competition authorities have role of advocacy for competition both with the executive branch and, in some cases, with the legislator. In its policymaking role, its case selection it cannot be fully isolated from the political context. And it should not be.

As a law enforcement agency, a competition authority is subject to hard accountability through the judicial process. This is important and, far from creating a tension, this dimension is a guarantor of independence because judicial oversight of the application of the law has the effect of pushing a competition authority to adopt procedures that would withstand judicial scrutiny and indirectly preserve the integrity of the system. In the UK, the Office of Fair Trading introduced Case Decision Groups in 2012 to create a separation between the team carrying out the investigation into a Competition Act infringement (the case team) and

80 Where a designated body makes a complaint to the CMA that any feature, or combination of features, of a market in the UK for goods or services is or appears to be significantly harming the interests of consumers, the CMA must publish a reasoned response within 90 days, setting out what, if any, action it proposes to take in response. Such action could include enforcement action under competition (or consumer) law, agreeing voluntary changes with the industry, launching a market study, marking a market investigation reference or recommending action by the government, a regulatory body or other organisation. CMA, *Guidance: What are super-complaints* (7 May 2015). Designated super-complainants include the Campaign for Real Ale (CAMRA, which in 2009 sought to trigger a market investigation reference focusing on the "beer tie"), the Consumer Council for Water, the Consumers' Association (more commonly known as Which?), the General Consumer Council for Northern Ireland, the National Association of Citizens Advice Bureaux and the Scottish Association of Citizens Advice Bureaux. Enterprise Act 2002 (Bodies Designated to Make Super-complaints) Order 2004, SI 2004/1517.

81 Kovacic (n 17).

82 Jenny (n 2) 164.

those who decide whether that infringement has occurred. The procedural tool was designed to reduce the risk of confirmation bias and improve the quality of the decision-making process. This system which has been maintained and adjusted by the CMA provides another layer of independence in Competition Act cases.[83] Independence in decision-making becomes as necessary as that of the judiciary to which it is subject. It is for that reason that even in jurisdictions where the appointment mechanism for the leadership of the agencies is overtly political (such as the US),[84] enforcement can be – to a large extent – insulated from political interference. In other words, intense judicial oversight acts as a counter-balance to the political nature of the agency leadership selection. This is, of course, not a complete answer, because the intensity of public enforcement can be affected by political considerations and judicial oversight would not have an impact of those important aspects.

Accountability for a competition authority also has a "soft" dimension. By "soft" accountability I refer to the ability of Parliament and the executive to request that a competition authority explains its action in completed matters and discuss general trends in policy which may influence the authority's independent view on case selection and prioritisation over which, as we have seen above, they enjoy a considerable degree of discretion. Soft accountability is inevitable and even desirable in a democratic process but needs to be coupled with solid mechanisms of protection from all pressure points (from appointment to funding, conflicts and cooling-off periods applying to activities post-term) and with a political culture that values the ultimate independence of the authority.

83 Currie, Chisholm and Jarvis (n 27), 18 and CMA, *Competition Act 1988: Guidance on the CMA's investigation procedures in Competition Act 1998 cases* (2014), paras 9.11–13.14.

84 In the United States the appointments of the top antitrust officials emanate from the president. The Antitrust Division of the DoJ is led by the Assistant Attorney General for Antitrust (AAG). The AAG is appointed by the president and confirmed by the senate. Beneath the AAG sit six deputy AAGs, selected by the DoJ (in practice, the AAG is understood to make the final decision). The Federal Trade Commission (FTC) comprises five commissioners, who are nominated by the president and confirmed by the senate. Each commissioner serves a seven-year term. The president chooses one commissioner to act as chair-person. No more than three commissioners can be of the same political party. Beneath the commissioners sit the directors of the three FTC Bureaus (Competition, Consumer Protection and Economics). Each of these is appointed by the chairperson. The chairperson also appoints deputy directors.

What is the Scope for Choice and Competition in Schools?

ALLAN FELS AO AND DARRYL BIGGAR*
Universities of Melbourne, Monash & Oxford
Australian Competition and Consumer Commission

Abstract

Investment in education accounts for a sizeable fraction of total government expenditure in OECD countries. But, historically, the scope for competition in primary and secondary education services has been tightly constrained, if not eliminated entirely. In principle, as in other sectors, competition in education services could be a key driver of productivity and innovation in education, with potentially substantial long-term impacts on economic and social welfare. In this essay we identify the goal of equality of opportunity as a key driver of government involvement in education, and we explore the steps that must be taken to ensure that competitive market forces remain consistent with this objective. We identify two issues in particular – the 'topping up' problem and the 'cream-skimming' problem, which must be carefully addressed in future pro-competitive reforms. Overall we remain positive about the scope for encouraging competitive forces in education services.

---

* Dr Darryl Biggar is the Special Economic Advisor (Regulatory) for the Australian Competition and Consumer Commission and the Australian Energy Regulator. His interests include the economic foundation of competition law, the theory of economic regulation, and the design of electricity markets. He previously worked for the Competition Division of the OECD. He has a PhD in Economics from Stanford. Prof Allan Fels AO is the former chair of the Australian Competition and Consumer Commission, and former dean of the Australia and New Zealand School of Government. He is currently a professorial fellow in both the Institute of Applied Economic and Social Research and in the Melbourne Law School at the University of Melbourne, an honorary professor in the Faculty of Business and Economics at Monash University and a visiting professor in the School of Social Sciences at Oxford University. He has a PhD in Economics from Duke University.

I. Introduction

This paper focuses on some key issues regarding the scope for choice and competition in education.[1] A key finding is that while there appears to be scope for expanding the role of choice and competition in many OECD countries, there are also some significant, often ignored, limitations on the scope for choice and competition if a major goal of education policy is to promote "equality of opportunity".

II. Choice and Competition in the Education Sector

Most governments are heavily involved in funding education services, especially in primary and secondary education.[2] In addition, in most countries the government is not merely the primary funder of education, but the primary provider of education services. Furthermore, in many countries competition in education services is not actively encouraged. In fact, in many cases, competition between government education providers is often deliberately and strictly limited, particularly by granting each education provider a limited geographic monopoly over the provision of education services to children within each school's zone.[3]

Why? Is there something about the provision of education services which requires a restriction on competition? Is conventional in-the-market competition somehow in opposition to the objectives the government is trying to achieve?

We will look first at the underlying economic problem (or "market failure") which gives rise to a need for government intervention in the first place. As we will see, that underlying economic problem provides a motivation for substantial government subsidies for the education sector. We next explore the issues that arise when we try to introduce competition in a context of material government

---

1 This paper draws on two wider papers by Professor Allan Fels and Dr Darryl Biggar, "The Role of Choice and Competition in Education" (CRESSE Conference, Greece, 2018) and "Competition in Public Markets" (OECD Global Forum on Competition, Paris, 7–8 December 2017) <https://one.oecd.org/document/DAF/COMP/GF(2017)7/en/pdf> accessed 8 July 2020.

2 As Milton Friedman observes: "Education is today largely paid for and almost entirely administered by governmental bodies or non-profit institutions. This situation has developed gradually and is now taken so much for granted that little explicit attention is any longer directed to the reasons for the special treatment of education even in countries that are predominantly free enterprise in organization and philosophy. The result has been an indiscriminate extension of governmental responsibility", Milton Friedman, "The Role of Government in Education" in Robert A Solo (ed) *Economics and the Public Interest* (Rutgers University Press 1955). OECD data shows that public spending on education varies between 2.5 and 5.0% of GDP across OECD countries.

3 School zones do not eliminate competition between schools entirely. Many parents are able to choose where they live on the basis of the local school. Such forms of school competition may contribute to social segregation and may undermine equality of opportunity (if more desirable schools are located in areas which are more expensive to live).

subsidies. We conclude with a checklist of issues that must be addresses if we are to increase the scope for reliance on choice and competition in education.

1. Why are Governments Involved in Education?

Why are governments so heavily involved in the provision of education services? In asking this question, we in no way intend to call into question the need for government action in the education sector. We merely seek to make clear that rationale so that any proposals for enhanced reliance on choice and competition can be carefully designed so as not to threaten the underlying objectives of government intervention in the first place.

We will focus in this paper on the "core" education sectors of primary, secondary and (to an extent) tertiary education.[4] To what extent can these services be provided in normal competitive markets?

Education is, of course, an investment in human capital. The decision as to the amount of education to purchase is similar to other investment decisions – how much consumption to forego in the short term in order to increase consumption in the long term. Investment in education is large relative to lifetime income, and consumers may be short-termist or myopic in their perspective. Perhaps there might be a tendency for consumers, left to themselves, to underinvest in education. But this might argue for a government information campaign to promote the benefits of investment in education, or a government-imposed requirement to purchase a minimum number of years of education. Why do governments typically heavily subsidise education services, and why do most governments directly provide these services themselves?

There are three common rationales offered for government involvement in education:

1. There are economic and political *spillover effects*:

- A tax dividend effect – if education results in higher income in the future individuals are not able to capture all of the benefits due to the effect of taxes. A government subsidy upfront may offset the distorting impact of taxes.[5]
- A productivity spillover – according to this theory, education increases the productivity of the individual, but also increases the productivity of individuals with whom that person interacts.[6]

---

4 Many secondary, ancillary or discretionary forms of education are a normal consumer service delivered in relatively normal consumer markets. For example, many children take lessons in a musical instrument, train in a sport or obtain tutoring outside of the regular classroom. Many older people take lessons in art, writing, computing or history. There are a few issues of quality assurance and accreditation, but these issues are not obviously insurmountable, and there are typically a large number of competing providers for these services. We will put these "secondary" forms of education to one side.

5 See Nicholas Barr, *The Economics of the Welfare State* (5th edn, OUP 2012), 271. A related idea is that government subsidisation of education may increase employability, reducing the tax burden from payments to the unemployed.

6 *ibid*, Box 11.2.

- A democratic spillover – having an educated citizenry allows the population to understand and participate in public decision-making and democratic processes, which leads to better democratic outcomes overall. As Stiglitz observes: "A society in which everyone can read functions far more smoothly than a society in which few can read".[7]

Stiglitz expresses some scepticism about the magnitude of these spillover effects, especially compared with the size of the benefit the individual receives from education:

> There is… a large private return to being able to read, and even in the absence of government support, many individuals would learn this and other basic skills. Indeed, most individuals would go far beyond that. The question is: Given the level of education that individuals would choose to undertake privately were there no government subsidy, would further increases in education generate any significant externalities? There is no agreement concerning the answer, but the case for government support based on these kinds of externalities – at least for advanced industrial economies like the United States – seems, at best, unproved.[8]

2. *Capital market imperfections*. Although it is theoretically possible for citizens to borrow to invest in education against their future lifetime income, in practice (due to moral hazard and asymmetric information) such contracts are difficult to enforce. As Stiglitz notes: "Private lenders are not, for the most part, willing to lend to finance education… Hence those lacking funds of their own (or funds from their families) would be denied access to higher education without some assistance from the government."[9]

Governments may have a comparative advantage in using the tax system to compel students to repay loans. But this is an argument for government provision of educational loans as opposed to subsidies. Many countries have a system of government-backed lending for education services, particularly for higher

7 Joseph E Stiglitz, *Economics of the Public Sector* (4th edn, W. W. Norton Company, Inc 2015), page 401. Hayek similarly notes that: "In a country with democratic institutions, there is the further important consideration that democracy is not likely to work, except on the smallest local scale, with partly illiterate people." Friedrich A von Hayek, *The Constitution of Liberty* (University of Chicago Press 1960). There are also links between education and fertility (lower levels of fertility are associated with higher levels of education) and links between education and mortality (especially infant mortality). There may also be links between education and mobility of the population, and links between education and flexibility of the workforce: "Individuals with lower education levels typically have higher unemployment risks, less stable jobs and more difficulties in facing the economy's demands for ever-increasing flexibility and to cope with technological transitions." OECD, *Equity and Quality in Education: Supporting Disadvantaged Students and Schools* (OECD 2012), 24.

8 Stiglitz (n 7), 401.

9 Stiglitz (n 7), 402. See also Barr (n 5), 277.

(tertiary) education.[10] But such systems typically operate alongside, instead of in place of, direct government funding and provision of primary and secondary education services.

3. The desire to promote *equality of opportunity*.

Stiglitz explains this last concept as follows:

> At the elementary and secondary levels, parents make decisions [about investments in education] on behalf of their children. Although most parents may view expenditures on their children altruistically, investing in their children as long as the returns are sufficiently high, some parents may not do so. Under a system of privately financed education, the children of such parents might receive an insufficient education. Thus, a rationale for public support of primary and secondary education is provided on distributional grounds: there is a widespread belief that children's access to education should not depend on their parents' financial ability or their sense of altruism. Indeed, such distributional concerns provide the strongest motivation for a public role in education more generally – for the financing of elementary and secondary education and for the extensive financial support for higher education.[11]

The LSE economist, Nicholas Barr, puts it like this:

> Equity is taken to imply that children A and B should have an equal *opportunity*... to acquire an education of equal quality and duration, irrespective of whether, for example, A comes from a middle-class family and B from a disadvantaged background... This definition of equity does not mean that individuals can necessarily obtain as much education as they want. However, it implies that, if individuals A and B have similar tastes and abilities, they should receive the same education, irrespective of factors that are regarded as irrelevant".[12]

There is some suggestion that promoting equality of opportunity may be more than a fairness or equity issue; it may also promote economic growth. The UK economic consultancy Oxera argues that the absence of social mobility results in foregone economic benefits due to underexploitation of the human capital potential. Specifically, Oxera notes:

> Social mobility is widely considered to be intrinsically good. Decoupling an individual's prospects from their social status or

10 For example, in Australia there is a Higher Education Loan Program (HELP). Similar programmes operate in New Zealand.

11 Stiglitz (n 7), 402.

12 Barr (n 5), 268.

> family background is a key pillar of fairness and social justice. While this perspective has filled philosophy textbooks and opinion columns, what is less well understood is the role that social mobility plays in boosting productivity and economic output... Even a modest increase in the UK's social mobility – for example, raising social mobility to the average of Western European countries – could increase gross domestic product (in the long term) by around 2%, through better job matching. This is equivalent to £39bn per year in today's prices. Improving social mobility further – to the average across all European countries – could lead to an even more substantial increase of £50bn. This improvement is not instant; it takes time for policies that increase social mobility to translate into improved job matching. But once achieved, it is permanent.[13]

For the purposes of this paper, we will assume that a primary motivation for government involvement in education is to promote a degree of equality of opportunity.[14] This motivation gives rise to government subsidisation of at least the core primary and secondary education services – to ensure that all citizens have access to a certain quantity and quality of education services regardless of their background or income.

2. Is Competition Between Educational Institutions Even Feasible?

In principle, if it were possible to harness the forces of competition in education without compromising the objectives above, education might be delivered like many other services, with a wide range of competing educational institutions meeting the needs of a wide range of students, innovating to develop new educational techniques, making efficient use of new technology and other inputs, responding to the changing desires of parents and the needs of the broader community, and doing so with the minimal claim on government resources. But to what extent is this vision in conflict with the objectives identified above? To what extent can we rely on choice and competition to deliver desirable outcomes in the education sector?

First let's address the question whether effective competition between education service providers is even feasible. To answer this question we will address the

---

13 Oxera, "Agenda: Hidden Talent: The Economic Benefits of Social Mobility" (research report for the The Sutton Trust, July 2017). Similarly, OECD (n 7), 24: "Underdeveloped human capital hampers productivity growth and limits the effective and full use of resources."

14 The OECD expresses it like this: "Equitable education systems are fair and inclusive and support their students to reach their learning potential without either formally or informally pre-setting barriers or lowering expectations. Equity as fairness implies that personal or socio-economic circumstances, such as gender, ethnic origin or family background are not obstacles to educational success. An equitable education system can redress the effect of broader social and economic inequalities. In the context of learning, it allows individuals to take full advantage of education and training irrespective of their background.", ibid, 15.

brief checklist mentioned earlier: Is there (i) scope for a number of competing service providers; (ii) which have both the willingness and ability to respond to financial incentives to improve performance; and (iii) do customers (or their parents or guardians) have the information they need to make a choice between service providers; and (iv) the willingness and ability to make a choice in their own (or their children's) best interest?

In principle, an assessment of the scope for competition in education services requires a formal competition analysis – that is, an analysis of the product and geographic dimensions of the market, barriers to entry and exit, and other factors such as transparency of prices and quality, vertical integration and barriers to customer choice. Such a full analysis is beyond the scope of this paper. We merely make the following observations:

There do not appear to be inherent structural barriers to achieving effective competition between educational institutions in most large towns and cities. In particular, there do not seem to be overwhelming economies of scale or scope in the provision of traditional primary and secondary education within a reasonable geographic market. Most urban areas are able to sustain many traditional educational institutions within any given 5–10 kilometre radius.[15] But even this radius is too far to walk; if competition is to be effective, consideration may need to be given to how students who make a choice of school will be able to travel to that school, perhaps by ensuring access to public transport.

The range of sizes of different schools that we can observe in operation suggests that relatively small schools (with fewer than, say, 200 students) are able to coexist and compete with quite large schools (with more than, say, 1,000 students). It therefore appears that, with the exception of relatively small towns, most urban areas should be able to sustain active competition in education services in most areas, even without students having to travel very long distances.[16]

In order to for choice and competition to be effective in improving overall outcomes, schools must have the incentive and ability to respond to market conditions, and to adapt and innovate in response to financial incentives. Historically, in countries where the education sector has been dominated by government providers, the scope for individual schools to exercise autonomy, independence and innovation has often been strictly limited. Government schools have historically not had either the incentive or the ability to respond to market conditions.

In other sectors, of course, private, for-profit firms typically have strong incentives to adapt and innovate, where doing so will increase the overall stream of profits.

---

15 This may not apply to "specialist" schools, such as schools that focus on music, drama or elite sports, for which the catchment area could be substantially larger.

16 Barr (n 5, 278) summarises: "There is no reason why schools in cities should not act competitively… But a rural school may have a local monopoly and, if run to maximise profits, would under provide."

We not see any particular reason why private for-profit firms would not have the same incentive in the education sector. Across the OECD, of the 12% of students who are enrolled in private government-dependent schools, around 8% are educated in for-profit schools.[17] This figure increases to over 50% in the case of Sweden, and in Turkey 7 out of 10 students in the private system attend for-profit private independent schools.[18]

But for-profit schools remain the minority, and in many OECD countries do not exist at all. Across the OECD the majority of students enrolled in private government-dependent schools attend not-for-profit institutions – either religious not-for-profit schools or other non-religious not-for-profit schools. There may be good reasons why not-for-profit institutions survive and thrive in the public services. For example, where quality is difficult for customers to measure, a commitment to a not-for-profit structure may provide an assurance and implicit commitment to customers that quality will not be cut *ex post*.

The effectiveness of both for-profit and not-for-profit structures depends on the quality of the governance and oversight. High-quality governance is typically easier to ensure in the case of a for-profit structure, where the owners have a direct financial incentive in the performance. But some of these incentives for high-quality governance could, in principle, be reproduced where the members of the school board have a direct personal interest in its success, such as parents who have children at the school.

A full discussion of the merits of for-profit and not-for-profit firm structures in the education sector is beyond the scope of this paper.[19] We merely note that, whatever structure is chosen, for competition to be effective education service providers must be willing and able to adapt and respond to market conditions, to meet the needs of customers, and to compete to attract students.

For choice and competition to be effective it is essential that schools not only have the incentive and ability to adapt. In addition, underperforming schools must be allowed – and indeed must be required – to exit the market. No matter how profitable and innovative their product offering, new entrants (with entrepreneurial skills) will be deterred from entering the market if incumbents are able to persistently earn a below-market cost of capital. Failing schools must be allowed to exit the market. There is a question how this applies to not-for-profit schools. Not-for-profit institutions (which are typically not subject to the threat of takeover) may be immune from the normal capital market disciplines. Among other things, not-for-profit institutions may be able to persistently earn

---

17 OECD, *School Choice and School Vouchers: An OECD Perspective* (OECD 2017), 6.

18 ibid.

19 See, for example, Timothy Besley and James M. Malcomson "Choice and Competition in Public Service Provision" (2016) STICERD Research at LSE, Paper No. PEP 29.

below-market returns on invested capital. This could in principle act as a barrier to entry. These questions remain to be explored.[20]

Of course, competition does not deliver desirable results unless the customers are willing and able to make choices in their own or their children's best interest. In our view, the majority of parents are willing and able to make an effective choice of schooling on behalf of their children. However, some parents do not have the capacity or the desire to do so and, in these cases, special support is required. In particular, parents with limited education or ability to make an effective choice may require special support in the choice of school for their children. Otherwise there is a risk that disadvantage may become entrenched from one generation to the next, undermining equal opportunity objectives.

There is likely to arise something of an information problem. Consumers are likely to have difficulty in observing the quality of the education provided – even for those consumers who have attended a particular school it can be hard to judge the relative quality of education (i.e., the counterfactual – how would the outcomes be different if I had attended a different school?). In any case, the quality of the education may be a personal or idiosyncratic experience (would the outcome be different if I attended the same school but was assigned different teachers, or met different classmates?). It can be even harder assessing the quality of education at a school without any direct personal experience.

The results obtained by students in standardised testing are relatively easily obtained. But such measures are only, at best, imperfect measures of the quality of education, since such results depend in part on the *ex ante* or intrinsic ability of the students and not solely on the quality of the teaching. In the absence of good measures, parents may be tempted to measure quality on the basis of easily-observable factors such as the quality of a school's physical facilities, which are not necessarily related at all to the quality of education. Alternatively, parents may make decisions on grounds such as where the other members of their child's friendship group are going. Barr notes:

> Knowledge of the nature of the product is certainly not perfect. Children (the immediate consumers) are not well-informed. In a market system decisions are therefore left to parents, at least for early education. But parents are likely at best to be only partially informed about such things as the quality of teaching… and the characteristics of the other children in the class.[21]

---

20 The issue of competition between for-profit and not-for-profit organisations is complex. See, for example, Richard A Hirth, "Competition Between For-Profit and Nonprofit Health Care Providers: Can it help achieve social goals?" (1997) 54(4) Medical Care Research and Review, and Rune Stenbacka and Mihkel Tombak, "Competition Between For-Profit and Nonprofit Health Care Suppliers and Quality" (21 August 2015).

21 Barr (n 5), 276.

This information asymmetry problem gives rise to the need for independent objective review, assessment and accreditation services. These services could perhaps be provided by the market or, alternatively, could be provided by government. The OECD has been a major contributor to this work, carrying out a major study on the evaluation and assessment of school performance culminating in 2013, together with a number of country studies on evaluation and assessment frameworks in the education sector.[22]

In 2006, the UK government concluded that for choice-based systems to be successful in raising educational standards for all, the following conditions were required:

> – Parents – particularly, parents of disadvantaged children – need to be provided with high-quality information, guidance and advice about the options open to them;
>
> – Help with the costs of making choices, such as covering the costs of transport to alternative schools, should be provided to those who need it; ... and
>
> – Above all, early effective action should be taken to tackle failing or poorly performing schools and increase the supply of good schools. Ultimately, the greatest safeguard against adverse effects on social inequalities and segregation is to make sure there are more good schools... Evidence... suggests that where schools face no financial implications from not attracting pupils there is only a limited behavioural response to choice.[23]

In summary, achieving effective competition between schools may require specific government action, such as the provision of comparator information on school quality, provision of transportation services for students so that they can travel to the school of their choice, mechanisms to ensure that schools have the ability to respond to financial incentives, and action to ensure that underperforming schools are able to (and indeed required to) exit the market. Provided that these issues are addressed, there do not seem to arise insurmountable barriers to competition between schools. But can this choice and competition be made compatible with government subsidies and the government objectives for education set out above?

---

22 See OECD Review and Evaluation and Assessment Frameworks for Improving School Outcomes (2009–2013) <http://www.oecd.org/edu/school/oecdreviewonevaluationandassessmentframeworksforimprovingschooloutcomes.htm> accessed 12 February 2020.

23 Department for Education and Skills, *School Reform: A Survey of Recent International Experience* (research paper, 2006), 5. Another condition was a prohibition on cream-skimming: "Schools should be prevented from 'cream skimming'... by putting in place funding regimes that reflect the higher costs of teaching some groups and by using regulation and statutory guidance to prevent unfair selection". This issue is discussed further below.

3. Competition and Subsidisation of Education

In this section we discuss how the scope for choice and competition depends on how the government subsidies are paid. One approach to subsidising education might be simply for the government to pay a fixed amount to each family with school-age children, and allow them to spend this money as they see fit (including on non-education goods and services). As long as the existence or the size of the subsidy is independent of the decisions of the consumer, the normal forces of competition can operate with little or no distortion. Some support services, such as disability support services, are paid in this way.[24] Many governments make direct payments to support the income of low-income and vulnerable taxpayers. However there is a substantial risk that, given the choice, the parents of some children would choose to not spend the funds on education, but on some other services (such as alcohol). We will not consider this approach any further.

We will focus instead on mechanisms in which government education subsidies must be spent on education services. One approach, of course, is for the government to pay a fixed amount to a school selected by the student and his/her parents. We believe that this fixed-fee-for-service approach can be compatible with competition and can lead to strong incentives for efficiency, innovation and responsiveness.

These ideas are, of course, not new. Following Friedman,[25] many countries have considered, trialled, or adopted *school voucher* schemes under which customers have a choice of school and the government educational subsidy is paid directly to the educational institution chosen by the end-user. There is quite a large amount of literature assessing the effects and outcomes of these reforms.[26] These voucher schemes differ in:

- The amount of revenue that is implicit in the voucher – from some fraction of the total (per student) funding of a school to the full (per student) government contribution;
- Whether the revenue implicit in the voucher varies with characteristics of the student – in some schemes, students from particularly disadvantaged backgrounds, or with special needs, are given a loading, weighting, or index on the basic voucher;

24 For example, Birmingham City Council provides Direct Payments for disability and elderly support services. Under this approach, end-users are allowed to choose how to spend their care and support budget allocated by the Council. This example does not fit the model perfectly, since customers cannot retain any funds not spent on care services themselves.

25 Milton Friedman, *Capitalism and Freedom* (University of Chicago Press 1962).

26 See, for example, OECD (n 17) and Mark Dynarski and Austin Nichols, "More findings about school vouchers and test scores, and they are still negative" (2017) 2(18) Evidence Speaks Reports.

- The students that are eligible to make use of the vouchers – in some schemes, the vouchers are restricted to students who would normally attend disadvantaged schools.

School voucher schemes are an example of a fee-for-service subsidy payment. Provided the revenue associated with the voucher exceeds the marginal cost of taking an additional child, the voucher scheme, coupled with choice, gives rise to a high-powered incentive on schools to attract students and therefore to achieve high levels of productivity, innovation and responsiveness to the needs of customers.

But there are also problems with the fixed-fee-per-service model:

A. The Topping-up Problem

It is widely believed that access to education is a fundamental component of promoting equality of opportunity. It follows that education services should not be allocated on the basis of parental income or wealth. As noted earlier, Stiglitz comments that "there is a widespread belief that children's access to education should not depend on their parents' financial ability or their sense of altruism".[27]

However, where choice and competition between schools is permitted, it is highly likely that some schools will be in demand. These schools may choose to, or be forced to, limit enrolments. The natural mechanism to balance supply and demand in this context is to increase the price – in this case, the tuition fee. This implies charging an additional fee to the end-customer, over-and-above the government subsidy. We refer to this as "topping up". In fact, under a system of unrestricted competition between schools, many schools will seek to, or be forced to, ration entry through the price system. Some schools will be considerably more expensive than others. These may be the schools which provide the greatest life opportunities.

In this world, the outcome of competition is likely to be – at least to some extent – an allocation of places at the schools which offer the most opportunity to those with the greatest ability to pay. In fact, for schools which choose to limit enrolment, the supply curve is, in effect, inelastic. An increase in government subsidy would be expected to result in an equivalent dollar-for-dollar increase in the price for education. In the absence of further intervention, the provision of government subsidy coupled with the right to choose the educational institution undermines the objective of equality of opportunity.

This problem is described by the OECD as follows:

> Critics argue that allowing publicly funded private schools to charge tuition fees gives these schools an unfair advantage over public

27 Stiglitz (n 7).

> schools and undermines the principle of free school choice. Like selective admissions, imposing substantial add-on fees tends to skim the top students from the public sector and increase inequalities in education…
>
> Relatively little is known about whether there is a threshold of household contributions beyond which lower-income families will be deterred from choosing subsidised private schools. However, both simulations and empirical evidence confirm that public funding may fail to widen access to private schools unless it is accompanied by restrictions on tuition fees. If private schools invest public resources to improve their quality, rather than to broaden access, subsidies can exacerbate inequities across school sectors. This is one of the reasons why abolishing substantial add-on fees, along with offering targeted vouchers, can help reduce disparities in achievement between advantaged and disadvantaged students.[28]

Many countries that have chosen to implement a voucher system for school choice (such as Chile or Sweden) have explicitly sought to prohibit "top-up" funding. For example, following concerns about a lack of equity in Chile's education system, a major reform was carried out which prohibited the charging of "topping-up" fees:

> In order to address equity concerns, the regulations governing school choice were considerably strengthened in 2016. The Inclusion Law (*Ley de Inclusíon*) seeks to ensure that school choice is not contingent on families' ability to pay, student achievement or other potentially discriminatory factors. The law forbids the use of economic, social and academic criteria for admissions, eliminates shared funding (*financiamento compartido*, tuition fees and public subsidies for a single private school) and forbids public subsidised schools to make a profit.[29]

But prohibitions on parental contributions are not always easy to enforce. Schools which seek to ration entry can request a range of supplementary inputs that parents are expected to provide. The simplest approach is to ask parents to make a "voluntary" contribution to the school. Parents can also be expected to volunteer their time to the school. Although not as obviously discriminatory, such rules can have a discriminatory effect where low-income families have less leisure time to devote to volunteering at the school and where well-educated parents can offer more highly-valued inputs (such as tutoring students). This

---

28 OECD (n 17), 15.

29 ibid, 22.

problem arose in the case of New Zealand, following the introduction of its own school choice programme:

> Most schools expect parents to pay "voluntary fees" to contribute towards the cost of running a school. Locally generated revenue is significant as a source of school revenue at secondary level (for urban schools). Obviously, parents who have less income can less afford these "voluntary contributions", so schools with an intake of children from predominantly poor backgrounds receive significantly less funding from this source than those with children from better-off families. While it is illegal to discriminate against children whose parents do not wish to/cannot pay this voluntary contribution, when schools can choose their students it is likely to be a consideration in a principal's decision about whether or not to admit a student if they are poor.[30]

If rationing through price is explicitly prohibited, how are schools to balance supply and demand? One possible approach is to ration through waiting lists or through lottery. In our view, neither of these approaches is satisfactory. In some countries oversubscribed schools are allowed to ration through waiting list. However, in one study it was found that the children who attended the school were overwhelmingly born in the first half of the year, since children could be entered on the waiting list as soon as they were born. It does not seem satisfactory to ration access to education by the happenstance of birth date.[31]

Some countries with school voucher systems (such as Chile, mentioned above) explicitly prohibit rationing by schools that participate in the voucher programme. Schools that participate in the voucher programme are required to accept all applicants. This is a fairly drastic intervention, but in our view is not unreasonable. It is possible that some inputs to the provision of high-quality teaching (such as access to the best teachers) are in inelastic supply and therefore unable to be easily scaled. But, overall, it appears that many aspects of education can be replicated and scaled up as needed. We speculate that many schools should be able to expand enrolment without undue dilution of quality. Concerns about sudden changes in student numbers could be mitigated by requiring that students indicate their intention to enrol in the school a few years in advance. For example, the requirement to accept all applicants could be limited to those applicants who indicate their intention two years in advance. With these modifications, some of the problems of an open-access system can be mitigated.[32]

---

30 Julian Le Grand, *The Other Invisible Hand: Delivering Public Services Through Choice and Competition* (Princeton University Press 2007), 90.

31 What about rationing by lottery? This seems equally artificial. However, where an open-access policy is infeasible, could it be a second-best choice?

32 We acknowledge that these mechanisms are not perfect. There are likely to be situations where this approach is less than perfect, such as in communities which are experiencing rapid growth or decline, or in the case of families that are highly transient.

To summarise, if equality-of-opportunity goals are to be achieved, access to educational opportunities should not be allocated on the basis of parental income or wealth. Although we have no objection to some, modest level of school fees,[33] the ability of schools to ration access by charging above a minimum threshold would be expected to result in allocation of educational opportunities on the basis of parental income and therefore must be restricted. This will likely require active enforcement. We do not support allowing rationing by queuing or by lottery. Instead, we prefer a mechanism in which all participating schools are required to accept all applicants (perhaps with some notice period, to mitigate problems from large swings in numbers).

B. The Cream-skimming Problem

The other primary concern with encouraging school competition using vouchers, is that of cream-skimming: the incentive for schools to identify and deny entry to high-cost-to-educate students.

There is a wide difference in how much it will cost a school to achieve its desired objectives with different potential students. As long as the voucher is for a fixed fee, independent of the characteristics of the student, each school has a strong incentive to compete vigorously for students who can achieve their desired objectives at the lowest possible cost, and to actively resist taking students for whom achieving the desired objectives will be very high cost.

But what are the objectives that each school wishes to achieve? In a world of school choice and competition, the objectives of each school presumably reflect the desires of customers. What do prospective customers (students or their parents) look for in a school?[34]

Where schools are assessed primarily on the basis of graduating students' academic performance on standardised exams, the cheapest way for a school to achieve good outcomes is to select students with high innate ability. This results in quite strong competition for the very best students. Students of average ability may find the range of schools willing to accept them is limited, while students of low ability may find no opportunities at all. This system has a tendency to favour parents who have prepared their children well, perhaps through tutoring, at an early age. It therefore seems to conflict with the objective of equality of opportunity. Barr:

> We know that (a) performance is determined largely by socio-economic background, and (b) schools in greater demand can attract more pupils and hence more funds. A school achieves (b) by maximising the examination results of its pupils; it does so most

33 Here, by modest we envisage something like one to two weeks of average wages. However, where it is difficult to enforce a rather arbitrary limit it may be better to eliminate the fees entirely.

34 Barr (n 5), 268: "Since there is no single definition of a 'good' education, there is no unambiguous measure of output. We can measure test scores, but (a) such measures are imperfect even in their own terms, and (b) educational outputs are much broader than such technical benefits."

> cheaply and easily be selecting students from higher socio-economic backgrounds. Just as medical insurers seek healthy clients, schools seek potentially high-achieving pupils.[35]

This problem persists even if schools are assessed in other ways. For example, it could be argued that a better approach would be to assess schools on the basis of the *change* in the academic performance of students on standardised exams – that is, the difference in performance from the time when the students enter the school, to when they leave. Here the change in performance could be argued to be a measure of the "value added" of the school.[36]

But even when schools are assessed in this way, there remain very strong incentives on the part of the school to actively seek out students who have the greatest potential to increase their performance, and to actively resist enrolment by students whose performance cannot be easily improved. Some children will have a greater natural "teachability" than others: such children will be significantly less costly to improve their performance than other students, who may require special attention, longer school hours, or one-on-one tutoring to achieve the same increase in performance level. Some children may have behavioural problems that will require extra attention from the teachers or disrupt the learning of their peers. Under a system of choice and competition, schools have a strong incentive to weed out such children. Again, the system of choice and competition works most in favour of those who have characteristics associated with being easy to teach; those who are more costly will face fewer schooling options or none at all. This may conflict with the objective of equality of opportunity.

Several countries have found that, following the introduction of school choice and competition, there was more "sorting" (or segregation, or stratification) in the school system, rather than an improvement in overall performance. Barr summarises the experience with school choice reform in New Zealand as follows:

> Until the late 1980s, New Zealand had a system of public finance of a centrally planned system where (other than moving house) parents had virtually no choice of school, and where local education boards gave schools virtually no management discretion. Radical reform in 1989... gave parents some choice over their child's school and removed schools from the control of local education boards. In further reform in 1991, regulation of school admissions was largely abolished... The result – cream-skimming – was predictable. Segregation increased as schools tried to improve their competitive position by selecting students who were most likely to do well in examinations rather than by improving the quality of education

35 ibid, 292.

36 Here we will put to one side the complaint that standardised tests cannot measure all of the objectives of a well-rounded education.

> they provided. As a result, diversity of school performance widened. In response, legislation in 2000 restored criteria for admissions policies. Children were given the right to a place at their local school, and where there was excess demand for places at a school, admissions had to give preferences to siblings and children of employees; beyond that, places had to be allocated by ballot.[37]

The OECD summarises the evidence as follows:

> The international evidence suggests that schools that are selective in their admissions tend to attract students with greater ability and higher socio-economic status, regardless of the quality of the education the schools provided. Given that high-ability students are less costly to educate and their presence can make a school more attractive to parents, schools that can control their intake can wind up with a competitive advantage. Allowing private schools to select their students thus gives these schools an incentive to compete on the basis of exclusiveness rather than on their intrinsic quality. That, in turn, can undermine the positive effects of competition. The evidence also shows that selective admissions can be a source of greater inequality and stratification within a school system.[38]

How can this problem of cream-skimming be addressed? One possible approach is to more carefully differentiate students into different groups, and to match the funding revenue to the likely cost of educating each student.

Many countries identify particular student groups, such as immigrant children, children from non-English-speaking backgrounds or children with special needs, and provide extra resources to schools who accept these students. These extra resources might take the form of, say, extra teachers in order to reduce the student – teacher ratio. For example, in Chile, a 2008 law (the *Ley de Subvención Escolar Preferencial*) provides additional funding to primary schools who enrol socio-economically disadvantaged students. The additional funding can increase the funds per student by 50%. Schools participating in the programme cannot select students by ability or socio-economic background and cannot charge additional fees. This programme was expanded in 2011 to cover secondary schools. Around 85% of eligible schools participate in this programme.[39]

---

37 Barr (n 5), 294.

38 OECD (n 17), 15. The OECD goes on to emphasise that as well as selective admissions, competing schools may use selective expulsion policies to eliminate low-performing students (i.e., those that are more costly to bring up to a standard). The Guardian reports an example from the UK: "Grammar school 'unlawfully threw out' students who failed to get good grades", 30 August 2017.

39 OECD, *Education Policy Outlook: Chile* (OECD 2013), 8.

Ideally, systems of school vouchers should, by independent and careful measurement, identify the key characteristics of each child and establish the revenue associated with each voucher at a level that induces schools to actively compete to provide educational services to that child. However, this process is unlikely to be perfect. There may still remain some students which are of particularly high or uncertain cost, and which do not fit easily within any pre-existing revenue categories. Monitoring of the voucher scheme may help identify situations where such cases emerge, and develop new categories as required. As a backstop, however, it may also be necessary to rely on lower-powered cost-reimbursement contracts. We suggest that schools willing to take on such students could be compensated for their out-turn costs, subject to close monitoring and control over the expenditure decisions by the government.

Furthermore, there are likely to remain some regions (such as small remote towns) where conventional competition cannot be sustained. In these regions introducing school choice is neither feasible nor desirable. Instead the government may choose to contract for educational services, perhaps through a competitive tender. Coupled with careful monitoring and enforcement, a contract for educational services should be able to ensure a minimum quality of education even for children in remote areas where conventional competition is not feasible.

The experience to date with school vouchers has not yet been universally positive. A survey of four different school choice programmes in the US by the Brookings Institute reports that recent careful studies show that students who participated in the school choice programme to attend a private school experienced a decline in key test scores compared with their peers who did not attend private schools.[40] This difference is hard to explain. Perhaps the students who moved to private schools are motivated by factors other than test scores. For example, perhaps those students (or their parents) are seeking to avoid violence, drugs, or bullying in their present school, or believe that attending a private school will lead to better long-term outcomes (such as college attendance or career prospects, perhaps due to better "old-boy" networks) regardless of test results. There is a strong need for further research.

Finally, we note that introducing choice and competition in education may possibly conflict with certain other government objectives, such as social integration and cohesion. One of the possible benefits of education is that it is a mechanism for inculcating core national values or acculturation. Hayek observed that "the United States would not have become such an effective 'melting pot' and would probably have faced extremely difficult problems if it had not been for a deliberate policy of 'Americanization' through the public school

40 Dynarski & Nichols (n 26).

system".[41] The school system may also be a tool for building bridges across religious or socio-economic differences. Barr observed:

> Education can create cultural benefits in a variety of ways including greater tolerance of diverse views and increased civic engagement… A common experience (music, art, literature) may foster communication generally, both at the time and in the future. In addition, there may be neighbourhood effects: the mechanics of taking children to school, parent – teacher associations, and the like, bring people into contact and more foster shared attitudes locally.[42]

Our preliminary view is that these concerns are not overwhelming. With careful attention to the issues identified above, choice and competition in education should not increase segregation along socio-economic lines. It remains possible that allowing choice and competition between schools may foster segregation on, say, religious or ethnic lines (particularly if members of each community have a preference to send their children to schools which promote their own religious or ethnic values). These effects could, perhaps, be mitigated by requirements on schools that participate in the government funding programmes, such as a prohibition on religious teaching, or the requirement to follow a (basic) national curriculum.[43]

4. Enhancing Choice and Competition in the Education Sector

Where does this leave us? What is the scope for choice and competition in the education sector? Taking all of the above considerations into account, the following lessons emerge as guidance for the promotion of choice and competition in the education sector:

- For choice and competition to be effective at all, attention must be paid to the basic competition conditions. Action may need to be taken to actively encourage competition and efficient consumer decisions, including:
  - Ensuring that students can easily travel to alternative participating schools (perhaps through the provision of public transport).
  - Information about the quality of schools to help parents and students choose (as well as information on what to look for when choosing a school).
  - Further assistance in cases where parents are unwilling or unable to make a choice on behalf of the student.

---

41 Hayek (n 7).

42 Barr (n 5), 271.

43 At the same time, one of the claimed benefits of school choice systems is an opportunity to "reduce the risk of political indoctrination". Barr (n 5), 290.

- Schools should have sufficient autonomy to respond to competition:
  - Schools should have ability to make decisions over staffing, philosophy and mix of inputs.[44]
  - Any barriers to school entry or expansion should be removed.[45]
  - Schools that are not able to earn a normal return should be allowed to exit the market.
  - Whether or not schools should be allowed (or required) to be "for-profit" remains unclear.
- Careful attention should be paid to school admission requirements and obligations on parents:
  - Careful consideration should be paid to preventing participating schools from denying entry to prospective students – i.e., schools should be required to accept all applicants with a reasonable notice period.
  - Schools should be prohibited from charging more than a regulated limit for fees and charges.
- Careful attention should be paid to funding:
  - As far as possible, the funding level for each student should reflect the expected cost for that student. This implies tailoring the fixed fee according to identifiable characteristics. As far as possible, each participating school should have a roughly equal incentive to compete to provide the education of each prospective student.
  - As a backstop, some schools could receive cost-based reimbursement for some particularly high cost or otherwise unusual students, to ensure that such students are not excluded. This would be expected to be accompanied by close monitoring by the government.
  - As a backstop, governments will need to be closely involved in the procurement, monitoring and/or regulation of schools in areas where competition cannot be sustained.

In short: this discussion suggests that effective competition in education services is possible, despite the presence of government subsidies and the need to pursue the basic government objectives identified above. However, perhaps unsurprisingly, specific and relatively strong controls on that competition are essential.

---

44 As an example, in the UK, so-called "free schools" and "academies" are funded by the government but are not run by the local council. They can set their own pay and conditions for staff, change the length of school terms and the school day, and are not required to follow the national curriculum. Between 2010 and 2015, more than 400 free schools were opened in England, representing 230,000 student places.

45 This includes, for example, a rule which prevents the opening of new competing schools in areas where existing schools have surplus capacity.

Specifically, in our view, schools that receive government subsidies must not be allowed to compete on price, and probably should not be allowed to deny entry to any applicant. These are relatively severe interventions. In addition, the government must pay careful attention to differences in the cost of educating different groups of students. Such differentiation may be tricky. Although we consider that this is not inevitable, there remains a risk that promoting competition between schools will enhance social segregation and undermine, rather than promote, social cohesion. We remain hopeful that these problems can be overcome.

At the same time there are large potential benefits. In our view there remains significant scope for school choice to significantly enhance the incentives on schools to provide educational services as efficiently as possible, to innovate, to provide the variety of services that parents and students desire, and to respond to changing market demands. Although the flame of competition in education must be tightly circumscribed, it is by no means extinguished entirely.

Antitrust and the Clash of Sovereigns – Bringing Under One Roof: Extraterritoriality, Industrial Policy, Foreign Sovereign Compulsion, and (Bad) Applications of Law Against "My Country's" Firms

ELEANOR M. FOX*

New York University

Abstract

When sovereign conflicts arise in the course of antitrust litigation, the traditional response is to retreat to "comity." This article challenges the traditional response. It argues that we have been too quick to find sovereign clashes and too timid to recognize common ground that may counsel reaching out rather than reining in. This is especially true in the case of hard core cartels in view of the near-universal norm against them. The article proposes that world welfare should be relevant especially in the case off-shore hard core cartels, justifying jurisdiction where the cartel harms the enforcing nation but the harm is not literally direct. Further, it proposes principles of legitimacy and illegitimacy in cross-border enforcement.

---

* Eleanor M. Fox is Walter J. Derenberg Professor of Trade Regulation, New York University School of Law. She thanks Koren Wong-Ervin for her helpful comments. The author is honored to dedicate this essay to Judge Douglas Ginsburg, who has done so much to advance antitrust law and policy in the United States and around the world.

In the presence of a global economy and in the absence of a global competition law, sovereigns clash. A system of global governance without a global regime would naturally consider norms for nations' extended or restrained jurisdiction over acts abroad with local consequences. In fact, nations have developed their own rules, often haphazardly, and often traceable to older times when sovereign states were less economically porous and before the era of interdependence. This essay attempts to reexamine appropriate reach or restraint of national jurisdiction in an age of a global commons of competition.[1]

The essay is about extraterritoriality, but the canvas is larger. "Clash of sovereigns" is broadly conceived. The essay includes the problem of how to treat orders by foreign sovereigns to their own firms to violate another nation's laws (thus, the foreign sovereign compulsion defense). It includes the use by one nation of strategic industrial policy to resolve its own antitrust cases against foreign firms that do business on its soil, and even the misuse by one nation of laws or process that impose costs on a complaining nation's firms. The insight is: these are all part of a central problem – a clash of sovereign interests.

The essay is not concerned with the law as it is. Rather, it is an invitation to reconceptualize appropriate and inappropriate spheres for national enforcement. A nation need not use all of space available to it,[2] but should not use space that unreasonably intrudes on other nations' legitimate sovereign interests, and other nations' legitimate interests include the community of nations' common interest in preserving a global competition commons.

The essay argues that traditional analysis is outdated in five respects, and shows how the analysis can be brought into a paradigm fitting for the 21st century. First, traditional analysis contains a presumption against extraterritoriality. This essay operates on the premise that, in the many areas in which the effects of acts are commonly global, the presumption is an anachronism. Second, traditional analysis assigns to separate silos what is essentially the same problem. The essay unites sister problems. Third, in many cases of litigation against private firms, traditional analysis sees the private firms as the principal stakeholders whose interests should determine the reach of the law. This essay posits state interests as prime and suggests considering any resulting unfairness to a firm as a subsidiary problem to be solved. Fourth, traditional analysis includes a laundry list of

---

1 I use the terms "jurisdiction," "subject matter jurisdiction," and "reach of the law" interchangeably, and not in the sense that evokes procedural consequences of burden of proof and the time at which the issue must be raised. *See* Morrison v. National Australia Bank, Ltd., 561 U.S. 247 (2010), for the technical procedural usage in the United States.

2 If nations systemically do not use the available space, this might signal or accentuate under-enforcement of law necessary to preserve the global commons of competition. *See* for discussion of "*inadequate internalisation of external effects of* [mergers] *across jurisdictions*," Damien J Nevin & Lars-Hendrick Röller, *Institutional Design: The allocation of jurisdiction in international antitrust*, 44 Eur. Econ. Rev. 845 (2000). *See also* Herbert Hovenkamp, *Appraising Merger Efficencies*, 24 Geo. Mason L. Rev. 703, 705 (2017): "Recent empirical literature suggests that merger policy today is under deterrent."

factors to balance in the case of a clash. This analysis treats jurisdiction based on significant effects as presumptively legitimate, defeasible only in narrow circumstances. Fifth, traditional antitrust sees the sovereignty problem as a two-player-game. This analysis identifies the "global commons of competition" as a player.

From the earliest days, the extraterritorial problem was seen as involving a universe of two sovereign players, for example, Turkey and France (the *Lotus*),[3] or the United States and the UK (*British Airways/Laker*).[4] It is fitting at last to recognize the global commons of competition. The world has an interest in preserving the global commons, unclogged by anticompetitive restraints. In this sense the old standby comity cases *Timberlane*[5] and *Mannington Mills*[6] both literally and figuratively miss the bigger picture.[7]

I conceive a clash of sovereigns broadly. The clash might or might not be justiciable. It might be a question for policy resolution. It might go beyond antitrust law into antitrust policy, which interfaces with trade, freedom of trade, and due process.

I pose five fact problems. I test them each against four standards. Based on the analysis, I suggest norms for the world.

Here are the four standards I use as a way of organizing the analysis of the fact problems. The first will be recognized as widely known and commonly applied:

(1) The law of a jurisdiction may appropriately reach conduct or transactions that emanate from abroad when the conduct or transaction has a direct, substantial and reasonably foreseeable effect on its territory or its citizens.

(2) The enforcement action and relief should not be disproportionate to the interests of the enforcing state.[8]

---

3 S.S. Lotus (France and Turkey), 1927 P.C.I.J.

4 *United States v. British* Airways *(Laker)*. The United States dropped a criminal information suit against British airlines for a conspiracy to squeeze out maverick Freddie Laker to accommodate the British, who were privatizing British Airways and did not want to deal with the financial cloud of pending litigation. *See Justice Takes Wing*, The Economist, Nov. 24, 1984, at 15.

5 Timberlane Lumber Co. v. Bank of America, 549 F.2d 597 (9th Cir. 1976).

6 Mannington Mills, Inc. v. Congoleum Corp., 595 F.2d 1287 (3d Cir. 1979).

7 *See* Koren Wong-Ervin, Bruce H. Kobayashi, Douglas H. Ginsburg & Joshua D. Wright, *Extra-Jurisdictional Remedies Involving Patient Licensing*, CPI (Dec. 2016), https://www.competitionpolicyinternational.com/wp-content/uploads/2016/12/CPI-Wong-Ervin-Kobayashi-Ginsburg-Wright-Final.pdf, giving regard to world welfare in analyzing the appropriateness of extra-jurisdictional remedies not necessary to protect domestic concerns in cases involving patent licensing. The article argues for restraint in imposing extra-jurisdictional remedies, especially, but not only, in cases in which the substantive rule is not clear or varies across countries.

8 Wong-Ervin, Kobayashi, Ginsburg & Wright argue that the only appropriate antitrust interest of the enforcing state is the domestic consumer interest. This essay takes a broader view and suggests a stance

(3) When (1) and (2) are satisfied, the enforcement and relief are presumptively legitimate. A complaining nation has the burden to prove illegitimacy.[9]

(4) When the subject matter of the enforcement action is one in which there is a world common interest and consensus, as in eradication of world cartels, there is a global commons of competition and a world welfare interest in its preservation. In such a case the controversy is greater than the sum of the interests of the parties (or nations) in the dispute. The world welfare interest counts in determining appropriate reach and limits of national law.

I apply these principles to the five following problem sets: potash, input cartels, the Chinese vitamin C export cartel, Intel-Lenovo/Acer incidents, and China's enforcement against Qualcomm and its merger clearance conditionalities.

Individuals who are more trusting in markets and skeptical of government interventions would prefer different presumptions and would highlight businesses' interest in certainty as well as nations' interest in regulating their own commercial affairs.[10] Business certainty and sovereigns' regulatory interests are discussed below. My principal aim in this essay is not to fine-tune the principles and presumptions but to put a common roof over problems of sovereign clash. The four principles provide one methodology for organizing the facts, to which we now turn.

I. Potash – Directness

Potash is a mineral used in agricultural fertilizers. The world potash market is highly concentrated with reserves confined to Canada and Russia/Belarus. China is the largest buyer market in the world, and the US is second. The farmers in developing countries are, together, large users. The potash producers (seven of them) had a price-fixing cartel. It was an open and obvious export cartel in Canada, whose officials told the press in defense of the cartel: Saskatchewan (the province at the source of Canadian potash) depends on its potash exports for its economic development; its large profit tax on substantial profits (35%, which it got from the export cartel sales) returned revenue to the Saskatchewan territory.[11]

---

of tolerance: that it is for the state to decide what interests it protects; for example, it might include rights of entrepreneurs to unfettered markets. The limiting principle is, as developed below: The state must not unreasonably interfere with the rights of other states. It does unreasonably interfere when it imposes externalities for the sake of aggrandizing its own economic power.

9 What is legitimate and illegitimate is fleshed out through the case studies below.

10 *See* Josh Hazan & Douglas H. Ginsburg, *Extraterritoriality and Intra-Territorality in U.S. Antitrust Law* (June 13, 2016), New Frontiers of Antitrust, 7th International Concurrences Review Conference, Concurrences No. 3 – 2016, 32–38, https://ssrn.com/abstract=3042670.

11 *See* Brenda Bouw and Andy Hoffman, *Sask. weighs in on Potash deal*, The Globe and Mail (Vancouver, September 1, 2010). The Saskatchewan government, contemplating the possibility of a Chinese SOE

The cartel's modus operandi for sales into the United States was simple: The cartel members arranged for a price increase to certain foreign buyers (it was $20 per ton in May 2004); thereafter the price increase charged by each cartel member into the US was exactly the same. The US buyers sued. The defendants moved to dismiss on grounds that the US effect was not direct; therefore no jurisdiction. The district court denied the motion. A panel for the Seventh Circuit Court of Appeals reversed on grounds that the effects of the cartel agreement in the United States were not direct. Sitting en banc, the Seventh Circuit court vacated the panel ruling and held that the effects in the United States were sufficiently direct. "*Direct*" does not mean only "*immediate consequence*," the court said. Directness is a relative term that is integral with the phrase "*direct, substantial, and reasonably foreseeable*." The US effects of the potash cartel were clearly substantial and foreseeable; therefore less weight had to be put on directness. The court, by Judge Diane Wood, made the case for a flexible, instrumental construction:

> Foreign cartels, especially those over natural resources that are scarce in the United States and that are traded in a unified international market, have often been the target of either governmental or private litigation. The host country for the cartel will often have no incentive to prosecute it. Canada and Russia... would logically be pleased to reap economic rents from other countries; their losses from higher prices for the potash used in their own fertilizers are more than made up by the gains from the cartel price their exporters collect.... It is the U.S. authorities or private plaintiffs who have the incentive – and the right – to complain about overcharges paid as a result of the potash cartel, and whose interests will be sacrificed if the law is interpreted not to permit this kind of case.[12]

Potash is an anchoring example. The price-raising effect on the US market was substantial and foreseeable. It was not indirect. The selling country profited from the cartel and supported it – since it hurt only foreigners. A buying country – the US – had the incentive to punish the cartel.

The United States would handicap itself – and the big needy populations in developing countries, and undermine world welfare – by choosing a narrow construction of "direct." Canada's and Saskatchewan's interest in supporting Saskatchewan's taxpayers by export cartel profits should be entitled to no weight; government support was a frontal assault on competition itself (Canada has laws against cartels and applies them when Canada is injured). Enforcement in

---

takeover of a leading Canadian potash firm, which had the incentive to break the cartel and increase production, opposed the takeover, saying: "The fear is that the new owner's primary motive – to supply food and fertilizer for their populations – would conflict with the province's goal of supporting its people through higher potash prices." Ibid.

12 Minn – Chem, Inc. v. Agrium, Inc., 683 F3d 845 (7th Cir. 2012).

the US is proportionate to US interests and is important to exonerate them. Wanting cartel profits is not a legitimate justification. The world welfare interest is clearly on the side of the US enforcement.

Moreover, since every antitrust nation has an anti-cartel law, allowing US jurisdiction does not impair certainty regarding how to conduct business, and allowing, even expecting, harmed nations to condemn the cartel does not interfere with the exporting nation's right to regulate its own economy.

II. Foreign Input Cartels With Assembly Abroad

Motorola Mobility is a good example of enforcement against foreign price-fixers of inputs that are assembled into finished products abroad, where the finished products are sold to the world. The price-fixing agreement took place in Korea and Taiwan. Koreans and Taiwanese fixed the price of liquid crystal display panels and sold them at the illegally inflated price in China to Chinese manufacturer/assemblers, who incorporated them into smartphones in China and sold the smartphones to the world. They shipped 42% of the phones to the US; indeed, directly to their parent, Motorola Mobility, which had organized the LCD sales from Korea and Taiwan to its own Chinese subsidiaries. If Motorola Mobility and the United States sue the price-fixers (they did),[13] are the suits impermissibly extraterritorial? Do they create clashes that warrant deference to foreign sovereigns, either because Korea and Taiwan want to help their nationals (shield them from US liability) or because China might be offended by the "undercutting" of its emerging antitrust legal system?

We assume that Motorola Mobility has had to pay an inflated price, which it would have to prove to win its case, and we know that US buyers have to pay more for their smartphones; thus the price-fixing caused an anticompetitive effect in the United States.

Defendants claim that US public and private enforcement against the price-fixers creates a clash of sovereigns that warrants deference; that they are beyond reach of US law.

The chips were made for US phones. The effect in the US was foreseeable; the higher price to be paid by US buyers would predictably be substantial. The trajectory of the chips was reasonably direct (although degrees of directness could be and was a point of contention). The home countries ban price-fixing when it hurts their nationals. Providing a remedy in US courts is without question proportionate to US interests and important to exonerate them. The world welfare interest aligns with enforcement. Indeed, if China or the Chinese manufacturers

13 United States v. AU Optronics Corp., 778 F.3d 738 (9th Cir. 2015); Motorola Mobility v. AU Optronics Corp., 775 F3d 816 (7th Cir. 2015); cert. denied in both.

could not be counted on to sue, and if all nations into which the assembled product is sold adopted a hands-off approach for cartels of inputs into products assembled elsewhere, China would become the jurisdiction of choice for assembling – and laundering – price-fixed inputs, and global welfare would be much diminished.[14] As in *Potash*, neither the business certainty rule nor a sovereign right to regulate the home market is implicated. All relevant countries have an antitrust rule.

Defendants raise the possibility of double counting in damages and fines whenever more than one nation can assert jurisdiction over a set of practices.[15] This might be unfair (although probably not over-deterrent, for the various schemes of enforcement worldwide are significantly under-deterrent).[16] We simply need a rule of no double counting. Is it relevant that Korea and Taiwan would like to help their nationals price fix into America with impunity? Such a nationalistic contention would rub against the grain of a community of nations respecting one another's laws, let alone, against the global commons.

III. Chinese Vitamin C Export Cartel – A Foreign Sovereign Defense

The Chinese vitamin C makers fixed the export price of vitamin C to the United States. They admitted it. The price-fixing took place within the Chinese trade association, Association of Importers and Exporters of Medicines and Health Products. Trade associations in China were infused with the presence of government officials, who typically guided the firms in the interests of China; thus, the trade associations were not all private, as they are in the United States today (as opposed to the time of the New Deal and the oil companies' crisis cartel).[17] US direct buyers sued. The defendants pled foreign sovereign compulsion

---

14 The Court of Appeals for the Seventh Circuit dismissed the case by Motorola Mobility as impermissible under the Foreign Trade Antitrust Improvements Act of 1982. The court held that Motorola Mobility was not injured by the cartels' effect in the United States. If it was injured, it was injured by the effect in China. Moreover, the court thought Motorola Mobility had elected China as its forum when it created the Chinese subsidiaries. Also the court said that Motorola Mobility was presumed not injured by reason of the *Illinois Brick* doctrine – it was an indirect purchaser. The court's holding was questionable but not material to this essay, which is not concerned with the FTAIA and with the limits that nations put upon themselves but rather with constructing a framework for considering appropriate apportionments of jurisdiction.

15 In numerous cases the laws of a number of jurisdictions apply to the same conduct or transaction because numerous jurisdictions are affected. This is so in the case of mergers, abuse of dominance and cartels where effects cross borders.

16 *See* John M. Connor, *Sanctions In Antitrust Cases*, OECD Global Forum on Competition, Dec. 1–2, 2016, DAF/COMP/GF(2016)9. But *see* Wong-Ervin, Kobayashi, Ginsburg & Wright, *supra*, concerned with over-deterrence even of cartels in the event of double counting.

17 *See* United States v. Socony-Vacuum Co., 310 U.S. 150 (1940) (government officials were helping the oil companies ease their way out of the Depression, but this was no defense to the price-fixing).

and comity. Reacting to the lawsuit and primed on the US foreign sovereign compulsion defense which allows the defense only if the foreign government ordered the offending conduct, the Chinese Ministry of Foreign Commerce (MOFCOM) told the federal district court that it ordered the firms to fix their export prices. MOFCOM explained: The firms needed to adjust to a market economy, and wanted to avoid a US antidumping action. Did MOFCOM really order the firms to fix prices? The trial court submitted the issue to the jury. The jury found no, MOFCOM had not ordered the firms to fix their prices, and it returned a large award to the overcharged buyers. The Court of Appeals for the Second Circuit reversed. It held that comity required the court to accept China's word on its face (China's interpretation of its own law) and that the Chinese interests outweighed the US interests, and it dismissed the case. The Supreme Court held that China's interpretation was entitled to respectful consideration but was not conclusive, and it vacated and remanded.[18]

Chinese Vitamin C is not about extraterritoriality, but it is about a clash of sovereigns. The analysis applicable in the cases of extraterritoriality is equally applicable.

- Were the effects of the price-fixing direct, substantial and reasonably foreseeable? Yes, without question.
- Was the US enforcement proportionate to the interests of the United States? Yes, without question.
- Where did the world welfare interests lie? This was a naked cartel, not limited to the United States. World welfare lay with the enforcement.
- There was a conflict of sovereigns. How should it be resolved? China wanted to shield its firms from the US antitrust system. But so did Canada (in potash), and Korea and Taiwan (in LCD panels); they just did not say: "I order."

Why should a country's order to its firms (let alone its claim that it ordered its firms) to violate the regulating country's law be enough to differentiate potash and LCD and to immunize the price-fixers? What gives China a greater interest in shielding its firms from the US anti-price-fixing law than the interest of the US in enforcing its world-standard law against price-fixing?

The easy answer is, the US law makes this distinction.[19] But is this the law we want and should have? The foreign sovereign compulsion defense is meant to

---

18 Vitamin C Antitrust Litigation, 837 F.3d 175 (2d Cir. 2016), vacated and remanded sub nom. Animal Science Products v. Hebei Welcome Pharmaceutical Co., 585 U.S. – (2018).

19 The United States has a rule of law allowing as a complete defense a foreign sovereign order on its own territory, and it has a rule of law requiring courts to take at face value a foreign sovereign's interpretation of its own law. The case law on both points is thin. There are few precedents. A change in the law would be disruptive for business. But rules should be changed if they are bad rules and do not accommodate

provide only a narrow gateway to violators.[20] A firm cannot justify violating US law just because it was acting pursuant to its own government's policy and encouragement;[21] it must be ordered to do the anticompetitive act. The defense was intended to forego application of US law only in the rare case in which the foreign firms had no choice but to act in breach of the US law; they had to do the act even against their will to further their sovereign's policy.[22]

If China did order its firms to fix prices in violation of US law and the law of all antitrust jurisdictions including its own internal market rules, this was a frontal assault on US law and world norms. China's own domestic law not only prohibits price-fixing but prohibits government officials from ordering price-fixing.[23] Although there was a clash of sovereigns, the US and world interests easily outweigh China's.[24]

IV. Intel (EU): The Geography of Constituent Acts

Intel makes the chip that is inside most personal computers; it is "the nervous system" of the computer. Intel sells about 95% of all such chips in the world. AMD was its one competitor of significance. AMD had not been a strong competitor; its chip was not as good as Intel's; but finally AMD invented a great new chip. This event galvanized Intel. Intel put in place various strategies (or so the European Commission found) to try to keep the AMD chip from getting traction in the period that mattered the most – the first six months after launch. One set of Intel's strategies were "naked restraints," and the other, exclusivity (loyalty) rebates. The naked restraint category comprised calls from an Intel official to its biggest customers, some of whom had already signed contracts for the new AMD chip. The Intel official would say in effect: We want you to breach your contract with AMD. We will buy you out of the contract

---

to a changing economic environment. This essay is trying to examine what are the wisest rules for this economic age, on the supposition that if there are better rules we should find the way to adopt them.

20 *See* US Department of Justice and Federal Trade Commission Antitrust Enforcement Guidelines for International Enforcement and Cooperation, January 13, 2017, Section 4.2.2.

21 *See* Hartford Fire Ins. Co. v. California, 509 U.S. 764 (1993).

22 Would jurisdictions thoughtfully allow a foreign sovereign to give its nationals authority to price-fix and to do so no matter how high the firms fix the price? States of the United States do not have this power. California Retail Liquor Dealers Ass'n v. Midcal Aluminum, Inc., 445 U.S. 97 (1980). Moreover, under EU law, even when firms are compelled by the state to allocate quotas, they are not protected from EU anti-cartel law if they could have set the quotas in a more procompetitive way. Consorzio Industrie Fiammiferi v. Autorità Garante della Concorrenza e del Mercato (Italian matches), Case C-198/01, EU:C:2003:430.

23 *Vitamin C*, note 18 *supra*. *See* the Chinese Anti-Monopoly Law, Articles 13, 36.

24 *See* Eleanor M. Fox & Merit E. Janow, *China, the WTO, and State-Sponsored Export Cartels: Where Trade and Competition Ought to Meet*, *in* William E. Kovacic: An Antitrust Tribute 319 (Nicolas Charbit & Elisa Ramundo eds. 2014).

and give you a very good deal if you switch back to Intel and do not buy the AMD chip for six months. As for those customers not already in contract with AMD, Intel made an equivalent approach. It offered payments or rebates conditional on delaying the launch of the AMD chip. The customers accepted the deals. The big customers included Lenovo in China and Acer in Taiwan. Geographically, the relevant conversations and sales were between Silicon Valley and Beijing or Taipei. Both Lenovo and Acer agreed to Intel's proposition. They breached contracts with AMD or delayed the launch, and continued to use the Intel chip in their tablets and laptops. They shipped the finished product to buyers all over the world, including Europe. The European Economic Area accounts for about 32% of purchases of the devices with the chip inside. It is impossible to know which of the devices contained the diverted chips that went to Europe.

The European Commission found that Intel had violated EU's abuse of dominance law. The General Court affirmed. On appeal to the Court of Justice, Intel asserted among other things that the court (and the EU) had no jurisdiction over the Lenovo and Acer segments of the case. The European Court of Justice affirmed jurisdiction.[25]

Does the Intel problem pose a clash of sovereigns? It would probably not do so if the law were exactly the same on both sides of the ocean, in which case the EU enforcement would complement and boost the US law. But if the law is divergent (or if an enforcing jurisdiction should lack due process, especially if process deficiencies impugn the fact-finding), the US might be heard to complain. Substantively, the US argument would be: These are my companies. This was all about low pricing and competition. When AMD introduced its new chip, Intel had to respond. Intel responded by charging a very low price; but it was not below cost. This was competition itself.

Let us assume that Intel's challenged conduct had or threatened to have a significant anticompetitive effect. Assume that it marginalized AMD's new chip, which otherwise would have made great inroads; that a rule of law allowing Intel's conduct would chill innovative efforts by AMD and other possible challengers, who now see a rocky path for launching innovative products; that Intel's conduct kept the price of the Intel chip higher than it otherwise would have been, and that Intel's conduct had this effect all over the world, of course including Europe. At least, let us assume, this is a credible story and one that a court could reasonably uphold.

Did the European Court have jurisdiction over the Lenovo and Acer incidents? This is a matter of EU law, and should be unless the EU enforcement is an unreasonable intrusion into US space and world welfare.

---

25 Case C-413/14 P Intel v Comm'n, EU:C:2017:632, remanding the case to the General Court for reexamination of the anticompetitive effects of the conduct.

Until the EU *Intel* judgment, the European Court of Justice grounded extraterritorial jurisdiction on the question whether the offending conduct was implemented in the EU.[26] Intel argued that its conduct with Lenovo and Acer was implemented in China and Taiwan and was therefore impermissibly included in the case. When the case reached the Court of Justice, the Court took the occasion to enlarge the jurisdictional test. It endorsed a "qualified effects" test, asking whether the conduct was capable of having an immediate, substantial and foreseeable effect in the European Economic Area. The court held that it was.

Analysis of appropriateness of EU jurisdiction over the Lenovo and Acer segments would go as follows:

1. There is a substantial and reasonably foreseeable effect of the Lenovo/Acer chip-switch all over the world, including significantly although not uniquely in the EU. The question is whether the effect is immediate or sufficiently immediate (or direct).

   This is a world market offense. The EU is a significant part of the world market. If Intel harmed competition in the chip, the EU has a significant interest to exonerate. Moreover, the Lenovo/Acer incidents are pieces of a larger puzzle; they are part of a single, continuous infringement that (the European Commission found) was intended to foreclose Intel's sole significant competitor from the world market.[27] By filling out the picture rather than fragmenting it, the European Commission and then the courts could better appreciate the scope and effects of Intel's acts.

2. Is the enforcement action against Intel with regard to Lenovo and Acer disproportionate to the interest of the EU? The factors above (1) are equally relevant and would point in the same direction. However, if there is a significant question about whether the challenged acts underlying the two incidents are procompetitive or anticompetitive and if there is concern that the EU institutions will prohibit procompetitive conduct, the potential US interest in non-enforcement would become part of the equation and proportionality is less distinct.[28]

3. Let us assume that the European Commission has met the criteria of directness, substantiality and foreseeability and no lack of proportionality, then, according to the proposed standards, Intel has the burden to prove illegitimacy of the enforcement. How would it do so? It might induce the United States to file an amicus brief in European proceedings to say: The Lenovo incident is a matter between the US and China and the Acer

---

26 Cases C-89, 104, 114, 116-17, 125-129/85, A. Ahlstrom Osakeyhtio v. Comm'n (Woodpulp), EU:C:1988:5193.

27 *Intel*, General Court judgment at para. 260–273; ECJ judgment at para. 40–60. On appeal, only the Lenovo incident remained as a jurisdictional issue in the case.

28 *See* Wong-Ervin, Kobayashi, Ginsburg & Wright: Disagreement as to competitive merits should lead to restraint regarding extra-jurisdictional remedies.

> incident is a matter between the US and Taiwan. The EU has no direct connection. The EU's effect is derivative from the world effect. Indeed, it would be argued (given the different appreciation of what is anticompetitive according to two different substantive models): World competition is enhanced by freedom of firms to engage in competition just as Intel did.

There was no such US brief.[29] The theoretical arguments are still available. The clash of sovereigns is just under the surface.

If proportionality is questioned and there is no burden shift to Intel, the arguments are still the same. Underneath, there is a question of political philosophy and presumptions about how well markets work, what induces innovation, and how effective is antitrust intervention.[30]

The more aggressive reach of EU abuse of dominance law – and that of most nations as compared with US monopolization law – does create uncertainty for business. There is significant world debate about what is the better approach, even within the EU and the US. The *Intel* ECJ judgment on the substantive aspects of the case may signify a step toward more convergence. The enforcement by the EU is tightly related to EU's regulation of its own economy; but no one nation owns the problem. It is a problem of and for the world.

4. This is a world problem. On which side of the equation does the world competition interest lie? The answer depends both on the facts and on the point of view. Were Intel's acts an abusive use of leverage undermining an innovative challenger and thereby entrenching a dominant firm, or were they just low price competition?

These questions could hardly have been resolved at the point at which the European Commission asserted jurisdiction over the Lenovo and Acer incidents as it launched its investigation. Nor could they easily have been resolved as the case proceeded. This observer agrees with the European Court of Justice that the incidents were too integral with a common core to be ignored.

V. China: Qualcomm and Merger Remedies – Industrial Policy and Claims of "Bad Law"

Qualcomm owns the most important technology inside smartphones. Most of the smartphones are manufactured in China. The manufacturers complained about the high licensing fees. The Chinese competition authority, the National

29 Indeed, in the United States, the Federal Trade Commission opened an investigation against Intel, including more conduct than the European Commission challenged. The case was settled. Matter of Intel Corporation (2010), decision and order at https://www.ftc.gov/sites/default/files/documents/cases/2010/08/100804inteldo_0.pdf. The United States is well known for a laissez-faire view of the offense of monopolization. *See*, e.g., Verizon v. Trinko, 540 U.S. 398 (2004).

30 *See* Wong-Ervin, Kobayashi, Ginsburg & Wright, urging restraint.

Development and Reform Commission, investigated Qualcomm's practices and eventually accused it of charging royalties based on a portfolio including expired patents, bundling non-essential patents with essential patents, forcing licensees to agree not to challenge the patents, and keying the royalty to the entire finished device, not just the value of the licensed technology. Some observers understand the case to be essentially a claim of excessive royalties. After a lengthy period of investigation in which Qualcomm complained of serious due process violations, Qualcomm settled, agreeing to exclude expired patents from its packages, reducing the royalty base to 65% of the finished product, among other things, and agreeing to pay a fine of nearly US$1 billion.[31] Soon after, it was announced that Qualcomm agreed to a joint venture with a Chinese firm.[32]

Glencore/Xstrata[33] was a merger of two Anglo-Swiss trading and mining companies with a relatively small percentage of sales of the relevant products in China. China cleared the merger on condition that the firms divest a copper company in Peru to a Chinese firm and that they continue to sell a specified amount of copper to China. The merger had no anticompetitive effect in China. It appeared to outsiders that the authority (MOFCOM) simply used the opportunity of the merger and the parties' need for Chinese merger clearance to extract conditions that would give China more copper.

The *Qualcomm* matter and the several merger clearances with conditions unrelated to competition problems have fed into an American claim that Chinese authorities are using the Chinese Anti-Monopoly Law to lower the value of Americans' intellectual property, to appropriate natural resources for China, and otherwise to advance its own industrial policy.[34] There is a clash of sovereigns, with US, and perhaps UK, Switzerland and others, wanting to protect their companies and their technological advantages from appropriation. How does the Chinese enforcement fare under the suggested framework?

The *Qualcomm* case raises no extraterritorial issues. The licensing was directly into China, and MOFCOM's remedy was not extraterritorial.[35] *Glencore/Xstrata* does not raise extraterritorial issues with respect to the vetting of the merger. It is common cause today that a merger that has effects or even a sufficient stream of revenues into a country is subject to the jurisdiction of that country for

31 *See* China's NDRC accepts Qualcomm's rectification plan, Feb. 10, 2015, https://archive.eetasia.com/www.eetasia.com/ART_8800709736_499488_NT_92130273.HTM.

32 For Qualcomm's recent activity in China, see David Barboza, *How This U.S. Tech Giant Is Backing China's Tech Ambitions*, N. Y. Times, August 4, 2017.

33 *See* Hannah C. L. Ha & John M. Hickinz, *MOFCOM Orders Extraterritorial Divestiture of Key Mining Asset in Glencore/Xstrata*, Mayer Brown, May 6, 2013

34 *See* International Competition Policy Expert Group, *Report and Recommendations*, US Chamber of Commerce, March 2017, https://www.uschamber.com/sites/default/files/icpeg_recommendations_and_report.pdf.

35 *See* Wong-Ervin, Kobayashi, Ginsburg & Wright.

purposes of premerger notification and clearance. There were sufficient contacts with China to warrant investigation of the conduct (*Qualcomm*) and vetting of the merger (*Glencore/Xstrata*). But the merger relief was both extraterritorial and unrelated to competition.

Was the enforcement or relief disproportionate to the interests of the state? In the merger case, the relief was disproportionate to a Chinese antitrust interest. But the Chinese Anti-Monopoly Law requires the authorities to consider mergers' effects on "national economic development"; not just consumers. This is a broad industrial policy clause and it would be hard to claim that the relief was disproportionate to the nationalistic industrial policy interest. Since that is the case, the question becomes whether the relief excessively intrudes upon other nations' interests. It may do so. In the case of excessive intrusion, according to the framework suggested, China would have to justify, arguing that the relief was legitimate in view of the conflicting sovereign and world welfare interests. We revisit this question under "Legitimacy" below.

Is the action against Qualcomm disproportionate to China's antitrust interest? to its industrial policy interest in "*promoting the healthy development of the socialist market economy*" (AML Section 2)? Let us first examine the antitrust interest, for if that is satisfied we need not turn to the more amorphous industrial policy.

The charges that China made and settled against Qualcomm may not be outside of the mainstream of the antitrust laws of nations, even if they are contentious. The case is principally about tying, bundling, and using the leverage of patents beyond the bounds of the patent grant, leading to very high royalties. As China regulates its own economy, it has the right to draw the balance between competition and intellectual property in a way that favors competition (or lower rates) more than it favors protection of IP holders' exclusive rights[36]—as long as it applies its rules transparently and non-discriminatorily.[37] Its law prohibits excessive pricing – which US law does not. Its foray into this area is not illegitimate, even though attacking royalty rates of technology licensing as excessive is a complex project. If China were to apply a different rule of law to its domestic firms than it applies to foreign firms, it would then be discriminating against outsiders in violation of the rules of the World Trade Organization. This author does not know of evidence that China has discriminated in this sense in the *Qualcomm* case, even though there is a "feeling" that China was and is targeting high-tech American firms that have technology that China wants.[38]

---

36 The remedy for "bad law" is conversation; dialogue; trying to convince. As more Chinese firms become inventors and patent holders, China may gain the incentive to develop more IP-friendly law.

37 Given the international controversy as to what is the better rule, China should have a duty of restraint against imposing extra-jurisdictional remedies. *See* Wong-Ervin, Kobayashi, Ginsburg & Wright.

38 *See, e.g.,* Jacob Schlesinger, *Trump Administration to Begin Probe of Alleged Chinese Technology Theft*, Wall Street Journal (Aug. 12, 2017). The best approach for perceived targeting may be to

If, however, China has denied due process to outsider firms, it would fail to meet the test of presumptive legitimacy on that ground alone.

Legitimacy. This is the point of action in this problem. For the *Qualcomm* case: The possible points of illegitimacy are lack of due process and discrimination, if that could be proved. But illegitimacy is not proved by the arguments, standing alone: You (China) have sued "my" firm; you are applying "wrong" principles of law; as a result you are getting valuable US intellectual property cheap.

For *Glencore/Xstrata*: The relief on its face is excessively intrusive. It has no relation to competition and it appears that China is simply using antitrust as a hook to get resources it wants. This maneuver is inconsistent with the spirit of the WTO and China's WTO accession commitments to free and open export markets except in the case of explicit reservations (and China made no relevant reservations on its accession to the WTO). In a better world, China would be required to defend and justify its conditions. But there is no law to require it to do so.

Is there a world common interest in facilitating or preventing these enforcement actions and remedies? On which side does world welfare lie? World welfare lies against imposing costs on outsiders for strategic economic gains (*Glencore/Xstrata*). But, as to *Qualcomm*, world welfare includes freedom of experimentation in designing rules of law, including the competition/IP interface, as long as the nation applies its rules equally at home and abroad, and grants due process. Thus, in the one case there does appear to be excessive intrusion into the sphere of other nations, and in the other case (*Qualcomm*) (where there may be more at stake), the argument of illegitimate intrusion is difficult absent proof of lack of due process or discrimination.

VI. Observations and Conclusions

Let us now make observations from this set of problems.

First, "extraterritoriality": Extraterritoriality is not always a helpful term. Semantically it may imply illegitimacy, but most often a reach beyond borders when the effects of the actors' conduct are within the regulating nations' borders is perfectly natural and proper. A more constructive focal question is: Is the reach of a regulating nation's law excessive in view of the nations' legitimate interests and world welfare?

Second, world welfare is a helpful referent, especially useful in areas in which there is consensus. The anti-cartel rule is the paradigm.

---

merge antitrust complaints with similar complaints in other disciplines such as trade and to treat the matter as a political policy matter rather than an antitrust matter.

Third, actions that could give rise to claims of sovereign conflict are nonetheless legitimate when the conduct's effects within the sovereign nation's jurisdiction are direct, substantial and reasonably foreseeable, the enforcement is proportionate to the regulating nation's legitimate (not parochial) interests, and especially when the enforcement contributes to world welfare. In such a case, a complaining country should have the burden to prove that the action or relief is illegitimate because it is excessively intrusive into the sovereignty of the other.

Fourth, the *Qualcomm* problem. Enforcement would be illegitimate if it were discriminatory in the WTO sense or if due process had been denied.

Fifth, the *Glencore/Xstrata* problem. The use of industrial policy in antitrust is not itself illegitimate[39] but where it is part of a strategy to impose costs on outsiders, as by extracting intellectual property or desired resources in the course of antitrust enforcement but without any relation to competition policy, the strategy should be recognized as an illegitimate use of antitrust law. It violates the general cosmopolitan principle embedded in the WTO. But we are in need of articulation of a world norm. Work should be done to formulate such a norm. It could be done within the context of the International Competition Network or the OECD.

Sixth, the *Intel* problem. Strategies of multinational firms often encircle the world and belong to a common core. In the absence of world antitrust law, which we do not have and will not have for the foreseeable future, world welfare is presumptively enhanced by allowing a regulating jurisdiction to include in its case all parts of the problem. The alternative is to disintegrate the parts so that no jurisdiction can grasp the whole. Therefore, in this author's view, the Lenovo and Acer segments were a proper part of the EU case.

Seventh, *Chinese Vitamin C*. For the sake of the global competition commons, one nation should never be allowed to declare its firms immune from another nation's price-fixing law just because it says so. A rule allowing such a "naked" shield[40] is a perverse rule. The US foreign sovereign compulsion defense should be limited to sovereign commands that have an integral relationship with the foreign sovereign's regulation of its own economy.

Lastly, *Potash* and *LCD*. These should be simple cases. "Direct, substantial and reasonably foreseeable" is an iterative category. "Foreseeable" of course includes "intentional." When cartelists fix prices of goods or inputs intended to exploit markets abroad and they do so, public and private actions in the harmed market

---

39 For example, when South Africa imposes conditions on mergers that save jobs or build capacities of small suppliers, it is not the business of other countries to complain. South Africa undoubtedly judges that the conditions will return more benefits than costs, and it is willing to pay the costs. The transaction costs that fall on foreign companies seeking to do business in South Africa are mere by-products.

40 A "naked shield" implies that the nation has no reason for the order except to shield its firms from another nation's enforcement.

against the members of the cartel are fair game and good game. The alternative is a cartelized world; an offense to the global commons. Problems of double counting are properly separately addressed, and they should be addressed.

By elevating and dissecting the clashes of sovereigns, we may build a more coherent road for conceptualizing laws' reach, nations' restraint, and common cause.

Norms that Promote Long-Term Institutional Improvement in the Face of Leadership and Regime Changes

WILLIAM E. KOVACIC*

George Washington University Law School

Abstract

Judge Douglas Ginsburg's career is a gallery of extraordinary accomplishment and distinction. He excelled first as a professor and scholar, next as a civil servant in senior government leadership posts, and then as a federal judge. In recent years he has returned to his roots as a teacher and, in giving seminars on competition law to judges around the world, has added what may be the finest chapter of his professional life. The global increase in judicial acumen in antitrust economics and law may be Doug's most powerful, enduring contribution to this truly international discipline. To contemplate Doug's work across the span of over four decades provides an occasion to reflect on what it takes for a nation to build an effective legal system, including the construction institutions vital to the effective regulation of commerce. This paper reflects on one ingredient of this process of institution-building: the development of leadership norms that promote the long-term improvement in the ability of public bodies to perform regulatory tasks expertly. Doug Ginsburg's teaching of judges abroad is a powerful example of making investments that pay off over the long term – to improve the legal system in ways that may not be apparent until all of us are gone. How can we inspire public officials to make similar investments?

---

* Global Competition Professor of Law and Policy, George Washington University Law School; Visiting Professor, Dickson Poon School of Law, King's College London; Non-Executive Director, UK Competition and Markets Authority. The author is grateful for comments from participants in the 2018 Conference on Private and Public Executive Power at the University of Chicago Law School. The views expressed here are the author's alone. Contact: wkovacic@law.gwu.edu.

Preface

Judge Douglas Ginsburg's career is a gallery of extraordinary accomplishment and distinction. He excelled first as a professor and scholar, next as a civil servant in senior government leadership posts, and then as a federal judge. In recent years he has returned to his roots as a teacher and added what may be the finest chapter of his professional life. I work with lots of new competition law systems around the world. An urgent priority in these jurisdictions is to build the capability of the courts in antitrust economics and law. Judges expert in antitrust law have played a crucial role in building this capability, and none more than Doug Ginsburg. From continent to continent, his teaching has proven highly effective in giving judges the analytical tools and confidence they need to resolve antitrust cases skillfully. In my conversations with dozens of judges, Doug's positive influence emerges again and again. The global ascent of judicial acumen in antitrust economics and law may be Doug's most powerful, enduring contribution to this truly international discipline.

To contemplate Doug's work across the span of over four decades provides an occasion to reflect on what it takes for a nation to build an effective legal system, including the construction institutions vital to the effective regulation of commerce. This paper reflects on one ingredient of this process of institution-building: the development of leadership norms that promote the long-term improvement in the ability of public bodies to perform regulatory tasks expertly. Doug Ginsburg's teaching of judges abroad is a powerful example of making investments that pay off over the long term – to improve the legal system in ways that may not be apparent until all of us are gone. How can we inspire public officials to make similar investments?

I. Introduction

In 2008–2009, the Federal Trade Commission (FTC) conducted a self-study in anticipation of the one hundredth anniversary of the agency's formation in 2014.[1] The agency convened a number of public hearings and conducted interviews concerning the future direction of the FTC's competition and consumer protection work. The proceedings focused chiefly on possible refinements in the agency's organization and operations.

Frederick Hilmer provided one of the individual interviews. In the early 1990s, Hilmer chaired a study that triggered major economic reforms in Australia and the redesign of the country's competition and consumer protection regulatory

1 William E. Kovacic, Chairman, FTC, *The Federal Trade Commission at 100: Into Our 2nd Century* (January 2009).

system.[2] At the time of the interview, Hilmer was Chancellor of the University of New South Wales and taught business school courses, including executive education classes. I asked him what he regarded as the most important lesson he sought to impart to the executives. To paraphrase a bit, his answer went like this: "The good things that are happening today in your organization are probably the result of investments that your predecessors made years ago. When you go home each evening, ask yourselves this question: What steps did I take today to make my organization successful, 10 years from now?"

Hilmer's advice goes to the heart of a major challenge whose resolution can determine whether institutions rise or fall. Each day, the leadership of countless private and public institutions changes hands. The former head of the institution – an advocacy group, a charity, a company, a government agency, a professional society, a university, and others – departs, and a new leader arrives. Myriad questions involving the relationship of new leaders to old arise in these transitions. Do new leaders understand how their predecessors improved the performance and reputation of the institution? Do new leaders embrace helpful programs and practices that their predecessors nurtured or initiated? Do new leaders outwardly recognize their predecessors for good work done?

Here are two basic approaches that new leaders take towards their immediate predecessors. One approach can be described as "Even Better."[3] Here the new leader identifies the institution's valuable previous work and thanks predecessors for their contributions to the institution's good programs and processes. The new leader strives to build on the institution's healthy traditions and taking new steps to make the institution "even better." In this vision, the new leader is a member of a team in a relay race, where ultimate success depends on the performance of each team member in individual legs and on effective baton exchanges at the end of each leg.[4]

A second approach can be called "Dire Straits." Here the new leader portrays the institution's programs and processes as a shambles. The new leader pledges heroic efforts to reinvigorate the badly underperforming institution. In a Dire Straits transition, the new leader places heavy blame for the institution's failings on previous management. In one variant of this scenario, the new leader simply

---

2 National Competition Policy Review, NATIONAL COMPETITION POLICY (Government of Australia, Aug. 25, 1993) (Frederick G. Hilmer, Chairman).

3 I borrow the phrase "even better" from presentations that Lord David Currie and Alex Chisholm made to the staff of the newly formed Competition and Markets Authority (CMA) in 2014. The CMA was formed by combining two predecessor agencies with responsibility for UK competition policy – the Competition Commission and the Office of Fair Trading. Currie and Chisholm routinely praised the contributions of the predecessor bodies and expressed their aim of making the new institution "even better."

4 I borrow the relay metaphor from Deborah Majoras, who chaired the FTC from August 2004 to March 2008. Deborah Platt Majoras, Chairman, FTC, Opening Remarks at the FTC's 90th Anniversary Symposium (Sept. 22, 2004).

ignores the predecessor altogether. The predecessor vanishes from the institution's history, much like the Soviet-era party functionaries who fall out of favor and are blotted out of older photographs.

There are times when a new leader *should* adopt a Dire Straits approach because the institution *is* in dire straits. Some institutions fail so spectacularly – through feeble imagination, sloth, timidity, or outright corruption – that a new leader must clean house and adopt policies that repudiate the catastrophically bad choices that earlier leaders have made. Anything short of a clear break from the past might be perceived, by the institution's own staff and external observers, as acquiescence in the bad programs or processes that brought the institution to grief.

Even here, however, a wise newcomer might exercise some caution in singling out a predecessor to vilify as a scapegoat. The causes of horrific failures, upon examination, occasionally turn out to be more complex than one might think at first glance. Reconstructions of matters such as the Challenger space shuttle disaster[5] and the attack on Pearl Harbor[6] have revealed how a combination of forces, rather than misconduct by one or a few persons, caused a catastrophe. The Dire Straits approach is sensible only when extreme measures are necessary to rehabilitate a failed or failing institution. Even so, some nuance is warranted to identify and preserve pockets of capability that have generated good results, notwithstanding the largely dismal quality of an institution's work.[7]

---

5 *See, e.g.*, Diane Vaughan, The Challenger Launch Decision (1996). Professor Vaughan's study of the Challenger disaster rejects "conventional interpretations that focus on managerial wrongdoing" by NASA. Her research "reveals a more complex picture that shifts our attention from individual causal explanations to the structure of power and the power of structure and culture – factors that are difficult to identify and untangle yet have great impact on decision making in organizations." *Id.* at xv.

6 For example, the experience of military institutions provides many examples how simple initial conclusions can give way over time to more complex explanations for specific events. Inquiries conducted after the Pearl Harbor disaster of December 7, 1941 condemned the senior Navy and Army officers (Husband Kimmel and Walter Short) in charge of the Pearl Harbor naval base and Army Air Corp installations on Oahu. Memoirs of military personnel present at Pearl Harbor in late 1941 and subsequent study of previously classified records have revealed that fault for the disaster resided at least as much with Washington-based US military and diplomatic officials who failed, owing to organizational lapses and institutional rivalry, to warn the Hawaiian Islands commanders of the emerging dangers to their forces. *See* Edwin T. Layton, And I Was There: Pearl Harbor and Midway – Breaking the Secrets (1985) (discussing intelligence and organizational failures in the Washington, D.C. armed services and diplomatic corps that contributed to Pearl Harbor disaster). During the change of command process, the naval officer who replaced Kimmel (Chester Nimitz) did not excoriate his predecessor and instead treated him with dignity. Perhaps this was because Nimitz realized that factors well beyond leadership failures of Kimmel and Short had exposed the US forces to a surprise attack.

7 In 1969, two studies of the FTC damned the agency for weaknesses in leadership, recruiting, and program selection. Much of this criticism was well-deserved. Yet the often categorical condemnation of the agency in the two reports overlooked significant accomplishments that should have dictated a more nuanced assessment, or at least an explanation of how a manifestly misguided institution could occasionally do exceptionally strong work. The two studies of the FTC are evaluated in David A. Hyman & William E. Kovacic, *Can't Anyone Here Play This Game? Judging the FTC's Critics*, 83 Geo. Wash. L. Rev. 1948 (2015) (*FTC's Critics*).

This paper explores how one might develop norms that coax each generation of leadership to accept, in the ordinary case, an Even Better management philosophy. The paper approaches the topic in three parts. It begins by describing why an Even Better approach to leadership transitions can promote long-term improvements in an institution. The paper then examines why new leaders resort to variants of the Dire Straits approach.Th paper then presents techniques for building norms that promote recourse to the Even Better approach. This discussion relies heavily on methods that increase the historical awareness of new leaders about the institutions they are about to head.

The principal inspiration for the paper comes from my experience in working for and with economic regulators, mainly agencies responsible for competition policy and consumer protection policy, though the paper also draws upon examples from other institutions. The themes addressed here build on earlier work with James Cooper,[8] David Hyman,[9] and Marc Winerman[10] about the behavior of organizations and the people who lead them.

II. Why the Understanding and Recognition of Past Achievement Matters

For three basic reasons, the Even Better method to leadership transitions has greater capacity to improve an institution's performance. For many institutions, good programs today often build upon an accumulation of experimentation and implementation experience over time. For example, the FTC's modern litigation successes – including three straight victories before the Supreme Court from 2013 to 2015 in antitrust cases – arose from what Jonathan Nuechterlein has described as "a multi-decade FTC initiative focusing on a difficult and discrete area of competition policy."[11] The same can be said for the development from the 1970s to the present of Department of Justice (DOJ) criminal antitrust enforcement into a powerful element of US competition policy.[12] To summarily

---

8 James Cooper & William E. Kovacic, *Behavioral economics: implications for regulatory behavior*, 41 J. Reg. Econ. 41 (2012).

9 Hyman & Kovacic, *FTC's Critics, supra*; David A. Hyman & William E. Kovacic, *Why Who Does What Matters: Governmental Design and Agency Performance*, 82 Geo. Wash. L. Rev. 1446 (2014); William E. Kovacic & David A. Hyman, *Consume or Invest: What do/should Agency Leaders Maximize?*, 91 Wash. L. Rev. 295 (2016) (*Consume or Invest*).

10 Marc Winerman & William E. Kovacic, *Outpost Years for a Start-Up Agency: The FTC from 1921–1925*, 77 Antitrust L.J. 145 (2010); Marc Winerman & William E. Kovacic, *The William Humphrey and Abram Myers Years: The FTC from 1925 to 1929*, 77 Antitrust L.J. 701 (2011).

11 Jonathan Nuechterlein, General Counsel, FTC, Remarks at Administrative Law Review Symposium, 1–2 (Mar. 20, 2015).

12 This progression is recounted in Donald I. Baker, *The Use of Criminal Law Remedies to Deter and Punish Cartels and Bid-Rigging*, 69 Geo. Wash. L. Rev. 693 (2001).

reject or denigrate earlier work (and the leaders who oversaw earlier endeavors) is to overlook significant foundations for future success.

Second, a new leader's spoken appreciation of good work previously done can build the morale and productivity of managers and staff who have served the institution in an earlier period. I cannot offer a rigorous proof for the proposition, but my experience working in public and private institutions has indicated that staff derive satisfaction from their association with an institution that is well respected. Such employees are important to the institution's success under the new leader. Nothing good comes to the institution from belittling their past efforts on its behalf.

Third, a new leader's spoken appreciation for good programs and processes developed in the past helps enhance the institution's reputation in the eyes of important external audiences. Institutions develop "brands" that play a role in determining their success.[13] Public statements by top leadership constitute one means by which the brand is enhanced or degraded. A regulatory body with a good brand is arguably more likely to receive deference from reviewing courts and to receive a sympathetic hearing from legislators when it defends its request for an expansion of its budget or powers. An institution understood to be engaged in a conscious process of continuing improvement is more likely to inspire confidence than an institution guided by a series of leaders who routinely disparage past work but assert that they will right the sinking ship.

The Even Better approach does not entail a new leader's commitment to make no changes to the status quo. It contemplates that new leaders will be a source of vitality by bringing new ideas to the agenda and by taking the institution in new directions. New leaders can be an antidote to contentment with how things have been done (even in a very successful institution) and can provide a fresh set of eyes to see possibilities that others have overlooked. Anne Bingaman's tenure as Assistant Attorney General (AAG) for Antitrust during the Clinton administration in the 1990s demonstrates that the denigration of past accomplishments is not essential to making refinements or carrying out significant adjustments in the institution's organization, staffing, and programs. Bingaman was Bill Clinton's first appointee to serve as head of the Antitrust Division. Her speeches generously praised the work of Republican AAGs, including William Baxter and Douglas Ginsburg.[14] Bingaman also initiated major upgrades of the DOJ's leniency program and, in doing so, transformed the detection of illegal cartel agreements in the United States and around the world. Bingaman showed how a new leader can vocally embrace the good work the agency has done in the past and still add new ideas to the mix.

---

13 William E. Kovacic, Creating a Respected Brand: How Regulatory Agencies Signal Quality, 22 Geo. Mason L. Rev. 237 (2015).

14 See William E. Kovacic, *Politics and Partisanship in U.S. Federal Antitrust Enforcement,* 79 Antitrust L.J. 687, 705 (2014) (*Partisanship*) (describing Bingaman's speeches at DOJ).

III. The Appeal of the Dire Straits Narrative

Despite the advantages to the institution of an Even Better approach to leadership transitions, various forces may press new leaders to embrace variants of a Dire Straits message. Four impulses stand out.

1. Poor Historical Awareness

A new leader may overlook good work the agency has done in the past, or understate the contributions of earlier leadership to current success, through ignorance of the institution's history – why it was created, what it has done, and what forces shaped its program over time. Some new leaders come to their institutions with deep knowledge of the institution's history, but others do not. Deep expertise in a specific field and keen historical awareness are not prerequisites for individuals to ascend to high leadership positions. A person who knows little about an institution's past may be prone to embrace simplistic portrayals of what the institution has done.

2. Self-Aggrandizement

A longstanding aphorism for performers doing live comedy is "Never follow a funny comedian." A funny comedian raises the expectations of the audience. By contrast, a bad comedian enables a good comedian who is next in the queue to excel by comparison. Part of the intuition of this ancient advice is that external observers grade on a curve; the current performer will be judged partly by how external observers assess the quality of the previous performer and later performers.

In some instances, the external observer is perfectly capable of judging whether a performance was successful. The jokes either made them laugh or had no effect. The audience may be less able to tell what accounted for a good performance. A number of factors might shape the success or failure of a live comedy act: the performer's skill in presentation, the writer's ability to generate good material, the wisdom of a manager in guiding the performer through a progression of appearances to refine their craft, or the pure luck of having a receptive audience rather than a collection of sullen drunks. In any event, the audience can assess for itself whether the act was funny, even if it cannot discern precisely all the sources of its success.

Evaluating an institution can be a more difficult task. In a number of instances, it may be hard to assess how well the institution is executing its mandate. Is an antitrust agency doing a good job of merger enforcement – clearing procompetitive or benign transactions, but blocking or modifying harmful deals? Is an anticartel program deterring the formation of new cartels? Are antitrust agencies making sound judgments about prioritization and project selection? In all of these areas, it may take a long time – perhaps decades – to know if the agency is performing effectively.

Suppose an institution is widely regarded as generating good outcomes. A further difficult question remains: what caused the good results? Was it the skill of middle managers and the professional staff, who would have achieved a beneficial outcome regardless of who led the agency at the time? Was the good outcome mainly a product of wise decisions taken by top leadership in an earlier period? In attempting to answer these questions, it may be difficult to assign proper credit for the good results.

New leaders bent on self-aggrandizement will strive to magnify their own contributions to what appears to be good performance of the institutions. Credit-claiming can take several forms. An incumbent leader might denigrate the contributions of a predecessor – either by asserting that the predecessor did nothing of value (setting a low baseline against which to compare the incumbent) or denying predecessors credit for actions that helped yield the current success. Another technique is to exaggerate the significance of the agency's current initiatives, portraying new matters as policy breakthroughs when the matters in question do not advance the state of the art.

The desire of new leaders to elevate their own profile also can warp the institution's decisions about how much resource to allocate to current projects and how much to invest in building capability that improves future projects. This is the decision to "consume or invest."[15] A new leader motivated mainly by self-aggrandizement is likely to spent too much on consumption – in the form of launching new initiatives – and too little on investment whose positive impact on the institution's performance may not become apparent until well after that leader has departed. The emphasis on consumption also may tend to commit the institution to projects that exceed its capability to deliver good results. A leader preoccupied with credit-claiming will be concerned foremost with launching projects that capture attention, and less concerned with how the projects come to earth.

3. Incentives that Discourage a Long-Term Perspective

Credit-claiming and other forms of self-aggrandizement are not the only reasons a new leader may emphasize consumption over investment. A variety of external observers – academics, the bar, elected officials, and journalists, just to name a few – may evaluate an institution's performance by measures that encourage short-term consumption rather than long-term investment. In doing so, they encourage leaders to focus on the relatively short term, rather than viewing the immediate period of leadership in a longer continuum and taking decisions that seek to replicate and extend earlier success.

In the area of regulatory policy, activity-based measures of success prevail. The prosecution of a greater number of cases, for example, is often taken to be a

15 Kovacic & Hyman, *Consume or Invest*, *supra* note 8.

proxy for an agency's effectiveness. Investments that build agency capability for the long term, and enable the agency to take on more ambitious matters over time, tend not to generate headlines, speaking invitations, or expressions of gratitude by legislative oversight committees.

If the institution's stakeholders praise activity and regard investment indifferently, new leaders may consume considerably more than they invest. The environment that surrounds many public officials does not create robust incentives to make investments that improve their agencies over the long term. Anthony King and Ivor Crewe describe the condition in which top ministerial officials operate:

> [T]here is one incentive that they lack: to think a long way ahead, to contemplate seriously the probable consequences for future generations of whatever it is they do today. They may choose to think ahead. They may worry about future generations. They may even worry about their place in history, if they think that they may have one. But beyond their own consciences, they have no positive incentive, in the here and now, to do any of those things.[16]

As Hugh Heclo has observed, this point of view robs an institution of the capacity to see how institutions evolve and to understand the importance of investments that benefit the institution in the long term: "Nothing closes so many doors on real opportunity as opportunism. A person who is forever weighing the odds of immediate success can never believe in anything long enough to make it succeed."[17]

4. Partisanship

In the world of public institutions, partisanship can be a strong motivation to embrace a Dire Straits narrative.[18] Regime changes in which control of the executive branch moves from one party to another rarely take place on the basis of carefully balanced discussion of the policy preferences of the contestants. It is not common practice for presidential candidates to campaign by acknowledging the good work of their adversaries. The party on the outside does not seek the presidency by offering a few improvements on what is conceded to be a largely sound program. The outside party striving to get into the White House is likely to depict the current administration as craven, inept, and destructive.

A campaign that gains the White House by depicting the incumbent administration as charlatans likely will have spillover effects when it comes to appointments to federal agencies. If the party line in the campaign is that an agency was gravely deficient, it is unlikely that a new appointee to run that agency will soften the

---

16 Anthony King & Ivor Crewe, The Blunders of Our Governments 156 (2013).

17 Hugh Heclo, *The Spirit of Public Administration*, 35 PS: Political Sci. & Politics 689, 691 (2002).

18 William E. Kovacic, *Partisanship, supra* note 13.

message – at least not very much. The new leader instead will feel compelled to import the slogans and clichés of the campaign into the process of transition. This may be fueled by a transition report that recited endless flaws of the agency and credited previous management with few or no positive contributions.

In this way, partisanship accentuates the embrace of a Dire Straits narrative. The public agency was on the rocks, and the new leader promises to salvage the vessel and set it on a proper course. If the agency is lucky, new leaders gradually will come to realize that their predecessors did some good work, and the putatively derelict agency had some strong programs and processes in place. The new leaders may come to see that important elements of the status quo are worth preserving, if only because they will help generate accomplishments for which the new leaders and their party can claim credit. The new leader likely will dissipate time and agency resources reflagging these elements with the party's insignia, but at least they will survive and serve the agency well in the future. If the agency is unlucky, the new leader will destroy sound institutional features before awareness of their value takes hold, or because the icons of the previous management must be shattered as an end in itself.

IV. Even Better: Building Healthy Norms for New Leaders

How to gain greater acceptance for an Even Better approach to leadership transition? The discussion below identifies how greater historical awareness of an institution's origins and development can nurture greater acceptance of the forward-looking norm suggested by Fred Hilmer and captured in the Even Better approach to leadership transitions.

In 1979, as a junior attorney with the FTC, I attended a program of Economic History Seminars organized by Thomas McCraw for the agency. McCraw was in the midst of a research agenda that soon would yield hi masterwork, *Prophets of Regulation*.[19] For the FTC seminars, he enlisted Alfred Chandler, Robert Cuff, Louis Galambos, and Ellis Hawley to join him in examining the changing conceptions of the role of the state in the US economy from the late nineteenth century to the present.

These were eye-opening presentations. At the time, Congress and the courts were shoving back hard at the FTC for its efforts to carry out an ambitious agenda of competition and consumer protection programs developed in the 1970s. The seminars made us all aware of the sobering difficulties that the FTC had encountered since its creation in seeking to fulfill its mandate to ban "unfair methods of competition" and apply exceptional information-gathering powers to study business behavior. It would have been valuable for the agency's leadership to have attended such a seminar a decade earlier.

---

19 Thomas K. McCraw, PROPHETS OF REGULATION (1984).

The historians' seminar program turned out to be a one-off, though the FTC produced an edited transcript.[20] Each new generation of FTC leadership should study that transcript. Newly appointed leaders at the FTC and other economic regulators would benefit significantly from a short course that addressed the themes of the 1979 seminars and added others on the history of US economic regulation.

History and interdisciplinary inquiry mattered to McCraw and his fellow lecturers at the FTC seminars. Does historical awareness matter to the regulators? How has historical awareness informed the formation and implementation of regulatory policy in the United States and abroad? Do regulatory agencies today routinely (or occasionally) draw upon knowledge of their past, and the history of other regulatory institutions, to guide decisions about strategy, prioritization, project selection, and institutional reform?

In the discussion below, I consider the development and application of historical knowledge in the context of the US federal antitrust system concerning the work of the DOJ and the FTC. Antitrust is one of the oldest US federal regulatory regimes, and its origins, aims, applications, institutions, and effects have inspired a massive volume of commentary. A considerable amount of this work has a historical orientation – sometimes in a discussion of what Congress meant to achieve in adopting the antitrust statutes, sometimes in a review of the path of doctrine over time, and sometimes in examinations of what the DOJ and FTC have accomplished in different eras.

Does historical awareness make a difference in the work of the federal antitrust agencies? From my own first-hand observations, dating back to the mid-1970s, the answer is yes. The DOJ and the FTC have taken useful steps to reflect on their own experience, more recent and more distant, and to study the work of other regulatory institutions to guide current and future decision-making.[21] These measures have yielded better diagnoses of commercial phenomena, greater understanding of how specific initiatives affect economic performance, stronger processes for the selection and implementation of programs, and sharper intuition about what agencies do well and what they do poorly. US agencies are not alone in taking these steps. My work with regulators outside the United States reveals similar beneficial developments abroad, and multilateral bodies such as the International Competition Network have made "knowledge management" (which encompasses the development and application of institutional memory) a centerpiece of its work on policy implementation.

---

20 Office of Special Projects – Bureau of Competition, FTC, *National Competition Policy – Historians' Perspectives on Antitrust and the Business Relationships in the United States* (Aug. 1981).

21 These steps are described in William E. Kovacic, *The Importance of History to the Design of Competition Policy Strategy: The Federal Trade Commission and Intellectual Property*, 30 SEATTLE L. REV. 319 (2006).

For all the good trends, there is room for improvement. By reason of their effort and longevity, US agencies have an unparalleled base of experience. To adapt some modern jargon, the DOJ and the FTC have big antitrust data. For the most part, the agencies have not realized how deeper analysis of that data could improve project selection. At a more general level, the agencies have done less than they might to examine past experience to identify the characteristics of successful programs and to understand the causes of program failures. In these and other ways, past experience is an underexploited resource for policymakers.[22]

The discussion below describes the main focal points for historical study relevant to regulatory agencies; examines how historical knowledge can strengthen policy formation and implementation; and reviews how the US agencies use history. In doing so, the discussion identifies specific respects in which fuller historical awareness could help US federal antitrust agencies embrace an Even Better norm for leadership transitions.

1. Historical Analysis for Regulatory Agencies: The Relevant Focal Points

This section describes the types of knowledge that comprise the history of a field of regulation and a regulatory agency. It sets out the focal points of inquiry that can increase understanding about the origins of a regulatory regime and the behavior over time of the institutions entrusted with the regime's implementation.

The field of journalism provides a rough way to think about what we expect from a historical approach to studying regulation. In principle, the news reporter pursues positive inquiries. Reporters are urged to build stories around the following questions:

Who was involved?

What happened?

Where did the events take place?

Why did the events occur?

By contrast, columnists and editorial writers generally address normative questions. These include:

What do the observed events *mean*?

Are the observed events *good* or *bad* for us?

The writing of history, more recent and more distant, about regulatory agencies can be classified in a similar manner. Inquiries about the history or regulatory institutions also can be placed into two baskets: positive and normative.

---

22 *See* Edward J. Balleisen & Elizabeth K. Brake, *Historical Perspective and Better Regulatory Governance: An Agenda for Institutional Reform*, 8 Reg. & Gov. 222 (2014).

A. Positive Historical Inquiries

The positive inquiries involve the identification of what happened in a given period of time. Among the things that historians and policymakers might want to know are:

Activity Types and Levels

- How did the agency use its resources?
- What cases did the agency initiate? What kinds of cases? How were these cases resolved?
- What research programs did the agency pursue? Which studies did it publish?
- What advocacy activities did the agency undertake before other public institutions?
- Which conferences, symposia, or other forms of public consultation did the agency convene?
- How much did the agency invest in policy research and development to build institutional knowledge?

Organization and Operations

- How was the regulatory agency structured?
- How did the agency organize its internal operations?
- How did the agency take decisions?
- How large was the agency's budget?
- How many people did the agency employ, and in what capacities?
- How did the agency's structure and operational framework change over time?

Powers

- What was the agency's substantive mandate? How did that mandate change in a given period?
- What capacity did the agency have to collect information from business operators?
- What remedies could the agency seek for infringements? How did the agency use its remedial authority?

Motivations

- What explains the agency's behavior?
- What forces guided its choice of priorities, its selection of projects, its adjustments in process and organization?

Effects

- How did the agency evaluate outcomes?
- How did the agency's program affect economic performance?
- How did the agency's program affect business behavior?

B. Normative Inquiries

The second category of inquiry involves normative assessments. These include:

- Did the agency do the right things: did it apply its resources wisely?
- Did its programs achieve good substantive results? By which criteria should the quality of its resource allocation and the substantive results of its efforts be assessed?
- Did the agency do things the right way: did it use sound processes in its internal deliberations and in its engagement with external groups? By which criteria should its processes be assessed?
- What adjustments does experience commend?

2. Contributions of Historical Awareness to Agency Performance

What does a system of regulation gain by trying to answer these questions and apply historical knowledge to contemporary decision-making – to establish systematic approaches to do what Richard Neustadt and Ernest May have called "thinking in time streams"?[23] This section suggests how historical awareness can improve regulatory agency performance. The discussion also presents the limitations of historical research, including methodological obstacles and behavioral phenomena that require care when assessing the reliability of individual historical studies.

A. Learning

Learning is a vital source of proficiency for any institution, including regulatory bodies. I came to see the value of institutional learning vividly in three years with a law firm working for clients in the aerospace and defense industry. From 1983 to 1986, I worked extensively on projects for McDonnell Douglas, and I spent lots of time with engineers who designed and built aircraft and launch vehicles. Many of my counterparts had been with the company since the early 1950s; they had worked on five or more aircraft programs that had long production runs. One of my closest professional acquaintances had worked on

23 Richard E. Neustadt & Ernest R. May, Thinking in Time – The Uses of History for Decision Makers 247–70 (1986).

each of the programs that had made McDonnell Douglas a major supplier to the US Department of Defense and to armed forces around the world: the F-101, the F- 4, the F-15, and the F-18.

My McDonnell Douglas colleagues emphasized two points. First, the careful assessment of experience, good and bad, informed decisions about the next project. By studying what worked and what did not, the company achieved steady (and often spectacular) improvements in performance from one generation of aircraft to the next. The second point concerned the development of the judgment of the institution. One colleague told me that, in contemplating a new aircraft design, the company had well-proven solutions to 90% of the problems it would confront. The crucial issue was whether the design and production team could solve the 10% of the problems for which no immediate solution was apparent. For example, could the company achieve full-scale production of a now-experimental lightweight material that, if eventually available in large quantities and at acceptable costs, would dramatically reduce weight and enable the company to extend the range and payload of a new aerospace system? Past experience provided an invaluable guide to answering the question, both in terms of suggesting technical methods to reduce and resolve uncertainties, and in sharpening a more intangible institutional intuition about whether problem could be overcome.

In my time at the FTC, I saw this phenomenon at work in the agency's competition and consumer protection programs. One notable illustration concerned introduction, in 2003, of the Telemarketing Sales Rule, known as the Do-Not-Call (DNC) rule.[24] The introduction of the DNC regime required the FTC to overcome three significant obstacles: to overcome objections that the DNC rule, which enabled consumers to enlist the FTC's assistance in blocking unwanted telemarketing calls, impermissibly restricted commercial speech; to devise a system that could accurately register large numbers of telephone numbers (through 2018, the DNC registry included over 235 million numbers); and to withstand severe political opposition generated by lobbying from telemarketing service providers and their principal trade associations. The successful resolution of these issues was significantly brought about through careful application of 20 years of experience with consumer protection rulemaking; with litigation involving the compatibility with First Amendment free speech guarantees of FTC competition and consumer protection orders; and with repeated encounters with Congress over specific applications of the FTC's mandate.[25] Learning did two things: it showed the agency how to surmount specific obstacles associated with the DNC rule, and it informed the FTC's intuition about whether the DNC initiative would succeed.

---

24 Telemarketing Sales Rule, 68 Fed. Reg. 4580 (Jan. 29, 2003), codified at 16 C.F.R. pt. 310.

25 See William MacLeod, Elizabeth Brunins & Anna Kertesz, *Three Rules and a Constitution: Consumer Protection Finds Its Limits in Competition Policy*, 72 ANTITRUST L.J. 943, 964-67 (2005) (describing challenges FTC overcame in promulgating and implementing Do Not Call Rule).

B. The Limitations of Learning

In setting out the benefits of learning, it is necessary to identify problems that impede effective learning. Even a regulatory institution dedicated to making the fullest possible use of historical awareness confronts serious difficulties in determining what happened in the past, knowing why it happened, understanding its effects, and forming a judgment about whether past practice made things better or worse. These tasks involve tricky questions associated with the collection and interpretation of information.

The modern literature on behavioral economics and psychology has reminded us of forces that can warp historical analysis and render it meaningless, or harmful.[26] Here are just a few complications. The willing student of the past may be overwhelmed with information – even for a single regulatory agency. To take one example, there is an immense body of information about the FTC – agency decisions, orders, guidelines, speeches, rules, oral histories, collections of papers of key agency officials and influential outsiders, and an Everest of commentary on the institution. Even before facing hard questions of interpretation, the researcher can despair at the difficulty of creating a data set that consistently and accurately tracks the agency's activity over time. And we have not begun to try the FTC's work in context by comparing it with other regulatory institutions at home or abroad.

One common response to information overload is to resort to badly imperfect rules of thumb (heuristics). The historical inquiry can founder because the chosen methodological rules of thumb distort data collection terribly and yield unreliable interpretations. Confirmation bias can induce the researcher or the user of historical analysis to ignore or de-emphasize information and interpretations that contradict a preferred hypothesis. Any proponent of historical research as a guide to regulatory decision-making must acknowledge the frequency with which papers that invoke history to support policy prescriptions are engaged in what Daniel Ernest has called the search for "a usable past"[27] – a form of brief-writing that showcases favored authorities and sidesteps contrary or inconsistent decisions.

Even when researchers and the users of historical analysis try as best they can to control for confirmation bias, other behavioral phenomena can get in the way. Availability bias can cause the regulator to attach undue significance to a very salient adverse event – such as the loss of a major case in court. Rather than engaging in a dispassionate assessment of what went wrong and devising solutions to do better the next time, the agency may recoil from a specific line of endeavor entirely – and pass up valuable opportunities to intervene more wisely and effectively in that policy arena next time.

---

26 This literature and its implications for regulatory decision making are examined in James C. Cooper & William E. Kovacic, *Behavioral Economics: Implications for Regulatory Behavior*, 41 J. Reg. Econ. 41 (2012).

27 Daniel R. Ernst, The New Antitrust History, 35 N.Y. L. Sch. L. Rev. 879, 883 (1990).

3. Historical Research and Its Imperfect Integration into Policy

There is no single history of regulatory events – no single accounting of what an agency did, no single interpretation of an agency's behavior, and no single assessment of the worth of an agency's work. An agency exhorted to take fuller account of history might properly ask, "Which history?"

In no particular order, here are some of the difficulties associated with examining the past to guide future policy development. First, the data concerning what happened is often badly incomplete or not readily accessible. Accurate data on activity can illuminate important trends over time and raise questions for further study and interpretation. Examples include the dramatic decline in the federal government's prosecution of Robinson-Patman Act infringements – from dozens of FTC cases per year in the 1960s to a total of two cases over the past 20 years, and none since 2000.[28]

Competition agencies vary dramatically in how they collect and present data on activity.[29] Some agencies give more complete information for litigation matters (citations and links to the event that began a case, reports of decisions taken by the agency, and decisions issued by appellate bodies); others simply report aggregates of activity (e.g., in calendar year 2017, the agency commenced 11 matters involving vertical restraints). In many cases, to obtain an accurate idea of what has happened (not to assess whether what happened was worthwhile), the researcher has to compile a data set almost from the ground up – e.g., by reading agency press releases and external news accounts. A poverty of good data, and the general absence of widely accepted reporting norms, seriously impede good historical research regarding economic regulation. My minimum proposition here would be that better data reporting by the antitrust agencies would provide a more certain basis for tracking activity and for discussions, inside the agency and by the external competition policy community, about what the agency has done.

A second consideration related to data is how the agencies use data at their disposal to refine their enforcement programs. In the area of cartel enforcement, one could imagine that the DOJ would do reconstructions of cartel episodes to identify how the cartel was formed and managed: Who took the decision to form the collusive scheme? Did top management instruct subordinates to form the cartel, or send less direct signals that lower level managers should do what it takes to meet profit expectations? What mechanisms did the firm put in place to implement the cartel's plans? It appears that the chief imperative for a cartel prosecutor is to prove the fact of agreement and then move to the calculation

---

28 William E. Kovacic, *The Modern Evolution of U.S. Competition Policy Enforcement Norms*, 71 Antitrust L.J. 377, 410-15, 478 (2003).

29 William E. Kovacic et al., *How Does Your Competition Agency Measure Up?*, 7 Eur. Competition J. 25 (2011).

of punishment levels. This type of reconstruction of the cartel's operations does not appear to be a priority.

This is but one area for the development of what one might call antitrust analytics – the detailed study of an agency's experience base as a way of guiding future enforcement. The increasing attention to *ex post* evaluation is an encouraging manifestation of the agencies' interest in documenting initial expectations before the enforcement event and matching those expectations against observed market-place behavior after enforcement takes place.

Even if the data were perfect, a good deal of the result of a historical inquiry would turn upon interpretation and assessment. Here the skills of a professional historian – either an employee of an agency or an academic consultant – may be necessary to enable the competition agency to make a sound appraisal of the institution's past work and offer useful suggestions about future programs.

4. Historical Analysis: Gains from Fuller Application

This section describes areas in which regulators and their external "co-producers" – a term Allan Fels has used to describe institutions, such as university researchers, that can directly or indirectly enhance the effectiveness of regulators – can improve the base of historically relevant knowledge that can inform policymaking.

Generation of better, historically relevant, data and interpretation does not, by itself, ensure integration into policymaking. Presented below are suggestions for steps that regulators can take to build historical awareness more completely into decision-making.

As suggested above, historical awareness does play a part in federal antitrust agency decision-making. The relevant knowledge tends to reside in three places: (a) individuals who have been with the agency for a significant period of time, (b) policy-related offices such as the Office of Policy Planning and the Office of the General Counsel, and (c) external observers (e.g., academic researchers) whose work the agency draws upon from time to time, who join the agency for occasional short-term secondments, or who are retained to give advice on specific matters.

The agencies do not have a formal position of "historian," although some individuals in effect have fulfilled that role. From the early 2000s until his retirement in the 2010s, Marc Winerman functioned as the equivalent of an official historian and made major scholarly contributions to the literature on the agency's origins and early history.[30] The enhancement of the role of historical analysis in agency decision-making could be accomplished by making such a

30 A notable example is Marc Winerman, *The Origins of the FTC: Concentration, Cooperation, Control, and Competition*, 71 ANTITRUST L.J. 1 (2003).

role more formal – by recruiting a researcher to serve as "agency historian," placing the function in a body with responsibility for larger policy development. The Office of the General Counsel is one possibility, given its direct involvement in larger agency policy issues and the implementation of specific measures.

One way to increase historical awareness is for a jurisdiction to develop academic programs to teach new leaders about the origins and development of their institutions. For civil servants, the Australia and New Zealand School of Government (ANZSOG) provides one example of the type of program dedicated to improve public administration by, among other means, giving senior leadership courses in the history of regulatory policy. ANZSOG serves the governments of Australia and New Zealand by providing executive education for civil servants, assembling case studies that examine specific government programs, and performing research on public administration. A key focus of the organization is to capture learning from the experience of public bodies and make the learning accessible to new generation of agency managers.

The audience for historically oriented training should include the institutional stakeholders whose views also shape the behavior of the leaders of the institutions, including legislators and members of their staffs, leaders of civil society, academics, and journalists.. Better historical awareness might lead these stakeholders to evaluate leadership not simply with activity-based measures (e.g. the number of cases prosecuted) but also to credit leaders who give proper account to long-term investments.

V. Conclusion

Greater historical awareness might encourage new leaders to behave in ways that improve the performance of their institutions over time. A better appreciation for where an institution has been, and a fuller understanding of what forces have yielded good programs might serve to discourage a short-term orientation that disparages previous leadership and underinvests in improvements in capability. Learning from past experience is a crucial means by which institutions, including competition agencies, achieve greatness. A core lesson from this experience is that respect for past achievements and investments in building agency capability contribute significantly to building effective institutions. In the relay race that links generations of leadership, the aim of each leader upon arriving in a new post should be to understand what is good and preserve it, and, at the end of one's term, to hand off an institution that is better than it was before the leader arrived.

Fair Competition Versus Fair Competition Review System in China

SUSAN NING, TING GONG AND TIANJIE ZHANG*
King & Wood Mallesons

Abstract

Over the past three decades, China has made extraordinary economic progress in a relatively short period of time. Being an important source of such growth, the adoption of the socialist market system has been essential for the continuing development of China's economy. Fair competition plays a key role in the process of attaining a well-functioning market economy. In a recent official document, Opinions on Establishment of the Fair Competition Review System in the Development of Market System, which was issued on 14 June 2016, China's State Council[1] *confirmed the position on strengthening the roles of market and fair competition in the national economy.*

The Fair Competition Review System (FCRS) constitutes a significant part of competition policy in China, aimed at regulating the administrative monopoly and maintaining market competition. The FCRS is expected to help balance the relationship between the government and the development of a market-orientated economy. In this paper, we will fully discuss the FCRS from its background, content and latest enforcement records, as well as its similarities and differences with EU state aid rules, which we believe are one of the sources of inspiration for the design of the FCRS.

---

* Susan Ning is a senior partner and the head of the global regulatory compliance team at King & Wood Mallesons. Ting Gong and Tianjie Zhang are associates at King & Wood Mallesons.

1 The State Council is the chief administrative authority of the People's Republic of China. It is chaired by the premier and includes the heads of each governmental department and agency. For more information, see <http://english.www.gov.cn/statecouncil> (the official English website of the State Council of the People's Republic of China; access is available dated on August 24. 2020.).

I. Background

China's transition to a modern market system is still ongoing, and the legacy of a centrally planned and highly administered and regulated system still remains in some areas of the economy. This current administrative and economic management system gives central and local government bodies extensive powers to intervene and participate in markets relevant to the industries and geographical areas in their jurisdictions.

At the central level, government departments may provide targeted sectors (e.g. regulated industries) and enterprises with preferential treatment or protection at the expense of non-favoured enterprises with which they potentially compete. The use of such preferential treatment is evident not only in regulated industries (e.g. tobacco, post and telecommunications, construction, and machinery) but also in some non-regulated industries such as foodstuffs, beverages and real estate.[2] At local level, local governments create barriers to internal trade between regions, and protect locally owned or controlled enterprises. Regional monopolies and protectionism in China have resulted in excessive duplication of industries across provinces, with large numbers of local producers in industries such as automobiles and cement.[3]

Bureaucratic structure plays a significant role in influencing the allocation of economic resources in China, which in turn determines how monopolies arise in the Chinese market. Large incumbent state-owned enterprises have continuously retained the necessary strategic positions that favour their competitive position, sometimes leaving numbers of market participants less room in the market. Fully using the effectiveness of the "invisible hand" in the Chinese market requires regulatory functions to perform in an instructive and complementary manner. Domestic and foreign market participants frequently encounter the "visible hand" in the form of state-owned enterprises or administrative mechanisms overwhelmingly dominant in favour of a unified and centralised interest. In this environment, the state is unavoidably characterised as an administrator, a participant and a supervisor, simultaneously.

Such problems of administrative monopoly are well recognised in China, and are basic aspects of the relationship between the state and the market that China is seeking to reform. In November 2013, at the Third Plenum of the 18th Party Congress, China's top policymakers allowed the "market" to play a decisive role in resource allocation and to establish a "unified, fair, open and competitive market", which constitutes a major breakthrough in China's economic reform

---

2 Bruce M. Owen, Su Sun and Wentong Zheng, "China's Competition Policy Reforms: The Anti-Monopoly Law and Beyond" (2008) 75 Antitrust LJ 231.

3 ibid.

policy.[4] The recently issued *Opinions on Establishment of the Fair Competition Review System in the Development of Market System* (*Opinions*), which were issued on 14 June 2016 by China's State Council, thus represent major progress in the development of a competition policy.

II. Fair Competition Review System in the Opinions

The *Opinions* introduce the Fair Competition Review System (FCRS) by setting forth review targets, methods and standards to further supplement China's current competition law regime in order to attain a unified national market based on fair competition.

1. Review Target

According to the *Opinions*, the following items shall be subject to the FCRS: laws, regulations, administrative policies, administrative practices and all instruments that are issued from a public authority entrusted with administration tasks to manage public affairs, regarding the economic activities of a market player. However, given the administrative constraints, for the moment it is focused on areas that are frequently affected by competition restrictions and which have significant impacts on the national economy, such as rules related to market entry, industrial development, foreign investment, bidding, government procurement, and the code of business conduct and qualifications.

With regard to State Council administrative regulations and other policy measures, as well as local regulations, the relevant legislative authorities are required to conduct fair competition review during the drafting process. Without such prior review, the legislative measures shall not be submitted for approval.

2. Review Method

The relevant policymaking authorities shall conduct self-review according to the review standards, prior to being issued. The policies can only be issued then implemented if they do not eliminate or restrict competition, otherwise the policies shall not be issued unless they are adjusted in a manner consistent with the review standards. Such review shall be conducted in parallel with soliciting opinions from interested parties or consulting public comments when drafting. After the relevant policies are issued, they shall be publicly available according to the Regulation of the People's Republic of China on the Disclosure of Government Information. Currently, the FCRS adopts a "self-review" approach following the principle of "who made it, who reviews it". This takes the practical consideration that Anti-Monopoly Enforcement

---

4 An abridged English version of the Third Plenum Decision can be found in: China Daily, "The Decision on Major Issues Concerning Comprehensively Deepening Reforms in Brief" (*China Daily*, 16 November 2013) <http://www.china.org.cn/china/third_plenary_session/2013-11/16/content_30620736.htm>.

Authorities (AMEAs) or other third-party institutions sometimes may find it difficult to fully understand the background, objectives and contents of such policies, given the specialty that may be required by the relevant policy areas. Thus, self-review by the policymaker may best suit the need to balance between the protection of market competition and the attainment of policy objectives.

3. Review Standard

According to the *Opinions*, the review shall be conducted in a way to protect an integrated national market and fair competition, in particular, in accordance with four major standards and an 18-item "not-to-do" list.

The four major categories of standard are: Standards relating to Market Entry or Exit; Standards regarding Free Movement of Goods and other Production Elements; Standards regarding Affecting Manufacturing and Operating Costs; and Standards regarding Affecting Manufacturing and Operating Conducts.

These standards accurately address and then redress a variety of commonly seen forms of administrative monopoly in China, such as (falling within the scope of the first major category of standard regarding market entry or exit) relevant authorities setting out unreasonable and discriminatory conditions for market entry and exit, and obliging undertakings to deal with or to use goods and services provided by designated undertakings.

Under the second major category of standard, regarding free movement of key production elements, relevant authorities are prohibited from restricting the entry of non-local and imported goods or services into the local market, restricting non-local undertakings from joining the local tendering or bidding, or restricting non-local undertakings from investing or setting up subsidiaries in the local market.

The third major category of standard, regarding affecting manufacturing and operating costs, requires that the relevant authorities are prohibited from providing preferential policies or financial aids, in the form of tax or social security exemptions, to certain undertakings.

The fourth major category of standard focuses on state interventions in obliging undertakings to conduct certain monopolistic behaviours which fall within China's anti-monopoly law (AML). For example, authorities requiring undertakings to disclose sensitive information, to facilitate such information disclosure, or to regulate prices of goods and services beyond the legally prescribed scope of authority.

4. Timetable of the Review Implementation and Implementing Rules

The *Opinions* require that Chinese government departments at different levels shall conduct fair competition review during the formulation of policies and regulations, starting from July 2016. The FCRS will be proceeded in a step-by-step manner, given that such review would be a difficult and time-consuming process. The *Opinions* go further, requiring a regular evaluation mechanism to safeguard the due process for such review.

In addition, the *Opinions* require the National Development and Reform Commission (NDRC), the Ministry of Commerce (MOFCOM) and the State Administration of Industry and Commerce, together with the Legislative Affairs Office of the State Council, to separately issue implementing rules and specific guidelines regarding public supervision to complement the implementation of the review. These implementing rules are widely expected to function as essential guidance in the future implementation process of the FCRS.

III. Existing Instruments Against Administrative Monopoly in the AML

Chapter V of the AML is the existing instrument that fights against administrative monopoly, which is defined as the abusive conduct of one's administrative powers. To grant favourable conditions to preferred enterprises at the expense of others is a popular example for administrative monopoly.

Article 51 of the AML serves as the primary enforcement provision for Chapter V and, instead of directly granting AMEAs the power to punish government agencies for violating the AML, it establishes that AMEAs can only identify violations and propose corrective actions to the superior authorities of the agencies in question. The government officials who are directly in charge and/or other directly responsible public servants can be individually held liable and disciplined according to the AML. It is clear that AMEAs still cannot restrict administrative monopolies directly through the legal system: only superior government agencies have rights to rectify the administrative monopolies.

To date, the NDRC has published 10 cases about the antitrust enforcement against administrative monopoly, in which it has either imposed penalties on the undertakings concerned, or made suggestions to the relevant authorities to rectify the administrative measures in question.

Although the Chinese antitrust regime has continued to gain momentum with increased enforcement over recent years, we still see a comparatively limited number of cases against administrative monopoly. This may be partly due to the fact that the local governments enjoy extensive legislative powers and have issued local rules or industrial policies, the applicable scope, methods and impact of which may not appear to be consistent with the spirit of the AML. And some academics have stated that: "China needs to actively pursue other reforms necessary to control administrative monopolies. Otherwise, the most significant restrictions on competition in China's economy would be left intact."[5]

5 See Owen, Sun and Zheng (n 2) 258.

In view of the above, Chapter V of the AML is an *ex post* control over administrative monopoly, which is developed on a case-by-case basis and therefore requires a relatively longer time to realise such deterrent effects. The FCRS, on the contrary, is an *ex ante* review mechanism of all the government policies in place or in the future by the prescribed review standards and methods, and it is anticipated to play a crucial role in preventing administrative monopoly.

IV. The Powers of State-Owned Enterprises

Nowadays, although the role of state-owned enterprises (SOEs) has gradually been diluted in most economic sectors, SOEs still exercise very significant control in certain economic sectors.

SOEs have specialties, functions or particular missions in China's economic development. The specialties of SOEs have reflected in their ownership, organisation forms, operation mechanisms and multiple missions.[6] The functions of SOEs include: (1) fiscal function, increasing government income; (2) national defence, aiming to control strategic industries; (3) macroeconomic purpose, adjusting the social and economic structure and operation by way of national investment.[7]

The AML is to encourage competition, but it seems that the role and function of SOEs is contradict the spirit of the AML: it is also said by some academics that, on one hand, China wants to rein in the monopolistic power of SOEs through the adoption of the AML or maybe other competition reforms, on the other hand, it wants to retain the absolute control of SOEs in certain crucial economic sectors.[8]

In this regard, we can see that Article 7 of the AML tries to strike a balance between maintaining the dominant potion of SOEs in some crucial economic sectors and subjecting the SOEs in those sectors to the new antitrust regime. Article 7 of the AML stipulates:

> In the SOEs' controlled sectors concerning the health of national economy and national security and in sectors where state trading is authorised by law, the legal operations of the enterprises are protected by law, yet the government will supervise and regulate the prices of the goods and services provided by those enterprises to protect the interests of consumers and promote technology advancement.

6 Guohai Li, "The Particularity of State-owned Enterprises and the Enforcement of Fair Competition Investigation" (2017) 38(4) Journal of Jishou University 68–75.

7 ibid, 69.

8 See Owen, Sun and Zheng (n 2), 244.

> The enterprises referenced in the foregoing clause shall conduct business in accordance with the law, be honest, exercise strict self-discipline, and subject to the supervision of the public. Those enterprises shall not damage the interests of consumers by virtue of their dominate market position or exclusive trading status.[9]

In China, some SOEs may also carry the functions of an industry regulator. If any measure issued by a state organ, which favours certain SOEs and therefore has adverse effects on market competition, then the FCRS will be applicable. However, some academics proposed that, given the ambiguity of the status of SOEs and relevant industry regulators, the fair competition review over certain measures concerning SOEs shall be given to an external review party to ensure objectivity.[10]

V. Implementation of the FCRS

Since the *Opinions* were issued in June 2016, the FCRS has been gradually implemented at different levels, such as central ministries and local governments. According to the *Opinions*, the implementation of the FCRS has certain time limitation, which is (1) the departments of the State Council and provincial governments along with their departments should enact measures to carry out the fair competition review from July 2016; (2) provincial governments should implement the FCRS step by step in their respective administrative regions, and guide the city and county governments, along with their departments, to carry out the review.

On 5 May 2017, the first plenary meeting of the joint ministerial conference on fair competition review was held in Beijing. During the meeting, the current enforcement status was reported; relevant implementation regulation was reviewed and the next major working agenda was issued.

1. Current Enforcement at Central Level

Currently, the NDRC, MOFCOM, the Ministry of Industry and Information Technology (MIIT), the Ministry of Housing and Urban – Rural Development (MOHURD), the People's Bank and other departments have issued notifications on the implementation of the FCRS, which clearly define the internal review mechanism and procedures. The NDRC, as a pioneer, has issued an internal notice specifying that the drafting bureaus or departments shall go through the self-review process and a written document should be included together with the proposed

---

9 See Article 7 of the AML and Owen, Sun and Zheng (n 2), 244.

10 Guohai Li, "The Particularity of State-owned Enterprises and the Enforcement of Fair Competition Investigation" (2017) 38(4) Journal of Jishou University (social sciences edition) 72.

policies. Further, drafting institutions may consult with the Price Supervision and Anti-Monopoly Bureau, if deemed necessary.[11] Finally, the Department of Law and Regulations will check the procedure in its review of legality.

Furthermore, as mentioned above, on 5 May 2017, the first plenary meeting of the Joint Ministerial Conference has reviewed the Fair Enforcement Rules of the Competition Review System (Enforcement Rules). The Enforcement Rules are still being drafted and, from the currently available version, the FCRS may require more time to evolve.

If the Enforcement Rules clarify the review procedures, improve the actual binding power of the current structural review and even impose sanctions on the behaviours which severely damage market competition under specific circumstances, as well as incorporating government information publicity system, improving the transparency of the process and result of review, introducing third-party supervision, and using social resources to supervise the self-review, the FCRS will undoubtedly be more effective in practice.

2. Current Enforcement at Local Level

In terms of the enforcement landscape at local level, there are already 30 provinces forwarding the *Opinions* or issuing related implementation opinions in order to specify the mechanism and responsibility of the FCRS. The main provisions of the documents issued by local governments are quite similar, and generally include: (1) for proposed local regulations or documents issued by provincial governments and their general offices, the drafting departments should be responsible for the fair competition review and the legal departments shall be responsible for checking content or procedures; (2) for documents formulated by provincial government departments, the review process should be completed by the drafting departments; (3) for documents jointly formulated by various provincial government departments, the leading department should be in charge of the review; (4) the third-party evaluation should be involved in the review and the results should be disclosed to the public in due course. In addition, some provinces, such as Hebei, Shandong, Shanxi and Hunan, have established joint meeting systems or corresponding work coordination mechanisms.

As regards the actual implementation of the FCRS at the provincial level, 12 provinces, Shanghai, Hebei, Jiangxi, Hunan, Ningxia, Jiangsu, Shaanxi, Shanxi, Jilin, Heilongjiang, Liaoning and Sichuan, have embarked on a fair competition review of the policies and measures issued by the provincial governments.

As for the actual implementation of the review at the city and county level, based on our observation, some cities and counties are starting to implement the FCRS under the guidance of provincial government and the relevant departments.

11 ibid.

According to statistics, provinces such as Hebei, Jiangsu, Hunan, Sichuan, Guizhou, and Guangdong have guided more than 26 prefecture-level cities on the issuance of the implementation opinions and the deployment of the review work.[12]

In general, we note that implementation by local governments is more active than that of central ministries. To date, 30 provinces have issued or forwarded fair competition review documents and implemented the specific system.[13] Many provinces have started to guide lower-level government on the system construction and clean up possible non-compliant documents issued prior to the establishment of the FCRS.

A. An Empirical Case Study: The Detailed Rules for the Administration of Online Taxi Booking Business Operations and Services

On July 28th, 2016, the General Office of the State Council (at central level) issued the *Opinion on Deepening the Reform to Promote the Healthy Development of the Taxi Industry*, which sets out the basic regulation of ride-hailing services. On 27 July 2016, the Ministry of Transport, together with seven other ministries, implemented *Interim Measures for the Administration of Online Taxi Booking Business Operations and Services*, which took effect on 1 November 2016. China became the first country in the world to acknowledge the legitimate status of "online taxis". Later, the implementation rules were intensively introduced nationwide. By 21 August 2017, 133 cities had promulgated new regulations for online taxis.

The regulations for online taxis in various regions commonly prohibit non-local drivers and non-locally licensed vehicles from operating locally, and the size, displacement and age of vehicles are also regulated. These restrictions obstruct the free movement of services among various regions and establish a relatively high standard of entry for online taxi services. Pursuant to the 18 prohibitive criteria in the *Opinions*, since the regulations include an unreasonable standard of entry and limitations on the service provision, they are likely to be considered against the *Opinions*, unless there are adequate reasons to justify them as an exemption.

Some voiced that:

> according to the Opinion issued by the General Office of the State Council, ride-hailing companies are service providers and assume carrier's liability. That indicates drivers registered with ride-hailing companies are not service providers… and the restrictions made in the regulations are based on the social considerations to ease population pressure and to resolve traffic problems in cities.[14]

---

12 ibid.

13 ibid.

14 Wei Huang, Bei Yin and Wen Zhou, "The Competition and Regulation Issues of the Sharing Economy – An Analysis Based on China's Ride-hailing Services Regulations" *Competition Policy International* (Asia, 20 April 2017).

Currently, the restrictions imposed by local governments in regulations on ride-hailing are still under intensive debate. A competition lawyer even filed a request for administrative disclosure obligations to Beijing's transport regulator, the Beijing Municipal Commission of Transport, demanding the disclosure of fair competition review content for the new rules. The ongoing case provides a good opportunity to test the extent to which local governments are implementing China's fair competition review mechanism.

VI. The EU State Aid Serves a Good Reference for the FCRS

1. Similarities Between State Aid Procedures and the FCRS

Though there are obvious differences, China and the EU share certain similarities.

From a political perspective, Europe is characterised by unity in diversity ("*in varietate concordia*"). The European Union is a politico-economic union of 28 (27 after Brexit) Member States. Today the EU is approaching a federal state, with a powerful and centralised institution, the European Commission, on top and Member States at the bottom. China, on the other hand, could be qualified as "diversity within unity". China's constitution stipulates that China is a unitary state and the authority of local governments derives from central government. Local government consists of four levels, including 31 provincial level units (22 provinces, four municipalities and five autonomous regions).

Chinese law and legal tradition, in general, has historically always been strongly influenced by continental European law. In particular, the legal framework of China's AML is largely influenced by the EU experiences. Moreover, the question facing both the EU and China of how to balance central and local level in order to meet changing policy needs is very similar, and they have a shared goal of realising a unified internal market without any local blockades in the field of competition policy.

These similarities serve as a basis for a successful legal transplant, taking reference of the EU state aid rules in the construction of China's FCRS.

2. State Aid Rules in the EU

State aid is defined by the EU as interventions – including grants, subsidies, loans, guarantees and tax credits – that give the recipient an advantage on a selective basis, that have distorted or may distort competition, and which are likely to affect trade between Member States.[15] These are generally prohibited,

15 If a government measure constitutes state aid, such measure will be automatically prohibited by Article 107(1) of the Treaty on the Functioning of the EU, unless it is justified in accordance to Article 107(3).

but there is a broad exemption for horizontal industrial policies deemed to address market failures with relatively slight implications for trade. State aid has to be notified to and approved by the European Commission, whose decisions are subject to scrutiny by the EU courts.

To decide whether state assistance constitutes "state aid", four tests should be met: (1) the assistance is granted by the state or through state resources; (2) it favours certain undertakings or the production of certain goods; (3) it distorts or threatens to distort competition; and (4) it affects trade between Member States. If all four tests are met, it is illegal to provide aid without prior approval from the European Commission, unless an exemption applies.

For practical reasons, it is imperative to set priorities and identify the most restrictive regulations for the initial enforcement stage of the FCRS. For that purpose, the approaches adopted in the EU state aid regime, such as the "selectivity test" and the "private investor test", could serve as a good reference for China's enforcement authorities.

A. Selectivity Test

State aid control only targets those public interventions which specifically and selectively benefit one or more undertakings, such as to create a different treatment that in essence can be qualified as discriminatory.[16]

Further, this criterion of selectivity comprises not only the measures that legally single out its recipients (de jure selectivity), but also those that, albeit appearing neutral, in practice exclude certain companies from advantages that benefit others (de facto selectivity) or are subject to the discretion of public authorities (discretionary selectivity).[17]

According to settled case law, state aid measures are defined in terms of the effects they produce, not in terms of the objective they pursue implicitly or explicitly, it is always presumed that selectivity in the granting of aid will result in distortion of competition.[18]

B. Private Investor Test

The "private investor test" has been a cornerstone of the EU state aid control regime. To determine whether or not an aid granted by the state distorts or threatens to distort competition, the private investor test must be applied. The essence of this test is that when a public authority invests in an entity on terms

---

16 Andrea Biondi and Elisabetta Righini, "An Evolutionary Theory of EU State Aid Control" in Anthony Arnull and Damien Chalmers, *The Oxford Handbook of European Law* (OUP 2014).

17 ibid.

18 ibid.

and in conditions which would be acceptable to a private investor operating under normal market economy conditions, the investment is not a state aid.

This test would be illuminating in China when applying FCRS to certain investments by the state and assessing whether such investments are in line with FCRS requirements.

VII. Conclusion

The importance of market competition is increasingly well understood in China. As mentioned above, two features of China's systemic and policy environment raise issues for market competition: abuse of the administrative powers of government agencies, and policies to promote the development of particular sectors and firms. While these features exist in all modern economies, their extent in China is exceptionally large. Alongside the current enforcement of the AML, the introduction of the FCRS, conceived by the highest level of the Chinese government, represents a significant change in the government's thinking about the role of the state and its relationship with the economy.

The introduction of the FCRS has brought, for the first time, a systematically *ex ante* control mechanism into the competition enforcement landscape in China. With more resources provided to Chinese competition authorities to fight administrative monopoly, we expect a more vigorously development of China's market, with more fair competition among market participants. In view of the above, the establishment of the FCRS is indeed a milestone in China's efforts to create fair competition across the country's economy.

Balancing Incentives to Innovate in Upstream Wireless Technology Markets with Exit Concerns in Midstream Component Product Markets

JORGE PADILLA AND KOREN W. WONG-ERVIN*
Compass Lexecon
Global Antitrust Institute, George Mason University

Abstract

We consider the merits of recent complaints about the common industry practice in many technology industries, including the wireless industry, of licensing patents at end-device level (as opposed to at component-part level), and the use of the entire value of the end device as the royalty base for the calculation of compensation. We identify the exceptional circumstances under which mandating licensing at component level may be justified from a welfare perspective. We also explain why using the entire value of the end device as the royalty base is optimal.

---

* Jorge Padilla is Senior Managing Director at Compass Lexecon, Research Fellow at CEMFI (Madrid) and teaches competition economics at the Barcelona Graduate School of Economics. Dr Padilla has represented and still represents SEP holders (including Qualcomm) and implementers in various antitrust and commercial disputes related to the licensing of SEPs. The opinions in this paper are the authors' sole responsibility.
Koren W. Wong-Ervin wrote this article during her tenure as the Director of the Global Antitrust Institute and an Adjunct Professor of Law at George Mason University School of Law. The views do not necessarily represent those of her new employer or any of its clients.

I. Introduction

Competition enforcers in many jurisdictions have expressed concerns about enforcement actions and policies, e.g. the compulsory licensing of intellectual property (IP), that threaten to harm incentives to innovate in upstream technology markets, such as the market for the licensing of wireless technology. Yet, many appear to struggle with how to weigh and balance these incentives against concerns that certain downstream manufacturers, which may need access to that IP at reasonable prices, may exit the market if there is no intervention.

To be sure, the task of measuring and balancing potential harms to upstream incentives to innovate against potential downstream exit is complex. For example, while the large body of literature on the economics of innovation teaches us that measures that negatively impact the return on investment are likely to reduce incentives to innovate, determining how much of a reduction is likely to result in decreased incentives (and by how much) is incredibly difficult, if not impossible.

The complexity of this balancing exercise is increased in multi-layered vertical industries where (upstream) IP holders, (midstream) component manufacturers and (downstream) end-product manufacturers coexist. This is the case, for example, in the wireless industry, which is populated by owners of standard-essential patents (SEPs), chipset manufacturers and end-user device manufacturers. In industries like this, competition enforcers may not only worry about the terms and conditions under which patents are licensed, but also about the identity of the licensees. Specifically, they may be concerned about the implications of the common industry practice of licensing patents at end-user device level as opposed to at component-parts level.

Some have complained that this industry practice substantially forecloses competition midstream and may allow patent holders to set excessively high royalty rates downstream.[1] Some of these complainants, mainly chipset makers,[2] may demand component-level licensing. Others, mainly end-device makers,[3] may demand that royalties be calculated using the value of the component (and not the value of their end devices) as the royalty base.[4]

---

1 *See* Karl D. Belgum, *The Next Battle Over FRAND: The Definition of FRAND Terms and Multi-Level Licensing*, 39 New Matter 2 (2014) available at https://www.law.berkeley.edu/files/Belgum_Karl__IPSC_paper_2014.pdf. *See also* Federal Trade Commission v. Qualcomm Inc., No. 5:17-cv-00220-LHK (N.D. Cal. Jan. 17, 2017) (Federal Trade Commission's Complaint for Equitable Relief) available at https://www.ftc.gov/system/files/documents/cases/0038_2017_02_01_redacted_complaint_per_court_order_dkt.pdf.

2 Diana Goovaerts, *Intel, Samsung Back FTC in Its Lawsuit Against Qualcomm*, Wireless Week (May 5, 2017), available at https://www.wirelessweek.com/news/2017/05/intel-samsung-back-ftc-its-lawsuit-against-qualcomm.

3 *Id.*

4 A royalty payment typically comprises two components: a royalty base and a royalty rate. The royalty base is the unit base to which the royalty rate is applied. The royalty rate is the percentage that determines the proportion of the royalty base the licensor will receive.

In this paper we review these concerns and consider whether the proposed interventions – mandating licensing at component level and/or requiring royalties to be calculated using the value of the component as the royalty base – are justified on welfare grounds or whether, instead, they are likely to undermine investment incentives without leading to lower end-device prices and, therefore, are likely to hurt consumers.

Relying on the work of Layne-Farrar, Llobet and Padilla,[5] we find that mandating component-level licensing will not have a positive impact on competition unless the licensor is vertically integrated midstream, i.e. unless it is also a competitor in the relevant component market. A non-integrated licensor has no incentive to foreclose midstream (and/or downstream) manufacturers; on the contrary, it will benefit from more competition midstream (and downstream) as that will increase sales volumes and, therefore, royalty payments. Furthermore, provided royalties are negotiated efficiently, a non-integrated licensor will not be able to extract higher royalty rates by licensing at end-device level only.

Vertical integration is a necessary but not sufficient condition for intervention, though. First, as we demonstrated in an earlier paper,[6] a refusal to license at component level cannot and will *not* result in anticompetitive foreclosure, provided the vertically integrated licensor offers (a) contractual protection against component-level suits and (b) non-discriminatory terms to end-device manufacturers, i.e. it offers the same terms whether the licensee purchases its components or those of its rivals.

But what if the evidence shows component manufacturers exiting the markets even when the conditions listed above fail to hold? Does that suggest that anticompetitive foreclosure is possible even when conditions (a) and (b) hold? We do not think so. It is important to remember the typical cycles of entry and exit in markets in general and to determine whether a particular licensing practice is in fact the but-for cause of a departure in these normal cycles. Given that end-user device licensing has been the industry practice for as long as we can remember, and it is adopted by both vertically integrated and non-integrated licensors, it is not logical to presume that this industry practice actually caused any recent exit (or threat of exit). Rather, the logical assumption is that such an industry practice has nothing to do with possible midstream exit, which may instead be caused by a host of other factors, such as quality and strength of technology or an inherently risky business model premised on high volume sales at low profit margins.

---

5 A. Layne-Farrar, G. Llobet & J. Padilla, *Patent Licensing in Vertically Disaggregated Industries: The Royalty Allocation Neutrality Principle*, 95 Communications & Strategies, no. 3, 2014, at 61–84.

6 Jorge Padilla & Koren Wong-Ervin, *Portfolio Licensing at the End-User Device Level: Analyzing Refusals to License FRAND-Assured Standard-Essential Patents at the Component Level*, 62.3 Antitrust Bull. 494 (2017).

When (a) and (b) hold, an obligation to license at component level is bound to be detrimental to welfare. On the one hand, even if such an intervention does not affect negatively the magnitude of the royalty payments, it will increase transaction costs and, as a result, cause harm to investment and competition to the ultimate detriment of consumers. End-user device licensing allows for easy monitoring and enforcement and thus reduces the transaction costs of licensing. It also reduces the number of licenses required, thereby reducing costly technology identification and negotiation costs. The resulting increase in overall surplus benefits both patent holders (licensors) and downstream implementers (licensees). It also benefits midstream component suppliers and end-users, since the reduction in transaction costs will expand the demand for end devices and components. Market demand goes up because the additional surplus will increase the licensors' incentives and ability to invest as well as the licensees' operating margins, and hence their willingness to compete more aggressively.

Of course, the economic implications of mandating access at component level would be different if that intervention not only implies a change in the identity of the payer but if it results in a reduction in royalty payments. In that case, when conditions (a) and (b) hold, the intervention would necessarily reduce upstream incentives to invest without any offsetting procompetitive effect in the midstream and/or downstream markets.

Second, even if conditions (a) and (b) fail to hold, the risk of anticompetitive foreclosure needs to be balanced against the potentially adverse impact of compulsory licensing on the incentives to innovate. Relying on established principles in the economics of innovation, we believe that the decision to compel patent holders to license at component level would only be justified if, absent that intervention, all effective competition would be eliminated, thus preventing the emergence of new products for which there is potentially substantial demand. Our position in this regard is consistent with the position adopted by the European Court of Justice (ECJ) in *Magill*[7] and *IMS Health*,[8] where it stated that compulsory licensing is only justified under certain exceptional circumstances, which are equivalent to those identified in this paper.

We also find no welfare justification for mandating a narrow royalty base. More precisely, we find that *ad valorem* royalties based upon the price of the end-user

7 Joined Cases C-241/91 P and C-242/91 P, RTÉ and Independent Television Publications Ltd v. Comm'n, 1995 E.C.R. I-743, para. 54.

8 Case T-184/01 R, IMS Health Inc v. Comm'n, 2001 E.C.R. II-3193, para. 102. The order was confirmed on appeal by the President of the ECJ in Case C-481/01 P(R), NDC Health GmbH & Co KG and NDC Health Corp. v. Comm'n and IMS Health Inc., 2002 E.C.R. I-3401. IMS Health's appeal was discontinued following the withdrawal of the interim decision by the Commission in 2003 on the grounds that the appeal had no further object. *See* NDC Health/IMS Health: Interim measures, Comm'n Decision 2003/741/EC, 2003 O.J. (L 268) 69, and Order of the General Court in Case T-184/01, IMS Health Inc v. Comm'n, 2005 E.C.R. II-217.

device lead to more upstream and downstream innovation and greater welfare than royalties based on the price of the component, whether the latter take the form of royalties based on the price of the component, per-unit component royalties or per-unit end-device royalties.[9] As demonstrated by Llobet and Padilla,[10] in industries where components are used in fixed proportions, *ad valorem* royalties calculated on the price of the end device lead to lower end-device prices and greater sales of end devices by mitigating the double marginalization problem that characterizes all vertical industries, including all licensing markets.[11] The resulting increase in demand benefits upstream licensors, downstream producers and, likewise, midstream manufacturers. This effect is more significant in industries like the wireless industry where there are multiple upstream developers with complementary innovations.

The remainder of this paper is structured as follows. In Section II we briefly describe the "use-creation" trade-off that is at the heart of the economics of innovation and identify the exceptional circumstances under which compulsory licensing could be justified from a welfare viewpoint. In Section III we consider the competitive implications of the common practice in technology industries, such as the wireless industry, of licensing at end-device level rather than at component level. Then, in Section IV, we investigate the welfare implications of using alternative royalty bases in licensing negotiations. Section V concludes.

---

9 As a matter of economics, provided the overall royalty payment reflects the value of the technology, using per-unit component royalties (royalties based on the price of the component), or per-unit end-device royalties makes no difference in an industry where components and devices are manufactured in fixed proportions. This is precisely the case in the wireless industry where typically each end device embeds one component.

10 Gerard Llobet & Jorge Padilla, *The Optimal Scope of the Royalty Base in Patent Licensing*, 59.1 J. L. & Econ. 45 (2016).

11 The double marginalization problem can be explained as follows. Consider a licensing market with one licensor and one licensee. The licensor charges a royalty to the licensee and the licensee sets the price for the final product it sells, taking that royalty as given. Because the royalty charged by the licensor reduces the licensee's price – cost margin, the licensee will increase the price of the final product in response to an increase in the royalty. In effect, the licensee passes through a fraction of the royalty increase to final consumers in order to maintain its price – cost margin. Therefore, any increase in the royalty payment (and thus the licensor's margin) will trigger an increase in the price of the final product in order to maintain the licensee's margin. This double marginalization will result in a reduction in the quantity sold of the final product and will make consumers worse off. The double marginalization problem essentially arises because (a) the licensor sets its royalty with its profit margin in mind, but without fully taking into account the impact of its decision on the licensee's price – cost margin, and (b) the licensee sets the price of the final product in order to protect its margin without regard to the impact of that decision on the profits made by the licensor. This results in royalties and prices that are too high from a consumer welfare perspective. The problem can thus be mitigated (and possibly resolved) by aligning the incentives of licensor and licensee.

II. The Simple Economics of Innovation and Compulsory Licensing

Economists have discussed for years the optimal trade-off between the ability to use an invention and the incentives to innovate in the first place.[12] Because inventions and works protected by IP rights are non-rivalrous, one firm using a specific IP right does not diminish the ability of another firm to use the same IP right. Also, the cost of having another firm use an existing IP right is effectively zero. Thus, from a static welfare perspective, it is desirable to disseminate IP rights to every firm (or consumer) that has a positive valuation for it.

Of course, doing so would create a strong disincentive to innovate in the first place, to the great detriment of dynamic efficiency, which refers to the gains that result from entirely new ways of doing business. Economic theory and empirical evidence suggest that the promise of monopoly profits, at least in the short term, stimulates risk-taking behavior involving investment and innovation.[13] Indeed, given that most new businesses fail, monopoly profits can be the prize for winning competitions that most people lose.

Society must therefore strike a balance between the incentives for innovation (dynamic efficiency) and inefficiencies stemming from the exercise of market power (static efficiency). The pragmatic resolution of this trade-off is, in the first instance, the subject of IP law. In fact, the decision to grant IP rights for a limited period only already involves a balancing of the interest in free competition with that of providing an incentive for research and development and creativity. In order to ensure consistency with the balancing decision struck by IP law, there should be no obligation to license IP rights during that limited period of exclusivity granted by IP law unless a refusal to license, as a result of some other factor, causes the exclusion of competitors in a separate (or secondary) market. However, from an economic standpoint, the exclusion of competitors in a secondary market is a necessary condition for intervention. It may not be sufficient, because it is generally efficient to allow a company to retain its own facilities for its own use, even if that causes the exclusion of some competitors. While static efficiency may increase consumer welfare in the short run, economics teaches that the societal gains from innovation are an even greater driver of consumer welfare.[14]

---

12 *See, e.g.*, Koren Wong-Ervin & Joshua D. Wright, *Intellectual Property and Standard Setting*, 17 Federalist Soc'y Rev., 52, 53–56 (2016), https://papers.ssrn.com/sol3/papers.cfm?abstract_id=2878955.

13 *See, e.g.*, D.W. Carlton & K. Heyer, *Extraction vs. Extension: The Basis For Formulating Antitrust Policy Towards Single-Firm Conduct*, 4(2) Competition Pol'y Int'l 285 (2008).

14 Robert Solow won the Nobel Prize in economics for demonstrating that gains in wealth are due primarily to innovation – not to marginal improvements in the efficiency of what already exists. *See* Press Release, The Royal Swedish Academy of Sciences (Oct. 21, 1987), http://www.nobelprize.org/nobel_prizes/economic-sciences/laureates/1987/press.html.

As a matter of economics, compulsory licensing should therefore be restricted to those situations where the prospective social benefits of licensing are so large as to offset the negative effects of forced sharing on the incentives to innovate and create new IP. However, this balancing exercise is both complex and prone to produce errors. In practice this means that intervention must be limited to those circumstances where the procompetitive effects (static efficiencies) of compulsory licensing are greatest and the disincentive effects (dynamic inefficiencies) of the obligation to license are minimal or non-existent.

Economic theory tells us that the procompetitive effects of compulsory licensing are largest when **(a)** the requested IP is indispensable to compete, **(b)** the refusal to deal causes the complete foreclosure of the market, and **(c)** the refusal prevents the emergence of markets for new products for which there is potentially substantial demand. Economic theory also tells us that the disincentive effects of compulsory licensing are less significant when **(d)** the products to be developed by the licensors are not in direct competition with those of the IP holder. So compulsory licensing should be restricted to situations where conditions **(a)** – **(d)** hold.[15] These are precisely the "exceptional circumstances" identified by the ECJ in *Magill*[16] and *IMS Health*[17] to conclude that a refusal to license infringes competition laws.[18]

III. The Competitive Effects of End-Device Licensing Practices

As explained in the Introduction, some implementers and policy pundits have argued that the common industry practice of licensing patents at the end-user device level as opposed to the component-parts level should be regarded and dealt with as an anticompetitive refusal to license. In this section we explore under which conditions that concern is justified from a welfare perspective.

In order to do so, we consider a vertically disaggregated industry where three firms operate. A patent holder *U*, whose IP covers the component produced and sold by the midstream producer. A midstream producer *M*, which sells an input (or component) that is required to create the final product sold by a downstream supplier *D*. For every unit of the final product that *D* produces, it needs one unit

15 C. Ahlborn, D.S. Evans & J. Padilla, (2004) *The Logic and Limits of the Exceptional Circumstances Test in Magill and IMS Health*, 28(4) Fordham In'l L. J., 1109–1156 (2004).

16 *Supra* note 7.

17 *Supra* note 8.

18 Instead, in the US, at least with respect to refusals to license, courts have essentially concluded that US IP laws have already struck a balance between the use-creation trade-off, and that antitrust law should not second guess that balancing. *See, e.g.*, Data General Corp. v. Gruman Systems Support Corp., 36 F.3d 1147, 1186–89 (1st Cir. 1994), 125 F.3d 1195 (9th Cir. 1997).

of *M*'s intermediate product, for which M. charges s.[19] Finally, D, which sells a final product (or end device) to consumers according to a demand function $D(p) + v$; where p is the price charged to consumers for the final product and v is the extra willingness to pay for that product if it includes a component embedding the technology of the patent holder. Importantly, the patent holder is not vertically integrated midstream (or downstream).

The patent holder licenses both the midstream and downstream producers and charges them royalty rates r_M and r_D, respectively. The downstream producer's incremental cost of production is $c + s + r_D$, where c denotes the variable operating costs associated to the production of one unit of the final product. We assume that the royalty rates r_M and r_D are determined through efficient negotiations between the patent holder and the midstream producer and between the patent holder and the downstream producer, respectively. An efficient negotiation is one that reaches an outcome without delay and does not leave money on the table.[20]

1. The Royalty Neutrality Principle

Layne-Farrar, Llobet and Padilla[21] demonstrate that under the assumptions above, the downstream price and quantity are decreasing in the aggregate royalty rate, $r_M + r_D$, but are independent of how that royalty burden is split between the midstream and downstream producers. In other words, they find that consumer welfare is the same whether the patent holder licenses the midstream producer, the downstream producer, or both. They called this result the "royalty allocation neutrality principle." They show that this principle holds whether the component price s is set unilaterally by the midstream producer or it is the result of a balanced and efficient negotiation between the midstream and downstream producers.

What happens if the patent holder shifts part of the royalty burden midstream, raising the midstream royalty but lowering the downstream one so as to leave the aggregate royalty unchanged? It turns out that the intermediate price the midstream manufacturer charges the downstream party will rise to accommodate the increase in costs suffered by the midstream manufacturer. In other words, the midstream manufacturer passes on the additional royalty payment, exactly offsetting the cost-savings enjoyed by the downstream producer from the lower royalty rate. Alternatively, if the patent holder reduces the midstream royalty and increases the downstream one, leaving the aggregate royalty rate unchanged, the component price will fall in response to the midstream manufacturer's reduced

19 The intermediate product and the end product are thus consumed in fixed proportions: more precisely 1 to 1.

20 These assumptions require that (A1) no negotiating party enjoys an informational advantage (e.g. both the patent holder and the two producers have symmetrical information regarding the prices of the components and final product and the number of units of the component and final product sold); and (A2) the component price s and the final price p are flexible (i.e. not subject to regulation or other technical or economic limitations).

21 *Supra* note 5.

costs, so that it offsets the increase in the downstream royalty. That is, the component price s responds to changes in r_M and r_D that leave the aggregate royalty rate unchanged, and leaving $s + r_D$ unchanged.

This means that the incremental cost of production faced by the downstream manufacturer, $c + s + r_D$, is a function of the aggregate royalty rate, but independent of how that the total royalty burden is distributed between the two layers of production. This in turn implies that the price and the quantity sold of the final product are also a function of the aggregate royalty rate *only*, and not of the way that such rate is split between midstream and downstream producers. Because the quantity sold of the final product is a function of the aggregate royalty rate and not of that rate as distributed, the profits of the patent holder, which are equal to the product of the aggregate royalty rate and the number of units sold of the final product, will also be a function of the aggregate royalty rate *only*. As a result, the patent holder will be indifferent in choosing to license to the midstream producer, the downstream producer or both. Likewise, since the price of the final product is an increasing function and the quantity sold is a decreasing function of the aggregate royalty rate only, consumer welfare falls with the aggregate royalty rate, but is independent of how that aggregate royalty rate is distributed. In conclusion, when royalty rates are negotiated efficiently, the profits of the patent holder and consumer welfare are the same whether the patent holder licenses the midstream producer, the downstream producer or both.

Note, in addition, that the upstream patent holder has no incentives to foreclose the midstream and downstream manufacturers, as otherwise its technology would never reach the final consumers. This conclusion applies equally to many midstream and downstream producers. A non-integrated patent holder will maximize its royalty revenues when the midstream and downstream markets are competitive. The more competition in those markets, the greater the volume of sales and, therefore, the larger the royalty revenues accrued by the IP owner.

There is, therefore, no justification for requiring the non-vertically integrated patent holder to license at the component level. Mandating component-level licensing will not have a positive impact on competition and welfare unless the licensor is vertically integrated midstream, i.e. unless it is also a competitor in the relevant component (or chipset) market.

2. Conditions for Anticompetitive Foreclosure with Vertically Integrated Licensors

Is it justified to presume that when the decision to license at end-device level only is made by a vertically integrated licensor, that choice is necessarily driven by anticompetitive motivations? The answer is "no," as we proceed to explain, relying on the arguments developed by Padilla and Wong-Ervin.[22]

---

22 *Supra* note 6.

One possible concern would be that by refusing to license at component level the vertically integrated patent holder may, in effect, be bundling its component (the bundled product) with its patent portfolio (the bundling product) in order to monopolize the midstream component market. It is true that any end-device manufacturer that buys the vertically integrated firm's component simultaneously acquires a license to its patents, but, when it buys components sold by the licensor's non-integrated rivals it still needs to negotiate a license for the vertically integrated patent holder's patents. As with other bundling strategies, the use of this strategy by a vertically integrated IP owner might in principle marginalize or evict its non-integrated component rivals. That will be the case when end-device manufacturers find it more economical to purchase the bundle rather than mix and match, i.e. if the strategy involves a sufficiently large bundled discount. However, as demonstrated by Padilla and Wong-Ervin, this will not happen when the vertically integrated patent holder (i) does not assert its component-level patents and (ii) licenses its patents portfolio to downstream end-device manufacturers on non-discriminatory terms, i.e. offering the same terms irrespective of whether they source components from its own subsidiary or from the non-integrated rival.

Intuitively, when these conditions hold, the bundled product offered by the vertically integrated patent holder can be replicated at no greater cost for end-device manufacturers. They can mix and match the component sold by the non-integrated component supplier and the patent portfolio of the integrated IP holder, paying no more than for the bundle. This is because the patents (the bundling products) are offered on a stand-alone basis (i.e. outside the bundle) on competitive terms and, therefore, the end-product manufacturers can choose either the vertically integrated patent holder's bundle or create their own bespoke bundle by purchasing the component from a non-integrated component manufacturer and still license the patent of the vertically integrated patent holder at the same cost. As a result, the bundle is effectively constrained by the unbundled products and *vice versa*, hence bundling causes no distortion of the competitive process.

A related concern would be that the refusal to license could increase the costs of the vertically integrated patent holder's rivals in the component market because they would have to offer indemnification to its customers from patent infringement liability in order to compete with the vertically integrated patent holder effectively. It is easy to see, however, that a covenant from the vertically integrated firm not to sue at component level could resolve the issue, provided that manufacturers of end-user devices are licensed on the same terms irrespective of whether they source components from their own subsidiary or from a non-integrated rival. When that is the case, the component price of the vertically integrated firm is effectively constrained by the prices offered by the non-integrated component manufacturers, since the latter need not offer indemnification to their customers to be competitive. It follows that, under those circumstances, the decision not to license at the component level causes no distortion of the competitive process either.

IV. Comparing Alternative Royalty Bases

Licensing agreements between licensors and implementers typically specify a royalty payment (though some licensing agreements are royalty-free). The royalty payment is often calculated as the product of a royalty base and a royalty rate.[23] The royalty base can be determined in two main ways. First, royalties may be calculated by reference to the value of the sales of the entire final product incorporating the patented technology. Royalties calculated on this basis are known as *ad valorem* royalties. Royalties based on the net average selling price of the final product can be shown to have the same price and volume effects, and hence the same welfare impact, as royalties calculated by reference to the value of the sales of the final product. Second, royalties may be determined as a fraction of the value of the product components incorporating the patented technology. Importantly, when components and end products are sold in fixed proportions, the impact on final prices and volumes is identical whether royalties are calculated using the value of the components incorporating the technology as the royalty base, or if they are calculated using per-unit royalties – i.e. royalties determined as a fixed amount for each unit of the end product sold (or what amounts to the same for each unit of the component sold). Thus, component-value royalties and per-unit royalties will have the same welfare implications. This is because both types of royalties increase the licensee's marginal cost of producing and commercializing the final product.

An extraordinarily large proportion of mutual agreements between licensors and licensees set royalties based on the sales price of the entire final product. One of the most comprehensive surveys to date considered the licensing practices of CNET (Centre national d'études des télécommunications, later part of France Télécom R&D, now Orange Labs), and showed that out of the 225 licensing contracts involving CNET's patents, only nine contracts specified per-unit royalties, or royalties assessed against specific components of a final product, while the remaining contracts (96% of them) specified *ad valorem* royalties.[24] Similarly, using data collected between 1990 and 2012 from license agreements, Parr and Smith found that the vast majority (91%) of license agreements examined involved *ad valorem* royalties and only 9% involved per-unit royalties or component-level royalties.[25] Moreover, in a review of declarations to ETSI (the European Telecommunications Standards Institute) and announced patent licensing statements for LTE 4G communications standards, Stasik found that every announced rate was expressed as a percentage of the sales price of the end

---

23 *See supra* note 4.

24 Alain Bousquet, Helmuth Cremer, Marc Ivaldi & Michel Wolkovicz, *Risk Sharing in Licensing*, 16 Int'l J. Indus. Org. 535 (1998).

25 Russell L. Parr & Gordon V. Smith, Intellectual Property: Valuation, Exploitation and Infringement Damages – 2013 Cumulative Supp. (11th ed. 2013).

device.[26] Notably, the rates considered by Stasik were announced by innovators all over the world, including Huawei, Qualcomm, Ericsson, and Nokia. The *ad valorem* nature of most royalty payments has also been acknowledged by the courts. In *Lucent Techs v. Gateway*, the US Court of Appeals for the Federal Circuit noted that "sophisticated parties routinely enter into license agreements that base the value of the patented inventions as a percentage of the commercial products' sales price."[27]

The fact that an overwhelming number of licensing contracts are voluntarily set with *ad valorem* royalties strongly suggests that both licensees and licensors find *ad valorem* royalties mutually beneficial. Not everyone agrees, however. Some commentators have argued that in cases involving complex products, calculating a royalty base that is broader than the value of the components covered by the patent may overcompensate patent holders when the patent at issue covers only some components *and* the components covered by the patent are not the sole drivers of consumer demand for the product (even thought they might contribute to demand).[28] In our opinion, this allegation is conceptually wrong because it (i) presumes that royalty rates will be the same irrespective of the choice of royalty base, (ii) ignores relevant practical considerations that militate in favor of royalties calculated by reference to the price of the final product, and (iii) fails to consider the (efficiency) implications for end-product prices and innovation incentives and, hence, for consumer and total welfare. We explain each of these arguments in greater detail in the remainder of this section.

1. Royalty Rates Are Not Independent of the Royalty Base

The distinction between royalties calculated using the entire value of the product and royalties calculated using the value of the components that integrate the technology is, in principle, arbitrary. This is because, as noted above, a royalty consists of a royalty rate and a royalty base. The royalty rate is a simple percentage that identifies what proportion of the base the licensor receives. Since the royalty rate can be adjusted downwards as the base expands, the final royalty payment can be mathematically identical irrespective of the royalty base. As stated by the US Court of Appeals for the Federal Circuit, "there is nothing inherently wrong with using the market value for the entire product for the infringing component or feature, so long as the multiplier accounts for the proportion of the base represented by the infringing component or feature."[29]

---

26 Eric Stasik, *Royalty Rates and Licensing Strategies for Essential Patents on LTE (4G) telecommunication standards*, LES NOUVELLES – THE JOURNAL OF THE LICENSING EXEC. SOC'Y INT'L, 2010, at 114.

27 *Lucent Techs., Inc. v. Gateway, Inc.*, 580 F.3d 1301, 1338–39 (Fed. Cir. 2009).

28 Brian Love, *Patentee Overcompensation and the Entire Market Value Rule*, 60 STAN. L. REV. 263–294 (2007).

29 *Lucent Techs., Inc. v. Gateway, Inc.*, 580 F.3d at 1338–39.

Those who argue that *ad valorem* royalties may overcompensate the licensor thus fail to understand that the royalty rate will have to adjust in response to changes in the royalty base. To the extent commentators or manufacturers argue that the royalty base should be the value of an individual component with no adjustment to the royalty rate, they are simply advocating lower total royalties rather than presenting a position about the appropriate method of calculation.

2. Practicability

There are a number of practical circumstances that make *ad valorem* royalties easier to apply and prone to fewer errors and subjective calls than royalties based on the price or value of the components covered by particular patents. Most importantly, apportioning value, either within a product or to particular patents, is a highly difficult and subjective task.

First, it may not be possible to separate the product into distinct components. In products driven by innovative technology, the value for a customer comes largely from the bundling of different features. For example, smartphones contain a telephone, photos and video upload/download, email, calendar functions and a range of other features. Further, implementation of features also cut across components. For example, the battery, screen, speakers, microphone and certain chipsets (e.g., the processors, RF chipsets, memory chipsets, etc.) contribute to implementing many of the aforementioned features (and may or may not implement all or portions of patents utilized to implement such features). Bundling is of value to customers since it allows them to have all the features on one device. The interactions between the various components make the value of the final product larger than the sum of the values of the different components. On this basis, any attempt to apportion value would in fact under-reward the innovation in each and every component, thereby reducing incentives for firms to invest and innovate.

Second, ascertaining the value of each component is a subjective task. This is particularly difficult for components that are not sold in wholesale markets or are developed in house. The practical realities limit the usefulness of using the value of the components that embed the technology as the royalty base.

Third, the component in question might enable other components to function. For example, the high data transmission rates provided by 4G mobile communication standards, and the underlying patented technologies contained therein, enable several different applications in smartphones that consumers value. Again, determining whether one component enables value for other components and assessing the value that this externality contributes to the product involves strong, highly complex, subjective considerations. Moreover, the precise choice of the component used to calculate the royalty will be arbitrary as it will not capture the underlying externality. *Ad valorem* royalties therefore provide a more practical approach to calculating appropriate royalty payments when some components are pivotal for others to work.

Fourth, the value of the component that embeds a patented technology is, in most circumstances, not a valid proxy for the value of that patented technology. This is because the patent, while covering a particular component, imparts value beyond that particular component. Consider, for example, a chipset used within a smartphone. The chipset is a distinct component, which has a discrete cost. However, it would be wrong to use that cost as a proxy for value because that chipset controls and facilitates many different functionalities, and the value of those enabled functionalities greatly exceeds the cost of the chipset. Just as it is impossible to separate the product into distinct components, it is just as hard, if not more so, to describe a particular patent as covering a single component.

In short, practical considerations suggest that *ad valorem* royalties are likely to be superior to royalties based on component value, particularly in technology markets where final products are often complex and the result of multiple patented components.

3. Efficiency Considerations

Ad valorem royalties are superior to royalties based on component value, even when we set aside the practical considerations discussed above. *Ad valorem* royalties lead to higher consumer welfare than component-value royalties (and hence per-unit royalties), because they reduce the final product price, encourage investment and, therefore, lead to more output and innovation. These effects are compounded in the case of complex products containing multiple patented components.

This is shown in a model by Llobet and Padilla.[30] In that model, licensors and licensees are allowed to modify their strategic choices – i.e. the royalty rates, the price of the end products and their investment decisions – in response to a change in the choice of royalty base. The model is structured as follows: licensors and licensees first decide their investment levels. Then the licensors are assumed to set royalty rates to maximize their profits. Finally, the licensees, taking as given the royalty rates, decide the volume to be sold of the end product, which in turns determines the price in the final market. This model is set up to describe with particularity the behavior of participants in markets where licensors develop technology that is embedded in complementary components of a final product, and where the probability of commercial success of the invention of a licensor is a function of all licensors' investment decisions.

Using this model, Llobet and Padilla investigate which method of determining the royalty base leads to higher consumer and total welfare. In particular, they consider (i) the price and volume outcomes for the end product obtained and (ii) the level of investment made by the licensors and the licensees under each royalty base. Of course, consumers prefer lower prices and greater volumes and, all else being

30 Llobet & Padilla, *supra* note 10.

equal, consumers also prefer higher investment that brings products they value to the market. Llobet and Padilla find that *ad valorem* royalties yield higher consumer and total welfare. Specifically, they show that *ad valorem* royalties result in a relative reduction in the final product price and a relative increase in investment in R&D.

The use of *ad valorem* royalties reduces the problem of double marginalization that arises in markets involving vertically related firms where an upstream firm (here the licensor) sells an intermediate product (here the technology) to a downstream firm (here the licensee) who then sells a final product to consumers.

The double marginalization problem is more severe when the licensor uses per-unit royalties (or component-value royalties) rather than *ad valorem* royalties, because the licensee's incentive to increase the price of the product it sells in order to pass on the increase in its royalty burden is greater with per-unit royalties than with *ad valorem* royalties. As mentioned above, a per-unit royalty increases the marginal cost of the licensee. The licensee therefore has an incentive to increase the final price charged to consumers in order to maintain its margin. This incentive is smaller with *ad valorem* royalties, since an increase in the final price increases the value of sales and, given that the royalty base is given by this value, it also increases the royalty payment. The use of *ad valorem* royalties is therefore beneficial from a static welfare perspective: it results in an increase in the quantity sold in the final market and a lower price, both of which are beneficial for customers and society as a whole.

However, as explained in Section II above, consumer welfare is not only determined by short-run price and quantity outcomes, but also by the investment decisions made by firms in the long run. High investment in R&D leads to technological development, which results in new, better products valued by consumers in the market. This is welfare-enhancing for the customers and it is also beneficial for the industry.

Llobet and Padilla demonstrate that the expected return to investment for both licensors and licensees is greater when royalty payments are based on the price of the final product. Because *ad valorem* royalties mitigate the double marginalization problem, less economic surplus is wasted due to inefficient design of the royalty contract. While some of this economic surplus contributes to higher welfare for customers, some of that incremental surplus is appropriated by licensors and licensees. This increases their rate of return from investment and, hence, their incentives to invest.

This positive effect is even greater in the case of complex products using technologies from multiple licensors, since an increase in the amount each licensor invests has a positive impact on the other licensors' investment decisions. Since the success of a particular innovation depends on the investment made by all the licensors and licensees, when a licensor increases the amount it invests it creates a positive effect on all other investors, licensors and licensees, and hence causes an increase in overall investment both upstream and downstream.

V. Concluding Remarks

In this paper, we have carefully considered the merits of recent complaints against the common industry practice in many technology industries, including the wireless industry, of licensing patents at end-device level rather than at component-part level, as well as complaints against the use of the entire value of the end device as the royalty base for the calculation of compensation.

We conclude that practice will not produce anticompetitive effects unless a licensor that is unwilling to license at component level is vertically integrated midstream (i.e. in the manufacturing of components), refuses to offer contractual protection against component-level suits, and offers better licensing terms when the licensee purchases its components.

In our opinion, these necessary conditions are not sufficient to justify the decision to compel patent holders to license at component level because such a decision may result in an increase in transaction costs, reduce the return to investment and, therefore, undermine dynamic efficiency. Instead we believe that, consistently with other refusal to license scenarios, compulsory licensing at component level would only be justified if, absent that intervention, all effective competition would be eliminated, thus preventing the emergence of new products for which there is potentially substantial demand. Our position in this regard is consistent with the position adopted by the ECJ in *Magill* and *IMS Health*.[31]

Our conclusions regarding the concerns that royalty payments may be excessive when the royalty base used in licensing agreements is the entire value of the end device are even more drastic. We find no welfare justification for mandating a narrow royalty base. Such an intervention would harm static and dynamic efficiency because *ad valorem* royalties based upon the price of the end device lead to more upstream and downstream innovation, lower prices and greater sales than royalties based on the price of the component, whether the latter takes the form of royalties based on the price of the component, per-unit component royalties or per-unit end-device royalties.

---

31 *Supra* notes 7 and 8.

Due Process in Antitrust Proceedings and the Quest for Global Convergence

RANDOLPH TRITELL, PAUL O'BRIEN AND DANIEL MUHEME*

Office of International Affairs, US FTC

University of Liège

Abstract

Effective antitrust enforcement is predicated on the agency's provision of procedural fairness throughout the proceeding. There is growing recognition throughout the international competition community of common basic principles of procedural fairness in competition law investigations. As a leading proponent of procedural fairness norms, Judge Ginsburg has made valuable contributions to international dialogue aimed at advancing this agenda. This article uses a framework of concerns that Judge Ginsburg has identified to explore the growing consensus on: 1) timing of investigations; 2) the opportunity to be heard; 3) neutral decision making; 4) the right to confront evidence; 5) reasoned decisions; and 6) independent review. The article also identifies some of the leading international efforts including in the ICN and the OECD, to define procedural fairness standards and provide practical advice to competition agencies on how to implement them.

* Randolph Tritell is the Director of the Office of International Affairs (OIA) of the US Federal Trade Commission (FTC). Paul O'Brien is Counsel for International Antitrust in the OIA. The views expressed are those of the authors and do not necessarily reflect those of the FTC or any individual commissioner. Daniel Muheme is a lawyer at the Brussels Bar and a Research Fellow at the Liège Competition and Innovation Institute, University of Liège.

I. Introduction

Procedural due process can be described as the legal framework that safeguards the fundamental rights of parties involved in legal procedures, thereby helping to ensure that justice will be done. Due process serves as a gatekeeper for the proper application of legal standards and their impartial, independent, and objective application to the case at issue. Due process should be ensured for any party involved in antitrust[1] proceedings.

While there is no single, universal list of specific agency practices that guarantee perfect due process (even assuming agreement on the definition), there is now widespread recognition of its importance and growing convergence on many of the principles that should guide antitrust agencies and their process. Panels, articles, agency statements, judicial opinions, and indeed any discussion of agency process will inevitably include desirable concepts such as transparency, impartiality, fairness, engagement, predictability, and accountability. Debate continues over the scope, timing, dose, compatibility, discretion, and combination of these concepts but their status as universally cited fundamental objectives is a solid and promising start for the prospects of convergence on due process.

Due process guarantees emanate from constitutions, statutes, and treaties beyond the specifically antitrust context[2] and, as such, one can view the entirety of the exercise as protecting the rights of defense. Given the natural focus on the treatment of the subjects of proceedings, discussion of due process can easily become a catalogue of complaints or grievances about perceived procedural shortcomings, sometimes indistinguishable from criticism of substantive analysis. This would be a disservice to the existing opportunity to promote and encourage better practices in antitrust proceedings. There is a real need to proclaim the benefits of sound, consistent process just as vociferously as we point out the consequences and injustice of inadequate process. The recognition of the dual nature of effective due process in promoting both fair investigations for parties and informed investigations for agencies is a necessary step towards meaningful convergence – a step that has guided recent progress toward global convergence.[3] The OECD Competition Committee has recognized that "[t]ransparency and

---

1 The notions of "antitrust (law)" and "competition (law)" are interchangeable for these purposes.

2 For example, in the US, the principles of due process are engrained in the Fifth Amendment that prevents the federal government from depriving any person "of life, liberty, or property, without due process of law." In the EU, the principle of due process is enshrined the European Union Charter of Fundamental Rights, Article 41, Right to good administration, which states that "every person has the right to have his or her affairs handled impartially, fairly and within a reasonable time by the institutions, bodies, offices and agencies of the Union."

3 "It is sometimes suggested that adequate procedural rights only exist for the benefit of parties... However, it is now recognized that, in fact, procedural rights are also beneficial for agencies themselves and indirectly contribute to the legitimacy of competition law enforcement." Paul Lugard, *Procedural Fairness and Transparency in Antitrust Cases: Work in Progress*, CPI ANTITRUST CHRONICLE, June 2014, at 4.

fairness are not only essential requirements for the parties involved in a competition proceeding, but are also a key part of efficient and effective case management by the competition authority."[4]

The provision of due process often involves fundamental rights. Agencies should ensure that required processes are observed because they are legally obligated to do so. But the benefits of the provision of due process go beyond the obligation to the subjects of proceedings. Dialogue and engagement with parties helps agencies to better focus and develop their investigations. The internal commitment to test and retest relevant evidence and argument helps ensure the quality and accuracy of agency decision-making and outcomes in individual cases.[5] More broadly, consistent, predictable, and fair process reinforces an agency's credibility and overall enforcement mission with parties, the private sector, government, courts and tribunals, and the public.[6]

This paper explores a basic set of due process principles in antitrust proceedings as proposed by Judge Douglas Ginsburg, the recent history of due process discussions in international forums, and the prospects for future convergence.

II. Due Process Fundamentals

Judge Ginsburg has been an important and active voice in the discussion of due process in antitrust proceedings and its global convergence.[7] As a longtime federal appellate judge and former Assistant Attorney General of the Antitrust Division of the US Department of Justice, Judge Ginsburg brings a uniquely informed and thoughtful perspective to the discussion. In 2014, in a keynote address to an international audience at the International Competition Network's Roundtable on Competition Agency Investigative Process, Judge Ginsburg articulated six "due process concerns to consider": (1) the consequences of delay in resolving

---

4 OECD, Procedural Fairness: Transparency Issues in Civil and Administrative Enforcement Proceedings (2011) at 26.

5 See, for example, Edith Ramirez, FTC Chairwoman, Core Competition Agency Principles: Lessons Learned at the FTC, Keynote Address at Antitrust in Asia Conference, ABA Section of Antitrust Law and Expert Advisory Committee of the Anti-Monopoly Commission of the State Council (May 22, 2014), at 2; Roger Alford, Remarks at China Competition Policy Forum, Shanghai, China (Aug. 30, 2017): "Transparency also helps to ensure that we as enforcers get to the right answers, exposing our views to criticism and feedback."

6 Paul O'Brien, Krisztian Katona & Randolph Tritell, *Procedural Fairness in Competition Investigations: U.S. FTC Practice and Recent Guidance from the International Competition Network*, CPI Antitrust Chronicle, July 2015 (1), at 2, https://www.ftc.gov/system/files/attachments/key-speeches-presentations/obrien_katona_tritell_-_procedural_fairness_in_competition_investigations_7-2015.pdf.

7 See, e.g., Douglas H. Ginsburg & Taylor M. Owings, *Due Process in Competition Proceedings*, 11 Competition L. Int'l 39, 39 (2015): "The design of competition proceedings varies by jurisdiction, but each jurisdiction should aim to ensure due process for companies accused of a violation. The rule of law requires no less."

antitrust investigations; (2) a hearing before the actual decision-maker; (3) a neutral decision-maker; (4) the right to confront evidence; (5) a reasoned decision based solely upon the evidence; and (6) review by an independent tribunal.[8]

Given the tribute nature of this paper, we will use Judge Ginsburg's framework of concerns to explore the need for and scope of due process considerations in antitrust enforcement, and then present some of the existing and ongoing convergence efforts in this area. Judge Ginsburg's list of concerns falls squarely within the contours of the global discussion of due process factors. For example, a former Director General at the Directorate-General for Competition (DG COMP) at the European Commission spoke of due process in antitrust proceedings as including: (1) a reasoned statement of objections with an opportunity to respond; (2) access to the case file; (3) an oral hearing; (4) a reasoned decision on the merits; and (5) the ability to appeal decisions in court.[9] A former official of the Irish Competition Authority and the Hong Kong Competition Commission articulated three similar components of due process: (1) full disclosure to parties under investigation of the totality of the evidence and theories of harm; (2) the opportunity to respond to the alleged violation and the agency's findings; and (3) an independent and impartial decision-maker.[10]

1. Judge Ginsburg Concern No. One: Delay

Timing is a critical element of antitrust enforcement. Unnecessary delay of antitrust investigations can harm not only the companies and individuals under investigation, but also markets and consumers by delaying remedies or efficiencies. Judge Ginsburg frames this due process concern with the familiar phrase: "Justice delayed is indeed justice denied." Merger enforcement is often accompanied by tight and strict statutory deadlines to help ensure that deals remain economically viable while undergoing appropriate review. In contrast, agencies often do not have deadlines within which they must complete cartel and single firm conduct investigations. Investigations may progress at a deliberate pace that meets the needs of the agency, but can expose the agency to criticism. Where there are no mandatory deadlines, some agencies monitor their timing through internal procedures, such as projected timelines and goals, and some share such non-binding constraints with parties under investigation.[11] As with many due

---

8 Judge Douglas H. Ginsburg, Due Process in Competition Proceedings, Keynote Address at ICN Roundtable on Competition Agency Investigative Process (Mar. 25, 2015).

9 Alexander Italianer, DG COMP, Safeguarding Due Process in Antitrust Proceedings, Speech at Fordham Competition Law Institute, Annual Conference on International Antitrust Law and Policy (Sep. 23, 2010), http://ec.europa.eu/competition/speeches/text/sp2010_06_en.pdf.

10 Stanley Wong, *Thinking About Procedural Fairness of Competition Law Enforcement Across Jurisdictions: A Suggested Principled Approach*, Competition Policy International (Apr. 23, 2014).

11 For example, in the ASEAN Regional Guidelines on Competition Policy (2010), the Chapter on Due Process encourages competition agencies to "have internal procedures, such as timeline projections, in

process considerations, there is an outward-looking concern – the costs of undue delay imposed on parties, businesses, individuals, and industries – but also the internal concern of timeliness and investigative efficiency to help the agency focus resources on the most important cases.

Aside from the overall length of investigations, there are aspects of investigations that require attention to timing. Important investigative tools such as requests for information need deadlines to ensure that the agency receives relevant information in a timely manner during investigations. Likewise, agencies should consider the burden imposed by such requests and allow reasonable response times to help ensure thorough and thoughtful submissions. In advanced investigations in which agencies consider taking enforcement action, the value of the opportunity to respond to a statement of objection, complaint, or proposed agency order is directly tied to a reasonable response time.[12] An "opportunity" to respond that is measured in hours or single days can severely impair the value of the response and raise serious due process questions.

Timing can also affect the value of another prominent due process pillar – appellate review (discussed below).[13] If judicial review takes years and final decisions about the appropriateness of agency action come long after transactions or agreements are abandoned, conduct is modified, fines are imposed, and business and markets have moved on, the value of the review as a constraint on agency process and legal guidance to all is diminished.

2. Judge Ginsburg Concern No. Two: Hearing Before the Actual Decision-Maker

Judge Ginsburg focuses this concern on the value of having the decision-maker intimately familiar with the case – present at a hearing for the presentation of evidence, able to judge the credibility of witnesses and experts firsthand, and committed to reading the submissions from both sides. It is self-evident that an informed decision-maker makes better decisions, but it is an important pillar of due process that should not succumb to the complacency of a decision-maker that rubber-stamps the decisions of others or a process that shields decision-makers

---

order to ensure that decision are no unduly delayed." ICN GUIDANCE ON INVESTIGATIVE PROCESS (2018), §8.4, states, "Agencies should avoid unnecessary delay in enforcement. Agencies should meet all deadlines set by competition laws or agency rules and in the absence of such deadlines, set internal projections or working estimates to help avoid unnecessary delay, appropriate to the complexity and circumstances of the matter." https://www.internationalcompetitionnetwork.org/portfolio/guidance-on-investigative-process.

12 For example, DG COMP, ANTITRUST MANUAL OF PROCEDURES § 6.1.1. (51) (2012) states that "The time limit for the reply to the [Statement of Objections] will take into account both the time required for the preparation of the submission and the urgency of the case. The parties have the right to at least a period of four weeks to reply to the SO."

13 OECD, RECOMMENDATION OF THE OECD COUNCIL ON MERGER REVIEW (2005) states that "review of adverse enforcement decisions should be completed within reasonable time periods." http://www.oecd.org/daf/competition/oecdrecommendationonmergerreview.htm.

from their ultimate responsibility. A hearing that involves presentation and argument before the decision-maker not only strengthens decision-making in individual cases, but also fortifies an agency's legitimacy and adds to the credibility of an agency's actions.

Though presented as a safeguard for ultimate decision-making, this principle is broadly applicable across an investigation and, importantly, in the formation and consideration of the staff's recommendations. During an investigation, engagement by staff with the parties on theories of competitive harm and key pieces of evidence is essential to ensuring a proper understanding of the potential for harm.[14] As agency management and top officials are presented with findings for their independent decision-making, they should receive enough information to understand the factual, legal, and theoretical bases for the recommendations. They should review, understand, test, and question key evidence and theories with the agency staff and consider meetings with parties (and perhaps third parties) at key points during the investigation. These interactions among staff, parties, and agency management allow for the testing and retesting of the evidence and theories of harm, and ultimately improve decision-making and outcomes.[15]

In addition to the focus on the decision-maker and the value of an in-person presentation through a hearing, this principle encompasses the parties' perspective and the opportunity to be heard. The ability to be heard ensures that parties to antitrust proceedings have the opportunity to respond fully before the agency reaches its decision. Party and third-party perspectives help to properly test whether agency theories and allegations hold up to reality, as they have the expertise and incentives to challenge incorrect, weak, and untested assumptions about their businesses and markets. This should encompass the opportunity to respond to the alleged violations and claims, the facts, and the legal and economic theory applied.[16] These objectives can be achieved through different mechanisms, including investigative meetings with the agency as well as formal hearings or court proceedings, and can involve the opportunity to respond in writing and orally at a meeting or hearing.[17] The content and characteristics of hearings vary among legal systems and are often set by agency or court rules, but several common aspects are recognized as desirable. These include the ability to present

---

14 Section IV, "Engagement", of the ICN GUIDANCE (*supra* note 11) recognizes that "[i]nvestigations benefit from the open discussion of investigative theories with the parties and the explanation of competition concerns at key stages."

15 See Terrell McSweeny, former FTC Commissioner, Procedural Fairness in Competition Law Enforcement and the FTC Experience, Remarks at King's College, London (Oct. 23, 2015) https://www.ftc.gov/public-statements/2015/10/procedural-fairness-competition-law-enforcement-ftc-experience. Commissioner McSweeny explains the benefits of engagement with subjects of investigations at 7–8.

16 Wong, *supra* note 10, at 2.

17 Daniel Muheme, Norman Neyrinck, Nicolas Petit, *Procedural Rights in EU Antitrust Proceedings*, in 3 PROCEDURAL RIGHTS IN COMPETITION LAW IN THE EU AND CHINA 129 (Caroline Cauffman & Qian Hau eds., Springer 2016).

witnesses, arguments, and factual evidence, the ability to question and cross-examine witnesses, a format that allows the decision-maker to evaluate the strength of arguments and evidence from both sides, with adequate time for preparation and presentation, and transparent rules of procedure.[18]

3. Judge Ginsburg Concern No. Three: Neutral Decision-Maker

Another common and crucial notion of due process is that the decision-maker should be impartial. This is often articulated as having no direct, specific personal interest in the matter or relationship to any party.[19] This can be accomplished through ethics rules that prohibit conflicts of interest. Though focused on the decision-maker, the principle of impartiality is applicable to all agency staff; conflict of interest rules often govern appropriate participation in investigations, from staff to agency management and decision-makers.

This principle can also include the concept of separating agency investigation and decision-making to limit susceptibility to confirmation bias. Internal rules that delineate separate investigation functions or components from decision-making and prevent the ultimate decision-maker from having a significant role in the investigative stage can help accomplish this goal. Agencies use outside experts, separate legal services components, or internal review of the case by "fresh eyes" not involved in the investigation to create an objective, independent check on their decision-making.[20]

More broadly, neutral decision-making involves a process and commitment to pursue objective, consistent application of legal standards and decisions based on the facts. Commentary on this point also often emphasizes the desirability of pursuing, considering, and addressing both exculpatory and inculpatory evidence, and not simply focusing on that evidence that supports an alleged violation.[21]

4. Judge Ginsburg Concern No. Four: Right to Confront Evidence

The right to confront evidence is a fundamental aspect of due process, in the antitrust context and elsewhere. Depending on the system and the rules, this can include the ability to see the evidence collected and used during an investigation, to cross-examine witnesses or otherwise challenge evidence, and to offer evidence

---

18 See, e.g., ICC, Recommended Framework for International Best Practices in Competition Law Enforcement Proceedings (2010), § 2.4.16.

19 See, e.g., ABA Antitrust Law Section, Best Practices for Antitrust Procedure (2015) (ABA Antitrust Best Practices), https://www.americanbar.org/content/dam/aba/directories/antitrust/dec15_lipsky_tritell_12_11f.authcheckdam.pdf, § III. B.

20 See OECD, Procedural Fairness and Transparency: Key Points (2012), http://www.oecd.org/daf/competition/abuse/proceduralfairnessandtransparency-2012.htm, at 29; ICN Guidance at § 9.2, *supra* note 11.

21 See, e.g., ABA Antitrust Best Practices, *supra* note 19, § I.D.

or argument, including expert analysis, in explanation or rebuttal. This principle can be accomplished across several formats and stages of proceedings through written submissions, oral hearings, court proceedings, and even in meetings with agency staff and management during the investigation. While confidentiality protection may limit the ability to confront specific evidence during an investigation, it is generally understood that before a final decision is imposed in an antitrust proceeding, a party should be provided with access to the evidence relied upon as the basis for any case against it and an effective opportunity to respond.[22]

The opportunity to confront evidence incorporates an important prerequisite – transparency during an investigation. Without transparency, parties are incapable of exercising a meaningful right of defense. Transparency embraces non-discrimination towards parties involved in antitrust proceedings as well as accountability to the public, in order to achieve procedural fairness. A meaningful opportunity to respond presupposes notice from the agency to the party under investigation about the legal basis for the allegations, the legal and economic theories applicable to the case, and the factual evidence, subject to appropriate protections for confidential information. If parties are not apprised of the evidence and arguments against them, they cannot usefully respond to and properly test the allegations. This transparency is achieved most fully and formally through access-to-file procedures or discovery rules, but the principle can be applied to a certain extent (subject to confidentiality rules) and to a certain utility (depending on the discretion of the agency) earlier in (and throughout) an investigation, in the interaction and discussions between agency staff and parties.

Open communication between the agency and the subjects of investigations can enable more informed discussions on both sides and focus investigations on the significant areas of dispute.[23] The opportunity for parties to confront and rebut evidence, enabled by agency transparency about that evidence, facilitates an agency's ability to better understand the facts and arguments at issue, which, in turn, increases the ability to reach the right decision. Agencies can pursue engagement through status calls, regular face-to-face meetings, and the invitation to submit white papers on key issues.

Interaction and the ability to submit evidence and arguments that respond to agency positions can occur during all stages of an investigation. Meetings enable staff and parties to discuss timing, working theories, and the nature of the evidence obtained. They also can include exchanges between agency and party economists on how they view the market and interpret relevant data. Some agencies also make their decision-makers available for meetings, often after recommendations are submitted but before the agency reaches a decision. This

---

22 See ICN GUIDANCE, *supra* note 11, at 5.4.

23 See O'Brien, Katona & Tritell, *supra* note 6, at 3–4.

previews the more formal due process rules integral to official hearings or court proceedings and, importantly, helps agency decision-makers evaluate the arguments before a decision.

Agency transparency regarding its competitive concerns, and engagement with parties on its theories and nature of the evidence, allows an agency to reach its decision through a process of critical thinking and reflection.[24] Conversely, an unwillingness to engage leaves the other side speculating about competitive concerns, potential counterarguments, or even other agency motives, and ultimately hinders informed decision-making.[25]

The principle of transparency includes general transparency about applicable laws, policies, and practices. Parties should know and be able to understand an agency's procedures in order to be able to follow and participate effectively in antitrust proceedings. Accordingly, it is crucial for agencies to publish their substantive and procedural rules and guidelines together with procedures and criteria necessary to challenge the allegations and eventual decision.[26]

5. Judge Ginsburg Concern No. Five: Reasoned Decision

All of the careful due process safeguards that guide fair and informed investigation, analysis, and decision-making can be for naught if they are not observed in the agency's final decision and how it is communicated. Agency decisions should clearly explain the findings of fact, evidence relied upon, and the legal and economic theories underlying the conclusion.[27] A reasoned decision that substantiates its findings of fact is the primary record for appellate review, which is the important final check on agency process and decisions.

More broadly, a written, published agency decision, order, or legal challenge is a vital tool for agency transparency and influence, providing details on the agency's legal reasoning, theory of harm, and supporting evidence. Reasoned decisions are essential to guide compliant business conduct.

6. Judge Ginsburg Concern No. Six: Review by an Independent Tribunal

The final stop for antitrust process, as is common in many legal contexts, is appellate review by an independent tribunal. Courts play a central role in guaranteeing due process and thus the principle of appellate review is an essential

24 Ramirez, *supra* note 5.

25 See McSweeny, *supra* note 15, at 7–8.

26 See ICC Framework, *supra* note 18, at § 2.1.1; ABA Antitrust Best Practices, *supra* note 19, at § IV. B; ICN Guidance, *supra* note 11, at 4.4.3.

27 See, e.g., ICN Guidance *supra* note 11, at § II.4.2.

part of all due process frameworks. Appellate review of agencies' competition law decisions exists in most, if not all, jurisdictions that enforce competition law, and acts as a check on agency process as well as on substantive decisions.[28] Due process requires that the reviewing entity is independent of the competition agency, though the format may be a court, commission, or other type of adjudicative body, it may be a specialized competition tribunal or have wider jurisdiction, and the standard of review of findings of fact and conclusions of law may be more or less deferential. Criticism tends to focus on the timing, costs, and scope of appellate review, as each can affect the availability and utility of the review, though not its existence.[29]

III. Due Process Convergence

The provision of due process (and the related, overlapping, and similar concepts of procedural fairness, transparency, rights of defense, and natural justice) is a common foundation of legal systems around the world, derived from constitutions, statutes, and rules far broader than antitrust.[30] Indeed, Judge Ginsburg, practitioners, academics, and competition agency officials articulate and define a similar set of due process principles to guide the provision of due process in competition enforcement. However, identical principles do not necessarily equate to identical practices. While the concepts and goals of due process may be similar, how it is implemented by competition agencies varies among jurisdictions with different legal traditions and institutional frameworks. We next turn to the current state of due process development in the international antitrust enforcement community and its future prospects.

Academic, practitioner, and former FTC Chairman Timothy Muris has described the soft law convergence process as unfolding in three stages.[31] The first stage is the decentralized implementation of diverse processes and practices in different jurisdictions. The second stage involves experience sharing, identifying best practices, and building consensus. In the third stage, individual jurisdictions voluntarily "opt in to superior standards." The next sections discuss the evolution of due process standards, noting the progression through these stages toward increasing convergence around recognized good practice.

---

28 ICN Guiding Principles for Procedural Fairness in Competition Agency Enforcement (2018), Judicial Review/Appeals, https://www.internationalcompetitionnetwork.org/portfolio/guiding-principles-for-procedural-fairness/: "Competition agency enforcement proceedings should include the right to seek impartial review by an independent judicial body."

29 See, e.g., Lugard, *supra* note 3, at 4–5.

30 See *supra* note 2.

31 Timothy J. Muris, Competition Agencies in a Market-Based Global Economy, Remarks at the Annual Lecture of the European Foreign Affairs Review (July 23, 2002) https://www.ftc.gov/public-statements/2002/07/competition-agencies-market-based-global-economy.

1. Early International Efforts to Articulate Due Process Standards

There is no evidence of a period when competition agencies simply rejected due process, touted their non-transparency, sought to remain uninformed, and were openly unfair in their enforcement process. There are no agency official statements or speeches to cite for the "opposed" side of any due process debate. Instead, there has been an evolution or gradual awakening to the need for and value of due process in antitrust proceedings, similar to the advancement of the legal and economic underpinnings of competition law. It is apparent that due process, procedural fairness, and transparency have attracted increased attention in the global antitrust enforcement community in the last 10 years, and have thus achieved a "hot topic" status.[32] Why has that happened?

As with the transformation of all of that is considered "international antitrust," the reasons start with globalization and the widespread adoption of antitrust regimes. The familiar and straightforward formula is: more global business + more antitrust enforcers = more investigations that occur in parallel in multiple jurisdictions. As more companies and their counsel encountered different investigative processes around the world and agencies learned of each other's practices through enforcement cooperation, comparisons and sharing of experience were inevitable. These new data points were used to criticize agency practices that were seen as inadequate or lacking in due process, and to call for global convergence towards best practices. The leading statement on international cooperation in competition proceedings enshrines this story in its preamble, noting the importance of "the widespread adoption, acceptance and enforcement of competition law as well as the concomitant desire of... competition authorities to work together to ensure efficient and effective investigations and proceedings and to improve their own analyses" and the link to procedural due process, recognizing that "transparent and fair processes are essential to achieving effective and efficient co-operation in competition law enforcement."[33]

One of the earliest agency-led efforts to articulate desirable due process practices arose in the International Competition Network (ICN) in the context of its merger work. Founded in 2001, one of the ICN's first projects was an ambitious effort to draft consensual "recommended practices" on merger notification and review procedures. With the increase in the number of agencies that were reviewing mergers, the project's goal was to develop best practices around which agencies could converge, in order to rationalize the system and limit growing differences and burdens imposed on agencies and companies, particularly for

32 See, e.g., D. Danny Sokol & Andrew T. Guzman, Antitrust Procedural Fairness (2019).

33 OECD, Recommendation concerning International Co-operation on Competition Investigations and Proceedings (2014) http://www.oecd.org/competition/international-coop-competition-2014-recommendation.htm.

global mergers subject to review in many jurisdictions (affectionately referred to as the "multi-jurisdictional merger thicket").

In 2003 and 2004, the recommendations expanded from guidance on notification thresholds and filing requirements to include four due-process-related topics: conduct of merger investigations, procedural fairness, transparency, and confidentiality. The resulting Recommended Practices for Merger Notification and Review Procedures[34] were a major success for the new network, providing inspiration for dozens of member agencies to change or implement new rules and practices in line with these consensus global norms. The OECD's governing council used the ICN Recommended Practices as a basis for its own 2005 Recommendation on Merger Review, including the due process principles, further boosting the profile and reach of the principles.[35]

The ICN Recommended Practices (RPs) on due process in the merger enforcement context were far-reaching, thoughtful practices that have stood the test of time. They include, for example, provisions such as:

- Merger investigation procedures should include opportunities for meetings or discussions between the competition agency and the merging parties at key points in the investigation. RP VI.B.
- Prior to a final adverse enforcement decision on the merits, merging parties should be provided with sufficient and timely information on the facts and the competitive concerns that form the basis for the proposed adverse decision and should have a meaningful opportunity to respond to such concerns. RP VII.B.
- The competition agency should make certain that there are safeguards, or "checks and balances," ensuring that merger reviews are handled in a fair, efficient, and consistent manner, procedurally and substantively. RP VII.D.1.
- Merger review systems should provide an opportunity for timely review by a separate adjudicative body of a competition agency's final adverse decision on the merits of a merger. RP VII.E.
- Merger control regimes should be transparent with respect to, at a minimum, the jurisdictional scope of the merger control law, the competition agency's decision-making procedures, and the principles and criteria the competition agency uses to apply the substantive review standard. RP VIII.B.

---

34 ICN, Recommended Practices For Merger Notification And Review Procedures (2017), https://www.internationalcompetitionnetwork.org/portfolio/merger-np-recommended-practices.

35 See OECD Recommendation Merger Review, *supra* note 13. See, for example, A.3. that states "Merger laws should ensure procedural fairness for merging parties, including the opportunity for merging parties to obtain sufficient and timely information about material competitive concerns raised by a merger, a meaningful opportunity to respond to such concerns, and the right to seek review by a separate adjudicative body of final adverse enforcement decisions on the legality of a merger."

The next major agency-led discussion – and first to include all enforcement areas – on due process occurred from 2010 to 2012 in the OECD Competition Committee. The Committee held a series of three best practice round tables on procedural fairness, involving dozens of member agency submissions, culminating in a "Key Points" report in 2012 that described the discussions and included many agency-specific examples of the provision of due process.[36] The report found "a broad consensus on the need for, and importance of, transparency and procedural fairness in competition enforcement, notwithstanding differences between prosecutorial and administrative systems, and other legal, cultural, historical, and economic differences,"[37] providing a notable milestone on the road to greater convergence. The agreement of the broad group of governments that constitute the OECD supports the proposition that convergence on principles of fair process is achievable despite differences in legal systems, procedures, and institutional frameworks.

2. Current Standards for Due Process: Stage 2 Consensus-Building

Three collaborative entities – the International Chamber of Commerce, the American Bar Association Antitrust Law Section, and the ICN – have led the development of the current state of international consensus and aspirations for the provision of due process in antitrust proceedings. Their work includes: (1) the ICC Recommended Framework for International Best Practices in Competition Law Enforcement Proceedings, and Discussion Paper on Effective Procedural Safeguards, (2) the ABA Antitrust Law Section's Best Practices for Antitrust Procedures, and (3) the ICN's Guidance on Investigative Process and Guiding Principles for Procedural Fairness.

A. ICC Framework and Discussion Paper[38]

The ICC Framework is a set of practices and principles that promote due process and related concepts, covering transparency, engagement, confidentiality, due process/fairness, non-discrimination, accountability, and the role of the courts. They state the intention "to promote the adoption of procedural safeguards, directed at ensuring that due regard is given to the fundamental fairness of the processes by which competition authorities enforce their laws in an increasingly global context."[39] With an audience of competition authorities and government officials in mind, the ICC Framework emphasizes that due process can "strengthen vigorous, efficient enforcement of competition laws."[40] The 2017 Discussion

36 OECD Procedural Fairness and Transparency: Key Points, *supra* note 20.

37 *Id.*, Introduction at 5.

38 ICC Framework, *supra* note 18; ICC, Effective Procedural Safeguards in Competition Law Enforcement Proceedings, Discussion Paper (2017).

39 *Id.*, ICC Framework at § 1.2.1.

40 *Id.*, ICC Framework at § 1.2.2.

Paper on Procedural Safeguards complements the ICC Framework by setting out overarching principles of due process and guidance on agency duties.

B. ABA Antitrust Best Practices[41]

The ABA Antitrust Law Section's International Task Force produced its "Best Practices for Antitrust Procedure" in 2015, detailing procedures that promote impartial, efficient, and accurate antitrust decisions. Like past efforts, the ABA Antitrust Best Practices also emphasize their value to agencies in helping to achieve "basic competition goals," including enhancing the quality of enforcement. The proposed best practices cover six categories, five of which correspond to stages of antitrust proceedings: (i) investigation, (ii) asserting contentions of infringement, (iii) assessing contentions of infringement, (iv) first instance decisions, (v) review, and (vi) practices applicable to all stages. Thus, they address procedural fairness in the decision-making, as well as the investigative, stage of antitrust enforcement proceedings.

C. ICN Guidance on Investigative Process and Guiding Principles for Procedural Fairness[42]

The ICN Guidance reaffirms the OECD's 2012 aspirational statement that "[t]here is a broad consensus among ICN members regarding the importance of transparency, engagement and protection of confidential information during competition investigations." It then goes further by articulating specific practices that promote the provision of due process during antitrust investigations. The practices are presented under five "basic attributes of sound and effective competition enforcement": (i) effective agency investigation tools, (ii) transparency, (iii) engagement with the parties during an investigation, (iv) internal agency safeguards, and (v) the protection of confidential information.

The ICN Guidance is organized in six parts:

Part 1 addresses effective investigation tools and their fair and efficient use, including appropriate legal requirements and limitations on agency powers, and accompanying internal agency procedures and safeguards.

Part 2 covers transparency of competition laws, rules, policies, decisions, and enforcement practices to ensure that individuals and companies know what to expect of competition enforcement, and that the public has a basis to monitor consistency of enforcement.

Part 3 addresses transparency to parties during an investigation, notably informing parties of the legal basis for an investigation, the facts and nature of evidence gathered, and the theories of harm.

---

41 ABA Antitrust Best Practices, *supra* note 19.

42 ICN Guidance, *supra* note 11; ICN Guiding Principles, *supra* note 28.

Part 4 on engagement discusses the interaction between agency and party and the value of opportunities for parties to respond to agency concerns. The engagement section mentions "meetings or discussions between the agency and parties at key points of the investigation" and "early discussion of the evidence and working theories."

Part 5 introduces recommended agency safeguards for internal practices that support informed decision-making such as consistent procedures, case management, and thorough evaluation.

Part 6 covers the importance of the protection of confidential information obtained during an investigation and policies regarding its disclosure, including the disclosure to parties of confidential information relied upon as the basis for an agency's formal allegations.

The two-page companion document, the 2018 ICN Guiding Principles on Procedural Fairness, lists nine high-level procedural fairness ideals that serve as a universal frame of reference for appropriate enforcement process. The ICN Guidance and Guiding Principles are, to date, the most comprehensive agency-led guidance on procedural fairness during antitrust investigations.[43] Together, they provide a benchmark for agencies to assess the provision of due process during their investigations.

IV. The Progress and Prospects of Due Process

Competition agency process, timing, institutional frameworks, and specific investigative practices vary from jurisdiction to jurisdiction. Some two decades into the era of international antitrust enforcement, there is no set of universal procedural rules on the horizon. There is no serious call for a world antitrust tribunal or arbiter of antitrust process. This is unlikely to change and need not change in order to achieve meaningful convergence on due process. Indeed, all serious efforts to articulate principles and practices that promote due process have acknowledged the "different legal and institutional frameworks that impact the choice of investigative process," and that there can be "different approaches to achieving fairness" in antitrust proceedings.[44] Rather than attempt to prescribe specific sets of procedures or institutional frameworks, which can vary depending upon the design of each legal system, these recommendations are based on the proposition that good process be guided by consensus principles of fairness to ensure procedural due process.

Academic and former FTC Chairman William Kovacic refers to the development of competition policy as a continual work in progress. He views "best" practices

43 At the time of publication, the ICN was poised to complete a project to refine the ICN GUIDANCE and elevate it to "Recommended Practices," the ICN's highest normative work product.

44 ICN GUIDANCE, *supra* note 11, Introduction.

as suggesting the existence of fixed objectives at the end of a journey. Instead, he prefers that agencies aspire to "better" practices in line with the dynamic discipline of competition law enforcement, a drive to continuously change, adapt, and renew the law, policy, and process.[45] This is an apt paradigm for the future of progress on due process in antitrust proceedings. The former DG COMP of the European Commission likewise explained that "due process is not a rigid or static concept. It should evolve in parallel with the dynamic development of antitrust law: we need to constantly examine and improve our procedures."[46]

While we may still experience stage one decentralization and differences in procedural rules, the antitrust community has made great progress in articulating guiding principles and standards in such documents as the ICC Framework, ABA Antitrust Best Practices, and the ICN Guidance and Guiding Principles. They are clear evidence of stage two consensus-building.[47] They are non-binding, soft law tools that work by the power of persuasion, as agencies consider, evaluate, and decide for themselves whether to opt in. Work remains in their promotion and implementation.[48] The challenges of stage three adoption – shaping something as diverse and comprehensive as every antitrust agency's set of procedural rules – are daunting. Still, the history of international exchange, comparison, adaptation, voluntary adoption, and refinement that has accompanied antitrust instruments including merger notification procedures, substantive merger standards, leniency programs, and fining guidelines provides hope.

The impossibility of perfect harmonization does not and should not hinder convergence. Identifying and targeting rules that do not measure up to due process standards – rules and practices that unnecessarily prevent or ignore transparency, squelch engagement between agency and party, and deny opportunities for parties to exercise their rights of defense – is a worthwhile endeavor. Importantly, this endeavor and ongoing dialogue will continue to need contributions from across the antitrust community, including academic study, private sector comparisons and criticism, agency commitment and self-evaluation, judicial scrutiny, international organization leadership on articulating consensus standards, and governmental support. Organizations such as the ICN and OECD have room to draft more consensus recommendations on due process standards and, importantly, encourage their implementation. Practitioners and academics should continue to evaluate the impact of different rules, and, in particular,

---

45 William Kovacic, Achieving Better Practices in the Design of Competition Policy Institutions, Remarks before the Seoul Competition Forum (Apr. 20, 2004).

46 Italianer, *supra* note 9, at 4.

47 Paul O'Brien, *Procedural Fairness: Convergence in Process*, CPI Antitrust Chronicle, Nov. 2018.

48 For an example of a recent call for a multilateral framework on procedures with "core procedural norms and meaning compliance mechanisms" for implementation, see Makan Delrahim, Remarks on Global Antitrust Enforcement at the Council of Foreign Relations (June 1, 2018), https://www.justice.gov/opa/speech/assistant-attorney-general-makan-delrahim-delivers-remarks-global-antitrust-enforcement.

identify practices that they perceive as inadequate.[49] Agencies need to commit to consistent implementation of their rules, via staff training and internal manuals, guides, and other procedures. The elimination of divergent or erroneous outcomes that derive from inadequate rules that leave agencies uninformed, uninterested, biased, or unfair is a desirable goal, worthy of efforts to align antitrust process towards shared ideas of fairness and transparency.

Calls for greater due process in antitrust proceedings, such as those from Judge Ginsburg, recognize the immense value of predictability and fairness to parties and more informed decision-making and greater credibility to enforcers. Continuing to seek to realize Judge Ginsburg's goal of fairness throughout antitrust proceedings is well worth the effort, both because it behooves governmental entities to practice and be perceived as conducting their enforcement in accordance with due process standards, and because fair process benefits decision-making by agencies and, ultimately, the consumers they serve.

49 See, e.g., US Chamber of Commerce, *Adherence to ICN Guidance on Investigative Process: A Practitioner Survey* (2017), https://www.uschamber.com/report/adherence-icn-guidance-investigative-process-practitioner-survey.

PART III
Criminal Antitrust

Criminal Antitrust Trials: The Case for Economics

JOSEPH J. BIAL*

Paul, Weiss, Rifkind, Wharton & Garrison

Abstract

Despite the widespread use of economics in civil antitrust investigations and litigation, prosecutors frequently seek to exclude economic testimony at criminal trials when it goes to the issue of liability. This paper addresses the narrow but important question of the role economics can play in criminal trials for alleged violations of antitrust laws and concludes that this economic testimony is relevant and should be admissible. Just as in the civil context, economic testimony can help the trier of fact understand the evidence that both prosecutors and defendants offer, an increasingly critical function in light of the expanding nature of criminal price-fixing cases. Economic testimony on industry and other economic factors that is routine in civil cases can reduce the risk that ambitious investigations will result in false-positive criminal prosecutions, avoiding potential costs to the targeted companies and individuals. These costs can be quite significant, even leading to the type of anticompetitive consequences the antitrust laws seek to prevent in the first place. Given these costs, it is worthwhile to consider what role economic testimony can play in today's criminal antitrust trials.

---

* Joseph Bial is a partner with the antitrust group at Paul, Weiss, Rifkind, Wharton & Garrison LLP where he represents clients across a wide array of industries in high-profile litigation in federal district and appellate courts as well as investigations before state and federal regulatory agencies. In addition to his private practice, Joe has been an Adjunct Professor at George Mason School of Law and at the University of Alaska College of Business and Public Policy and taught the introductory Econometrics course for PhD (Economics) students at George Mason University. Prior to Paul, Weiss, Joe worked as an economist at the White House Office of Management and Budget, consulted and testified as an economic expert, and clerked for the Honorable Douglas H. Ginsburg of the US Court of Appeals for the District of Columbia as well as in the Alaska Supreme Court. Joe received his JD from the University of Chicago Law School and also holds a PhD in Economics from the University of Arizona.

Joe would like to thank Roberto Finzi for his helpful comments on this paper. He also would like to thank Eric Sega for his insight and assistance in preparing this chapter as well as Evan Goldstick for assisting in preparing this paper.

I. Introduction

This paper addresses the very narrow, but important, question of whether economics has a role in criminal trials for alleged violations of antitrust laws. Indeed, the question is even narrower than that, as economics is often used by prosecutors to prove the volume of commerce affected by the alleged criminal price-fixing and, as a result, the fine to be assessed. On the issue of liability, however, prosecutors frequently seek to exclude economic testimony on the basis that it is not relevant to proving (or disproving) an agreement among competitors to fix prices. There are many reasons, though, to permit such testimony on the issue of liability. As prosecution of alleged price-fixing expands – both in geographic scope (and, especially, internationally) and complexity – economics can be critical to helping the trier of fact understand the evidence offered by the government and by the defendant.

This paper underscores the increased risk that the Department of Justice's increasingly ambitious prosecution of industry-wide price-fixing actions may lead to an increase in false-positive criminal prosecutions. This phenomenon may stem in part from the implementation of the Corporate Leniency program, which generates broader and more extensive grand jury investigations,[1] but there is little doubt that the cost of false-positive prosecutions is potentially quite high. These potential costs, including the loss of efficiency in industries under investigation, are too high to ignore the benefit of permitting economic testimony on industry structure and other economic factors in criminal antitrust trials, as is already routine in the civil context.

This paper provides a background on the use of economics in civil antitrust cases, which is routine, and how similar use of economics would benefit the trier of fact in criminal antitrust cases. Section II addresses the use of economics in civil investigations by government agencies and its use in civil litigation. Section III addresses the issue of whether economic testimony is relevant in criminal price-fixing trials. I conclude it is relevant and should be admissible.

II. Economic Analysis is Commonplace in Civil Antitrust Investigations and Civil Antitrust Litigation

It is beyond dispute that economic analysis plays a critical role in the legal field of antitrust. For example, economists routinely provide input on merger-and-acquisition transactions to identify the extent of the relevant market that

---

1 Antitrust Div., US Dep't of Justice, Measuring the Value of Second-In Cooperation in Corporate Plea Negotiations, Address at the 54th Annual ABA Antitrust Section Spring Meeting (Mar. 29, 2006), at 4: "[T]he Division has had great success engaging in a strategy of 'cartel profiling' techniques aimed at ferreting out violations that sprout 'cartel trees' where one investigation will eventually give root to prosecutions in a half-dozen or more different markets."

is potentially affected by the transaction.[2] Economic analysis is similarly used to identify potential efficiencies, the extent of barriers to entry, proof of damages, and even the existence of antitrust injury and standing. The importance of economists for this work cannot be denied. Each of the federal agencies charged with enforcing the antitrust laws – the Antitrust Division of the Department of Justice (DOJ) and the Federal Trade Commission (FTC) – employs dozens of economists to support their legal work.[3] These same economists assist the agencies in their civil investigations and, in the event of litigation, may provide testimony or work with the testifying economist to further that important work.[4] The importance of economic testimony has become so central to many antitrust cases that some courts have gone so far as to remark that it is an *essential* part of the testimony before the court, and that the absence of economic testimony from an expert may be fatal to a party's case.[5]

---

2 Economists were instrumental in the development of numerous standard techniques used by agencies to evaluate the impact of transactions on the marketplace including, among others, the SSNIP test, Critical-Loss Analysis, and Upward Pricing Pressure analysis. *See* Dep't of Justice & Fed. Trade Comm'n, Horizontal Merger Guidelines, § 4.1 (2010) (discussing SSNIP); Russell Pittman, *Three Economist's Tools for Antitrust Analysis* (EAG Discussion Paper) Jan. 2017, https://www.justice.gov/atr/page/file/925641/download, (Pittman, an economist in the Dep't of Justice's Economic Analysis Group, discussing all three tools).

3 The Antitrust Division contains a Deputy Assistant Attorney General, who is typically an economist, as well as the Economics Analysis Group, which employs over 50 economists. *See* Economic Analysis Group Homepage, https://www.justice.gov/atr/about-division/economic-analysis-group (last visited Feb. 14, 2020); *see also* Diane S. Owen, *Economists in the Antitrust Division*, 1 CSWEP News (2016) at 7, https://www.justice.gov/atr/file/economists-in-the-antitrust-division/download. Likewise, the Bureau of Economics of the FTC is headed by an economist and employees over 70 full-time economists. *See* Bureau of Economics Homepage, https://www.ftc.gov/about-ftc/bureaus-offices/bureau-economics (last visited Feb. 14, 2020).

4 *See* Economic Analysis Group Homepage, *supra*: "EAG economists... play... a central role in enforcement efforts to protect competition and benefit consumers through low prices, high quality, and innovation;" Bureau of Economics Homepage, *supra*: "The Bureau of Economics (BE) has a proud tradition of providing scientifically sound, data-driven economic analysis that informs antitrust, consumer protection, and business regulation policy in the US. With a staff of approximately 80 PhD-holding applied microeconomists, BE plays an essential role in virtually all aspects of the FTC's mission;" *see also*, Owen, *supra* note 3, at 7: "As economists, most of what we do centers on specific civil investigations, either investigations into proposed mergers or investigations of a firm's business conduct (e.g., exclusive contracts, loyalty discounts); the Division's criminal price-fixing investigations don't rely on economic analysis to the same degree."

5 *See, e.g.*, Am. Exp. Co. v. Italian Colors Rest., 570 U.S. 228, 242 (2013) (Kagan, J., dissenting); Jeffrey May, *The US Supreme Court rules that an arbitration agreement did not prevent effective vindication of antitrust rights (American Express / Italian Colors Restaurant)*, 20 June 2013, *e-Competitions* June 2013, Art. N° 53371: "The agreement might block the claimant from presenting the kind of proof that is necessary to establish the defendant's liability – say, by prohibiting any economic testimony (good luck proving an antitrust claim without that!);" Virginia Vermiculite, Ltd. v. W.R. Grace & Co.-Conn., 108 f. Supp. 2d 549, 576 n.16 (W.D. Va. 2000): "However, as a practical matter and as discussed below, the plaintiffs' lack of any witness to testify about antitrust economics, or to rebut the defendants' economists, proves fatal."

1. Economic Analysis is Routinely Used in Cases Invoking the Rule of Reason

Many practitioners, whether they are in private practice or public service, understand and appreciate the relevance of economic methodologies to rule-of-reason analysis.[6] Initially set forth in the early 1900s,[7] the rule of reason became increasingly prevalent over time – coinciding with a diminished use of per se analysis – in situations where there are potentially significant procompetitive benefits from a restraint of trade. As courts better understood the facts underlying these cases from the perspective of economic theory, they became better able to incorporate economic analysis into their decision-making.[8] Had there been a blanket rule to forbid economic analysis, it is likely that prohibitions by courts of certain economic conduct would have persisted for years or even decades, as parties adhered to legal rulings that were at odds with the economic underpinnings.

Under the rule of reason, a defendant can argue a restriction is reasonable given market circumstances and economic effects (as opposed to per se analysis, which does not allow a defendant to avoid liability through justifications of efficiency or increased competition). Given the rule of reason's focus on market circumstances and economic effects, economic analysis became the dominant tool for

---

6 *See* Owen, *supra* note 3, at 7: "As economists, most of what we do centers on specific civil investigations, either investigations into proposed mergers or investigations of a firm's business conduct (e.g., exclusive contracts, loyalty discounts).... Every merger and conduct investigation has at least one economist on it from the outset, and complex or data-rich matters can have six or eight with different areas of responsibility divided up by interest and skills."

7 *See* Board of Trade of the City of Chicago v. United States, 246 U.S. 231, 238 (1918): "[T]he legality of an agreement or regulation cannot be determined by so simple a test, as whether it restrains competition. Every agreement concerning trade, every regulation of trade, restrains. To bind, to restrain, is of their very essence. The true test of legality is whether the restraint imposed is such as merely regulates and perhaps thereby promotes competition or whether it is such as may suppress or even destroy competition. To determine that question the court must ordinarily consider the facts peculiar to the business to which the restraint is applied; its condition before and after the restraint was imposed; the nature of the restraint and its effect, actual or probable. The history of the restraint, the evil believed to exist, the reason for adopting the particular remedy, the purpose or end sought to be attained, are all relevant facts."

8 Camden Hutchison, *Law and Economics Scholarship and Supreme Court Antitrust Jurisprudence, 1950–2010*, 21 Lewis & Clark L. Rev. 145, 147 (2017) (stating antitrust jurisprudence was transformed in the 1970s by focusing on economic efficiency, whereas prior antitrust jurisprudence was "ideologically based, doctrinally incoherent, and (worst of all) harmful to the American economy"); *see also* Continental T.V., Inc. v. GTE Sylvania Inc., 433 U.S. 36 (1977) (overruling prior precedent to uphold franchisor's limitations on franchisees because "per se rules of illegality are appropriate only when they relate to conduct that is manifestly anticompetitive"); Northwest Wholesale Stationers, Inc. v. Pacific Stationery & Printing Co., 472 U.S. 284 (1985) (refusing to apply the per se standard to an allegation of a concerted refusal to deal in the absence of market power and exclusive access to essential elements and in light of plausible efficiency justifications); Business Electronics Corp. v. Sharp Electronics Corp., 485 U.S. 717 (1988) (finding vertical price restraints are not per se unlawful unless they include an agreement with the distributor to adhere to a certain price or price level); Leegin Creative Leather Products, Inc. v. PSKS, Inc., 551 U.S. 877 (2007) (overruling prior precedent to establish that vertical price restraints should be analyzed under the rule of reason); David T. Fischer, Donald M. Barnes, *The US Supreme Court sets aside Dr Miles rule on resale price maintenance agreements as per se illegal replacing it with the rule of reason standard (Leegin Creative)*, 28 June 2007, *e-Competitions* June 2007, Art. N° 48820.

litigating and deciding antitrust cases that invoked the rule of reason.[9] In particular, the rule of reason usually requires an analysis that begins with defining the relevant market both in terms of products and geography.[10] Defining the relevant market in turn requires determining whether the defendant has "market power," that is, "the ability to raise prices above those that would be charged in a competitive market."[11] This requirement involves not only analyzing specific geographic prices for the identified product for the relevant period but also comparing those prices with a hypothetical "but-for" world in which the challenged restraint did not exist.[12] This level of analysis is far beyond a lay person's capabilities and even beyond that of experienced antitrust practitioners. Indeed, the analysis essentially requires the use of expert testimony by an economist.[13]

Over the years, rule-of-reason analysis has become more and more sophisticated, with courts even weighing in on interpretations of the antitrust agencies' Merger Guidelines and other economic analyses, such as the SSNIP test.[14] A SSNIP test, for example, determines whether a small increase in the price of an at-issue product could be sustained for a prolonged period or would cause consumers to switch to a substitute product. In other words, the SSNIP test calculates the producing firm's residual elasticity of demand, or how a change in price of the

---

9 *See, e.g.*, Abbott B. Lipsky, Jr., *Antitrust Economics – Making Progress, Avoiding Regression*, 12 Geo. Mason L. Rev. 163, 165 (2003): "[T]he rapid assimilation of microeconomics into antitrust thinking makes almost every antitrust controversy an exercise in microeconomic analysis;" Geoffrey A. Manne & E. Marcellus Williamson, *Hot Docs vs. Cold Economics: The Use and Misuse of Business Documents in Antitrust Enforcement and Adjudication*, 47 Ariz. L. Rev. 609, 614 & n.21 (2005): "Today economics is the primary tool for all aspects of antitrust analysis…;" *see also* The Antitrust Revolution: Economics, Competition, and Policy (John E. Kwoka, Jr. & Lawrence J. White eds., 5th ed. 2009).

10 See, e.g., Times-Picayune Pub. Co. v. United States, 345 U.S. 594, 611–13 (1953); United States v. Columbia Steel Co., 334 U.S. 495, 527 (1948).

11 NCAA v. Board of Regents, 468 U.S. 85, 109 n.38 (1984).

12 In addition to this market analysis, rule of reason cases also require the parties to analyze the competitive effects of the challenged restraint itself. The plaintiff must show the challenged restraint has (or likely will have) a substantial anticompetitive effect. *See, e.g.*, United States v. Arnold, Schwinn & Co., 388 U.S. 365, 374 n.5 (1967), *overruled on other grounds by* Continental T.V., Inc. v. GTE Sylvania Inc., 433 U.S. 36, 58–59 (1977). If the plaintiff can show anticompetitive effect, then the defendant must counter that showing with evidence the challenged restraint was for a legitimate business purpose. *See, e.g.*, Clorox Co. v. Sterling Winthrop, 117 F.3d 50, 59–60 (2d Cir. 1997). Procompetitive justifications include increasing output, introducing a new product to the market, creating operating efficiencies, improving product or service quality, widening consumer choice, and other benefits. As with the market analysis, showing these procompetitive benefits requires comparing the actual state of the market with a "but-for" world in which the challenged restraint does not exist.

13 *See, e.g.*, Am. Key Corp. v. Cole Nat'l Corp., 762 F.2d 1569, 1579 (11th Cir. 1985) (holding that "[c]onstruction of a relevant economic market or a showing of monopoly power in that market cannot… be based upon lay opinion testimony"); Va. Vermiculite, Ltd., 108 f. Supp. 2d at 576 n.16.

14 SSNIP stands for a "small but significant and non-transitory increase in price." *See, e.g.*, FTC v. H. J. Heinz Co., 246 F.3d 708 (D.C. Cir. 2001) (interpreting Horizontal Merger Guidelines); Delco LLC v. Giant of Maryland, LLC, No. CIV. 07-3522, 2007 WL 3307018 (D.N.J. Nov. 8, 2007) (interpreting SSNIP).

at-issue product affects the demand for that product. There can be no serious argument that a lay witness is an appropriate source from whom to elicit evidence about the proper manner in which to conduct a SSNIP test. It is the evolution of the marketplace, which has a far greater geographic (and often international) scope and more complexity in many industries, that requires more sophisticated economic analysis. The same is true, in many circumstances, of legal decision-making under per se analysis.

2. Economic Analysis is Routinely Used in Cases Invoking the Per Se Standard

In cases where price-fixing is alleged, courts typically proceed under the per se rule. The per se rule is invoked in cases for "agreements whose nature and necessary effect are so plainly anticompetitive that no elaborate study of the industry is needed to establish their illegality."[15] There is a question – not taken up rigorously in this paper – whether certain types of conduct alleged as "price-fixing" are more accurately characterized as "information-sharing" that should proceed under the rule of reason. Although there is a strong argument to be made that this should be the case, as a practical matter, most civil price-fixing cases (and all criminal price-fixing cases) are reviewed under the per se rule. Be that as it may, this should not be taken to suggest that economic analysis plays no role, or even a lesser role, in assisting the trier of fact with the determination of liability. (Generally, no party – plaintiff or defendant – would contest the relevance of economic analysis to calculating damages.) It is also the case that price-fixing cases have become broader and more complex in terms of geography and scope (e.g., well beyond narrow bid-rigging). Allegations of price-fixing now span the globe, often across numerous (dozen-plus) defendants and tens, hundreds or even thousands of products. The testimony of economic experts, as well as economic analysis itself, may assist judges and juries in determining whether such expansive allegations of cartel conduct can stand up to longstanding economic theory.

For example, price-fixing cases are ordinarily filed as class actions. If the case survives the inevitable motion to dismiss on the basis of the pleadings, then the parties turn to briefing of class certification. Although this stage of litigation was once skewed more toward the plaintiff class – meaning that plaintiffs could often satisfy their burden at class certification by advancing nearly any defensible economic model to show common impact – both the case law and changes to Rule 23 of the Federal Rules of Civil Procedure have set up a first round of expert reports to be submitted along with briefing of class-related issues.[16] Economic experts have now become central, for the plaintiff class, to

15 Nat'l Soc'y of Prof Engineers v. United States, 435 U.S. 679, 692 (1978).

16 *See* In re Hydrogen Peroxide Antitrust Litig., 552 F.3d 305, 322 (3d Cir. 2008), *as amended* (Jan. 16, 2009); Fed. R. Civ. P. 23(b)(3).

demonstrating how a model can show that the common issues predominate. As a practical matter, plaintiffs' economic experts will advance some variant of an overcharge model that shows that prices were elevated during the alleged price-fixing period.[17] Defendants' economic experts are often charged with critiquing the methodology employed by the plaintiffs' economic expert and, in some cases, advancing an alternative model. The common denominator of this back and forth, however, is that the modeling invariably requires an economist (or econometrician) to explain underlying methodology and its relevance to the case.

If a plaintiff class survives challenges to its motion to certify a class, economic analysis, and testimony by economic experts, continue to be relevant. Increasingly, for example, plaintiffs (and defendants in response) will submit reports that are more qualitative in nature, describing the economic landscape and conditions that are ripe – from the perspective of the plaintiffs – for the alleged collusion to take place. Of course, economic experts for defendants submit responses to the plaintiffs' experts demonstrating critical omissions or errors underlying the plaintiffs' expert reports (or their models). These responses often rely upon theories of industrial organization, auction theory, and other methodologies that are the province of economists – not of lawyers and certainly not of lay persons.[18] Nonetheless, courts have come to expect, and in many cases rely upon, such submissions in civil price-fixing cases.[19]

Without judging the merits of the various methodologies employed by economists (for plaintiffs or defendants), it is very clear – and, frankly, not controversial – that economic analysis is nearly as routine, or as routine, in civil cases invoking the per se rule as it is in rule-of-reason cases such as those described above.[20] The lawyers at the DOJ charged with carrying out the prosecution of criminal charges for violations of the antitrust laws, however, do not usually see it this way.

---

17 This modeling can become quite sophisticated, but plaintiffs' experts often use a model that will compare the alleged price-fixing period against a competitive "benchmark" period. Other methods, such as predictive models, can also be used.

18 *See, e.g.*, Branta, LLC v. Newfield Prod. Co., 310 F. Supp. 3d 1166, 1192–93, 1211 (D. Colo. 2018) (discussing an expert's testimony utilizing economic theory for auctions); Kleen Prod. LLC v. Int'l Paper, No. 10-cv-5711, 2017 WL 2362567, at 16 (N.D. Ill. May 31, 2017) (discussing an expert in industrial organization).

19 As mentioned previously, plaintiffs (and defendants) almost always rely upon economists for claims of damages (and defenses to such claims). This is also true in criminal antitrust actions where the government will often rely upon economic testimony to calculate allegedly affected commerce. We therefore do not take up the issue of damages here, as the use of economists is not particularly controversial in the civil and criminal contexts.

20 Although the facts of an actual conspiratorial meeting are not something economists are routinely called upon to assess, economists nonetheless can add expertise to the viability of an alleged cartel being effectively carried out (or not) by testifying about the characteristics of the relevant market and whether those characteristics are consistent with and conducive to collusive behavior. *See, e.g.*, Holiday Wholesale Grocery Co. v. Philip Morris Co., 231 F. Supp. 2d 1253 (N.D. Ga. 2002), *aff'd sub nom.* Williamson Oil Co. v. Philip Morris USA, 346 F.3d 1287 (11th Cir. 2003).

III. The Use of Economics in Criminal Antitrust Trials

1. DOJ's Opposition to Economic Testimony on Liability

Notwithstanding the obvious import of economic analysis to civil antitrust cases – including advocacy by the federal antitrust agencies – the DOJ routinely seeks to exclude economic testimony from the liability stage of criminal trials.[21] The argument advanced by the Antitrust Division is that, in a per se case, the government need only prove the existence of an agreement to fix prices or to restrict output.[22] As we discuss below, this desire to exclude economic testimony is readily confirmed in numerous cases around the country, as well as by members of the Division's leadership over the years. It is not a controversial position within the Division that, from the perspective of the government, economic evidence refuting the viability of a price-fixing agreement is "irrelevant."[23]

One problem with the government's argument is that its cases have grown increasingly complex as it has expanded its jurisdictional reach. The cases the government routinely prosecutes are not, for example, limited to surreptitious agreements between government contractors to rig bids – one of the classic forms of price-fixing.[24] In such cases, the covert nature of the agreement, the small number of participants and the precautions the participants take to keep the agreement secret are similar to conspiracies to rob a bank or to steal a car.[25] It is therefore unsurprising that the DOJ succeed in excluding economic testimony from those conspiracies.

One of the most recent attempts by the DOJ to exclude the testimony of economists came in the government's case against AU Optronics (AUO). AUO is a manufacturer of panel displays, most notably thin-film-transistor LCD panels that were alleged to have been the subject of a conspiracy that included no fewer than eight other manufacturers. Needless to say, the alleged conspiracy, which included allegations of information-sharing, extended far beyond garden-variety bid-rigging.

---

21 It is the DOJ's stated policy that it will not prosecute rule-of-reason cases (or even certain other per se cases) criminally so as not to chill procompetitive conduct. *See* Dep't of Justice, U.S. Attorneys' Manual, Title 7, § 1.100.

22 The DOJ alone has the ability to prosecute criminal offenses under the federal antitrust laws. *See* Dep't of Justice, Antitrust Enforcement and the Consumer (2015). The FTC has no such authority. *See id.*

23 *United States v. AU Optronics Corp.*, No. 3:09-cr-110 (N.D. Cal. Dec. 6, 2011) ECF No. 484 (Mot. in Lim. at 2): "arguments that justify restraints on trade – such as that they were necessary to avoid ruinous competition, that the defendants lacked market power, *that the agreement could not have succeeded*, or that the coconspirators acted with good intentions – are irrelevant in a per se case" (emphasis supplied).

24 William Kovacic, *The Modern Evolution of US Competition Policy Enforcement Norms*, 71 Antitrust L.J. 377, 421 (2003): "many criminal antitrust cases of the 1980s and early 1990s focused on abuses in public procurement."

25 Although beyond the scope of this paper, it is worth asking whether antitrust laws are even necessary to prosecute a bid-rigging conspiracy; rather, such conduct likely could be prosecuted under state criminal fraud statutes.

Yet, throughout the criminal case, the government sought to exclude AUO's experts from testifying. The DOJ's rationale? The well-worn claim that the evidence would be "irrelevant" insofar as it extended beyond evidence of (or lack thereof) and instead went to the viability of the agreement.[26] Here, it is worth noting that both plaintiffs and defendants submitted expert reports from economic experts in the civil case on the same issue of the existence of an agreement (for the plaintiffs) and the lack of such an agreement (for the defendants).

2. The Changing Landscape in Antitrust Criminal Prosecutions

Even accepting that the DOJ's arguments to exclude economic testimony have merit in some cases (such as the covert bid-rigging discussed above), these arguments are attenuated with the drastic expansion of the prosecutorial reach into other jurisdictions around the globe. Indeed, in the 1990s, the Antitrust Division made significant changes to its Corporate Leniency program specifically designed to expand its reach internationally. In particular, the Division placed a greater emphasis on "concentrating its enforcement resources on international cartels that victimize American businesses and consumers."[27] The Division characterized the changes to its Corporate Leniency program as a "Case Generator," resulting in "scores of convictions and over $1.5 billion in criminal fines."[28]

In the United States, a company that obtains corporate leniency may avoid criminal prosecution both of the company and of its employees. There is a catch, however, as only the first cooperating party qualifies for leniency. Along with the changes to expand the Division's reach internationally, it also encouraged participation in its "Amnesty Plus" program, which promises lower criminal fines for cooperating parties. Under Amnesty Plus, a company bringing a second cartel to the Division's attention "will receive amnesty, pay zero dollars in fines for its participation in the second offense," and none of its officers, directors and employees will be prosecuted in connection with the second cartel. To top it off, "the company will receive a substantial additional discount by the Division" for its participation in the first cartel. Although the Division's explanation sounds similar to a sales-circular in the weekend newspaper, it has had the intended effect: more corporate prosecutions and greater fines collected. The numbers bear this out, as well. Fines collected have sky-rocketed, increasing from

26 *See AU* Optronics, No. 3:09-cr-110 ECF No. 484 at 2–4. *See also* Symposium, *Delivering Remedies: The Role of the States in Antitrust Enforcement*, 69 Geo. Wash. L. Rev. 1004, at 1007 (Oct./Dec. 2001) (growth in treble-damage litigation in the 1960s triggered by bid-rigging in heavy duty electric equipment industry).

27 Antitrust Div., US Dep't of Justice, The Modern Leniency Program After Ten Years: A Summary Overview Of The Antitrust Division's Criminal Enforcement Program, Address at the ABA Antitrust Section Annual Meeting (Aug. 12, 2003).

28 *See id.*

$48 million for the period 1970 to 1979 to $9.7 billion for the period 2009 to 2018.[29] Moreover, out of 144 fines levied since 1995 that exceed $10 million, 135 have been for cases that are international in scope.[30] And indictments of individuals, both US and foreign, as well as the length of sentences, have risen dramatically.[31]

IV. An Argument for the Admissibility of Economic Testimony

The point of the discussion in this paper is not to criticize the government's expansion of its prosecutorial reach – if that expansion does not itself result in false-positive prosecutions that chill economic activity – but rather to call into question the government's opposition to the use of economic testimony in criminal antitrust trials.[32] As cases become more complex, and the economic underpinnings of the government's theories less certain, economic testimony can be very helpful to the trier of fact. This benefit is precisely what we have seen in the civil context throughout the years. Lawyers are ill-equipped to handle some of the heavy lifting that goes along with defining markets and proving concentration and harm to competition. Courts have certainly realized this in the civil context. Furthermore, even a cursory review of many of the largest cartel cases over the past decade demonstrate that they look nothing like the simpler (factually speaking) bid-rigging cases where the use of economic

---

29 *Compare* Antitrust Div., US Dep't of Justice, The Evolution of Criminal Antitrust Enforcement Over the Last Two Decades, Speech at the 24th Annual National Institute on White Collar Crime (Feb. 25, 2010) at 5, https://www.justice.gov/atr/file/518241/download *with* Dep't of Justice, Total Criminal Fines & Penalties, https://www.justice.gov/atr/total-criminal-fines (last visited March 22, 2019).

30 Dep't of Justice, Sherman Act Violations Yielding a Corporate Fine of $10 Million or More, https://www.justice.gov/atr/sherman-act-violations-yielding-corporate-fine-10-million-or-more (last visited July 8, 2020).

31 Dep't of Justice, Average Prison Sentence In Months, https://www.justice.gov/atr/criminal-enforcement-fine-and-jail-charts (last visited July 8, 2020); Evolution Speech, supra note 29, at 9; *also id.* at 1: "Since the mid-1990 [*sic*], the Antitrust Division has uncovered and prosecuted dozens of international cartels, secured convictions and jail sentences against culpable U.S. and foreign executives, and obtained hefty corporate fines."

32 This article does not consider the efficacy of the Corporate Leniency program in eliciting truthful testimony. However, it is worthwhile to consider how the incentives – and disincentives – of the program influence its results. Indeed, some practitioners believe that an individual in a managerial role targeted for a white-collar crime – complete with threats of occupational termination, crushing monetary fines, and extended prison sentences – is more likely to implicate an innocent co-worker or competitor than a hardened criminal is to implicate an innocent associate. *See* Leslie W. Jacobs & Geoffrey S. Mearns, *Lessons from United States v. True: Effective Use of Expert Testimony in Defending Criminal Antitrust Cases*, 13 SPG Antitrust 48, 50–51 (Spring 1999); *see also* Ronald A. Cass, *Overcriminalization: Administrative Regulation, Prosecutorial Discretion, and the Rule of Law*, 15(2) Engage, (July 2014) at 20, (large potential penalties and high litigation costs may induce defendants to "accept quite harsh punishment, even when they believe they've done nothing wrong"); Ellen Yaroshefsky, *Ethics and Plea Bargaining: What's Discovery Got to Do with It?*, 23(3) Criminal Justice (Fall 2008) (general discussion of innocent persons pleading guilty).

testimony is far less clear. Instead, many cases now rely on innuendo, information-sharing, industry trade-association meetings and other evidence that is at best uncertain and in some instances demonstrably procompetitive.

Economists are ideally placed to shed light on industry structure, including how industry participants may interact with one another and how such conduct may impact prices. Economists have written books on this topic. It is the subject of seminal articles in the leading economic journals. Moreover, this topic is highly relevant to claims of cartel conduct. To confirm this latter point, one need look no further than the fact that economists routinely testify about the feasibility (or lack thereof) of cartel cases in civil antitrust actions. By depriving the finder of fact of economic testimony in criminal antitrust cases, defendants are left to defend themselves with a hand (or hands) tied behind their backs. This deficiency is exacerbated by other prosecutorial methods that government lawyers routinely rely upon in criminal antitrust cases. For example, indictments are nearly always "bare bones," and almost certainly would not stand up to pleading standards in civil antitrust actions.[33] Also, the government routinely opposes issuing a bill of particulars, which requires the government to set forth significantly more information about its legal theory. Indeed, the government's handbook for prosecuting antitrust cases specifically states "the Division typically opposes requests for bills of particulars on the ground the indictment provides the defendants with a basic statement of the charges against them."[34] Permitting defendants to introduce economic testimony to defend against the government's case helps level the playing field and provides the trier of fact a critical source of evidence in a criminal antitrust case.

To deny the trier of fact this evidence is to risk the false positives that I have mentioned previously.[35] These false positives can be either the prosecution of procompetitive conduct or even the over-prosecution of limited anticompetitive conduct. Unnecessary prosecutions will result in over-deterrence, which not only can have a significant impact on the targeted companies and individuals but also the industry at large. For example, unwarranted or excessive penalties can lead to higher consumer prices or stifled product innovation, ironically the very thing the Division sought to prevent by prosecuting a cartel case in the first place.[36] These anticompetitive effects can result from companies overinvesting in

---

33 *See* Bell Atlantic Corp. v. Twombly, 550 U.S. 544, 556–57 (2007) (holding that a well-pled complaint, in satisfaction of Rule 8(a)(2) of the Federal Rules of Civil Procedure, and in the context of a Section 1 claim, must have "enough factual matter (taken as true) to suggest that an agreement was made" and that such allegations must cross the line from possible to plausible).

34 Dep't of Justice, Antitrust Division Manual, ch. IV, 68 (5th ed. 2012).

35 Cato Institute, Cato Handbook for Policy Makers (8th ed. 2017): "another inevitable consequence of overcriminalization has been more governmental errors."

36 One economist defined the optimal fine to be "equal to the social cost of the crime adjusted for the probability of non-detection." *See* Bruce H. Kobayashi, *Antitrust, Agency and Amnesty: An Economic Analysis of the Criminal Enforcement of the Antitrust Laws Against Corporations*, 69 Geo. Wash. L. Rev. 715, 726 (2001).

compliance programs or over-monitoring their employees for fear the company may violate the antitrust laws.[37] This inefficient use of corporate resources can result in increased production costs, which in turn can lead to increased prices to consumers.[38] Additionally, investigation targets who find themselves subject to massive criminal fines will have to make hard choices internally with respect to future capital allocations, including foregoing expansion, cutting payroll, freezing employee salaries, and increased prices to the consumer.[39] All of these negative consequences stand together with the fact that a false positive also can result in unjustly imprisoning a human being in the federal corrections system for months or even years.

These false positives can reverberate through civil litigation as well. Corporations that face criminal prosecution by the Division but are unable to defend themselves through expert testimony from an economic expert may decide it is better to plead guilty than take their chances at trial. That guilty plea now is prima facie evidence of the facts set forth in the plea, subjecting those corporations to civil suits in which the penalties could approximate or even exceed those levied in the criminal cases. Thus, companies in fact face a type of double jeopardy when it comes to a criminal conviction, and it is this sort of over-deterrence that has long been documented in the United States (and not just with respect to antitrust).[40]

V. Conclusion

There can be no doubt that criminal prosecutions of antitrust violations have become much broader in scope, both geographically and for the alleged conduct at issue. At the same time, there is a continued opposition by prosecutors to the introduction of economic testimony in criminal antitrust trials – the same type of testimony that is commonplace for the very same cases in civil antitrust trials. Economic testimony in these increasingly complex antitrust prosecutions can help the trier of fact understand the economic landscape and the likelihood (or lack) of a successful price-fixing cartel as alleged by the government. As discussed above, there are significant costs to false-positive prosecutions – in antitrust, just as in other areas of the law. By allowing economic testimony to be presented, courts can help ensure a balanced trial on the relevant facts at issue.

---

37 *See id.* at 736: "A fine that exceeds this level will cause the private return to monitoring and compliance to exceed the social return, and will result in overcompliance."

38 *See id.*

39 *See id.*; *see also* W. Robert Thomas, *The Ability and Responsibility of Corporate Law to Improve Criminal Fines*, 78 Ohio St. L.J. 601, 610–11 (2017) (discussing how excessive fines can also lead to bankruptcy).

40 *See, generally*, Paul J. Larkin, Jr. & Michael B. Mukasey, *The Perils of Overcriminalization*, The Heritage Foundation (Feb. 12 2015) (discussing overcriminalization generally).

Tuna Tales: The Antitrust Tsunami

TIMOTHY CORNELL AND JOHN FRIEL*
Clifford Chance

Abstract

Most everyone ensures their house is clean before inviting others in. That concept applies equally to a party contemplating a strategic transaction, the prospect of which will invite the government of one or more jurisdictions to visit each party's corporate "house." As the below-described events portray, an unclean house – one beset with compliance failures such as cartel conduct that violate the antitrust laws – can quickly turn the tide on a pending transaction and instead leave parties to the prospective deal faced with exposure to criminal penalties, prison time for executives, the inability to sell unwanted assets, diminution of corporate value (indeed, including bankruptcy), and significant business disruption.

What follows is the story of a merger gone awry – so far awry that even industry participants who were not parties to the planned deal faced criminal antitrust prosecution and the end of their careers. One was convicted of criminal price-fixing in December 2019, and now faces a prison sentence and a significant monetary penalty. Meanwhile, the companies were left with massive criminal penalties, tarnished reputations, and oppressive legal bills. And, of course, the potential merger never came to fruition; instead one of the companies has filed for bankruptcy, and will soon be forced to liquidate its assets.

We end our tuna tale with some key takeaways for parties contemplating strategic transactions.

---

* Tim Cornell is a partner and head of Clifford Chance's US antitrust practice. John Friel is a partner at Clifford Chance.

I. The Cascading Implications of Collusion

1. Prologue: Conglomerates Take Hold of Tuna

Canned tuna is an undifferentiated, commodity product. Three producers of canned tuna and other packaged seafood products – Bumble Bee, StarKist, and Chicken of the Sea – dominate their marketplace, together holding 73% of the market, with the remainder fragmented between smaller companies and private-label products.[1]

During their rise to a triopoly, each of the three market leaders was acquired by large conglomerates and/or private equity firms.

- **Bumble Bee** was founded in 1910, when a group of seafood canners came together to create the Columbia River Packer Association. Over the next century, Bumble Bee went through a series of transactions and ownership changes before landing as a portfolio company of United Kingdom-based private equity firm Lion Capital.[2] In late 2010, Lion Capital acquired a majority stake in Bumble Bee from Centre Partners Management for US$980 million. When that deal was announced, Lion Capital was "excited about the opportunity to acquire one of North America's best-known consumer packaged goods companies and a portfolio of brands that enjoy unrivaled positions with US and Canadian consumers."[3] Over the next several years, Lion Capital sought new opportunities for Bumble Bee, including the acquisition of Anova Food LLC, and a partnership with Sapmer SA to deliver sashimi-quality frozen tuna to North American restaurants and food retailers.[4] Lion Capital also explored the possibility of merging Bumble Bee with one of its competitors in order to take advantage of economies of scale and improve its competitiveness in the market.
- **StarKist** began as the French Sardine Company, established in 1918. StarKist's later owners included the H.J. Heinz Company and Del Monte. Dongwon Industries of Korea acquired StarKist in 2008 for US$363 million. At least for some part of the time period at issue here, StarKist was the largest seller of canned tuna in the United States.[5]

---

1 Amended Complaint & Demand for Jury Trial, *In re* Packaged Seafood Products Antitrust Litigation, No. 3:15-md-02670-JLS-MDD (S.D. Cal. May 23, 2016), ECF No. 147.

2 *Id.*

3 *US: Lion Capital funds buy Bumble Bee Foods*, Just-Food (Nov. 5, 2010), https://www.just-food.com/news/lion-capital-funds-buy-bumble-bee-foods_id113103.aspx.

4 Mike Allen, *New Partnership Puts Bumble Bee Foods in Premium Food Arena*, San Diego Business Journal (Mar. 5, 2014), https://www.sdbj.com/news/2014/mar/05/new-partnership-puts-bumble-bee-foods-premium-food.

5 Amended Complaint & Demand for Jury Trial, *supra* note 1.

- **Tri-Union Seafoods LLC**, operating under the brand name "Chicken of the Sea," started in 1914, when the company was created as the Van Camp Seafood Company. In 2000, Thai Union Group, a conglomerate based in Thailand, acquired Tri-Union. Thai Union Group became the world's largest canned tuna producer, capturing approximately 18% of global canned tuna production.[6]

Ownership by conglomerate parents and private equity funds can put significant pressure on a business to perform. Such pressures can be exacerbated when the parent is seeking to sell the business in the short term. Indeed, under such pressures, management can become focused solely on short-term numbers.

2. Act I: A Conspiracy Develops

Despite few competitors, the prepackaged tuna industry was not particularly booming around 2010. Prices of canned tuna were steadily decreasing. The industry faced a supply glut as the supply of skipjack tuna – the primary tuna used for canned tuna – increased. The oversupply problems were compounded by a simultaneous decline in canned tuna demand.[7] Indeed, packaged tuna consumption had been on the decline since 2004.[8] Contamination fears contributed to the decline.

Faced with decreasing prices and continued pressure to remain profitable, the three major tuna manufacturers decided to work together. The three competitors agreed with one another to (1) decrease the size of the cans in which they sold tuna, (2) list price increases for canned tuna, (3) limit promotional activity so as not to upset agreed-upon market prices, and (4) not offer tuna products labeled as "FAD free," which the competitors believed would decrease profits by cannibalizing sales of the products they sold that were subject to the price-fixing conspiracy.[9] According to court filings, the agreements between Bumble Bee, StarKist and Chicken of the Sea occurred through a mix of bilateral conversations, emails, phone calls, and in-person meetings between senior executives and sales personnel at each company.[10]

Like most cartels, the canned tuna conspiracy included a means to monitor and punish those that did not abide by the illegal agreement. The conspiracy was

---

6 *Id.*

7 *Id.*

8 Plaintiffs' Third Consolidated Amended Complaint for Violation of the Sherman Act, 15 U.S.C. sec. 1, *In re* Packaged Seafood Products Antitrust Litigation, No. 3:15-md-02670-JLS-MDD (S.D. Cal. Apr. 17, 2018), ECF No. 923.

9 Amended Complaint & Demand for Jury Trial, *supra* note 1.

10 *Id.*; Brief for Plaintiff, United States v. Lischewski, No. 3:18-cr-00203-EMC (N.D. Cal. Aug. 6, 2019), ECF No. 246; Plea Agreement, United States v. Starkist Co., No. 3:18-cr-00513-EMC (N.D. Cal. Nov. 14, 2018), ECF No. 24.

enforced through so-called "jabs" – calls between company executives to address circumstances where one of the competitors failed to abide by the terms of the parties' agreement.[11]

Multiple factors may have led to the ill-fated decision by the parties to conspire. Profit pressure, as described above, may have been one. Another may have the incestuous nature of employment in the industry. According to private plaintiffs, of the 58 executives eventually implicated in the conspiracy, approximately one-third had held executive positions at a competitor at some point in their careers.[12] Also facilitating collusive behavior were the companies' joint operations and packing agreements, which plaintiffs claimed afforded opportunities for information-sharing and avenues through which parties could communicate to monitor adherence to the conspiracy.[13] Such frequent interaction between competitors can often lead to coordination and information-sharing, and form the basis of cartel conduct.

In addition to their joint agreements, the competitors also met frequently at trade association meetings. In 2008, members of Bumble Bee, StarKist and Chicken of the Sea gathered at the Infofish Conference in Thailand. Shortly thereafter, each reduced the size of their tuna product from six ounces to five ounces.[14] In 2009, Bumble Bee, StarKist and Chicken of the Sea formed the National Fisheries Institute and the International Seafood Sustainability Foundation, an organization chaired by Bumble Bee's CEO Christopher Lischewski.[15] Prosecutors later argued that the companies used such trade associations to further their conspiracy.

The collusive conduct described here, surprisingly, was not well hidden from public view. Beginning in 2008 (the year the alleged conspiracy began), Bumble Bee's CEO Lischewski made several public statements regarding pricing that private plaintiffs later argued could be considered "signaling" to competitors.[16] Then, the companies in 2011 began a practice of using announced list prices, and followed each other in increasing the price of canned tuna on those list prices.[17] For each list price, the competitors "agreed on whether to take a list price increase, the amount of the list price increase, the announcement date of

---

11 Amended Complaint & Demand for Jury Trial, *supra* note 1.

12 Second Consolidated Direct Purchaser Class Complaint, *In re* Packaged Seafood Products Antitrust Litigation, No. 3:15-md-02670-JLS-MDD (S.D. Cal. May 29, 2017), ECF No. 334-1 Appendix A; Plaintiffs' Third Consolidated Amended Complaint for Violation of the Sherman Act, *supra* note 9 (listing the employees that were employed by at least two of the three major canned tuna producers).

13 Amended Complaint & Demand for Jury Trial, *supra* note 1.

14 *Id.*

15 *Id.*

16 *Id.*

17 Amended Complaint & Demand for Jury Trial, *supra* note 1; Brief for Plaintiff, *Lischewski*, *supra* note 11.

the list price increase, and the rationale the conspirators would give their customers for the list price increase."[18] Rarely can there be clearer evidence of price-fixing than list prices agreed by competitors in the same marketplace.

The conspiracy appears to have been vast and far-reaching within each of the three participating companies. To date, the individuals implicated in the legal proceedings surrounding the conspiracy have included senior-level managers with titles like CEO, CFO, COO, Chairman, Controller, Regional Sales Manager, Vice President of Operations, Senior Vice President of Sales, CEO of US Operations, Head of Human Resources, Vice President of Retail Sales, and more. The implicated individuals included employees of the three companies as well as of their respective parent companies.[19]

3. Act II: The Merger

While Lion Capital was building Bumble Bee's profits, it was also looking to sell the business.

Lion Capital found a buyer. On December 19, 2014, Thai Union, the parent company of competitor Chicken of the Sea, announced it had reached an agreement to acquire Bumble Bee from Lion Capital for US$1.5 billion.[20] In press releases, Thai Union announced that it planned to raise US$400 million through the issuance of new shares in order to finance the transaction. Together, the combination of Chicken of the Sea and Bumble Bee would have captured approximately 40% of the market and have only one remaining significant competitor: StarKist.[21] But, before the deal could be consummated, the two companies needed to convince competition authorities around the world to approve the transaction, which would be especially difficult given the size of the transaction and the two brands' respective shares of the market.[22] Indeed, it was not long before the deal raised antitrust eyebrows.

As part of its investigation of the proposed transaction, the Antitrust Division (the Division) of the US Department of Justice (DOJ) issued a Second Request (see below definition), seeking various documents relating to, among other topics, competition in the marketplace. Those documents became the eventual downfall of the deal and led to much more.

---

18 Brief for Plaintiff, *Lischewski*, *supra* note 11.

19 Second Consolidated Direct Purchaser Class Complaint, *supra* note 13.

20 Amended Complaint & Demand for Jury Trial, *supra* note 1.

21 *Id.*

22 At the time, estimates showed that Bumble Bee had 28% of the US packaged seafood industry, while Chicken of the Sea had 20%, and StarKist had 30%. In 2013, StarKist had 36%, followed by Bumble Bee with 25% and Chicken of the Sea with 13%. This disparity in market share may have helped precipitate Chicken of the Sea's parent to look for an acquisition opportunity.

4. Act III: The Conspiracy Is Uncovered

It was not long before the authorities' review of the proposed transaction took a back seat to more pressing antitrust issues. As the Division reviewed the documents supplied by the merging parties, it uncovered evidence of anticompetitive practices between Chicken of the Sea and its competitors. On July 23, 2015, while the merger was still pending – and just before Thai Union was expected to publish a stock offering to fund the transaction – news broke that the Division had issued subpoenas focused on more than the competitive implications of the transaction: an investigation of potential criminal collusion in the packaged seafood industry, including by the parties to the proposed deal.[23] In response to the news, Thai Union announced that it was postponing the planned share offering intended to raise money to finance the deal, pending further details on the Division's investigation. The writing was on the wall, and in December Thai Union announced that it had formally abandoned its acquisition of Bumble Bee.[24]

Unfortunately, the break-up of the deal was just the beginning of the tuna saga. Soon after the Division's investigation into Chicken of the Sea came to light, media reports revealed that Bumble Bee and StarKist had also received subpoenas relating to the Division's antitrust investigation.[25]

The news of the Division's investigation led almost immediately to a panoply of civil class action lawsuits against the three companies by consumers seeking damages under state and federal antitrust and consumer protection laws. Olean Wholesale Grocery was the first to file its class action against the tuna companies, submitting a complaint on August 3, 2015 on behalf of a purported class of consumers who had purchased packaged seafood directly from at least one of the defendants.[26] Other wholesalers of tuna soon followed with class suits of their own, including PITCO Foods[27] and Affiliated Foods[28] (both of which sought to represent the same purported class as Olean). Certain major wholesalers "opted out" of these class actions and filed their own individual lawsuits, the most notable of which was Wal-Mart, which according to its complaint bought and resold at least a quarter of all prepackaged tuna purchased in the United States

---

23 Amended Complaint & Demand for Jury Trial, *supra* note 1.

24 Press Release, Dep't of Justice, Chicken of the Sea and Bumble Bee Abandon Tuna Merger After Justice Department Expresses Serious Concerns (Dec. 3, 2015), https://www.justice.gov/opa/pr/chicken-sea-and-bumble-bee-abandon-tuna-merger-after-justice-department-expresses-serious.

25 Amended Complaint & Demand for Jury Trial, *supra* note 1.

26 Olean Wholesale Grocery Cooperative, Inc. v. Bumble Bee Foods LLC, Tri-Union Seafoods LLC, and Starkist Company, No. 3:15-cv-01714-JLS-MDD (S.D. Cal. filed Aug. 3, 2015).

27 Pacific Groservice Inc. v. Bumble Bee Foods, LLC, No. 3:15-cv-01791-WQH-JMA (S.D. Cal. filed Aug. 13, 2015).

28 Affiliated Foods, Inc. v. Tri-Union Seafoods, LLC, No. 3:15-cv-03815-DMR (N.D. Cal. filed Aug. 20, 2015).

during the period of the conspiracy.[29] The wholesaler actions were followed by class actions asserted on behalf of individual plaintiffs who claimed to have indirectly purchased packaged seafood products (e.g. from a grocery store).[30] All told, over 70 class and individual actions have been filed against the tuna producers, seeking hundreds of millions of dollars in damages.

In the meantime, the Division's criminal cartel investigation continued. In order to protect the confidentiality of its investigation, the Division sought and obtained judicial stays of discovery in the civil litigation (a measure intended to shield potential grand jury witnesses from a company under investigation from evidence relevant to a potential indictment against them). The agency continued to gather facts, eventually pursuing criminal cases not only against the companies, but also against certain executives allegedly responsible for the companies' participation in the conspiracy.

5. Act IV: The Aftermath

The US District Court for the Northern District of California ultimately found executives from Bumble Bee, StarKist and Chicken of the Sea engaged in a conspiracy to fix shelf-stable canned tuna prices, in violation of the Sherman Act.[31] Bumble Bee agreed to plead guilty to the conspiracy in May 2017, agreeing to pay a fine of US$25 million.[32] Starkist agreed to plead guilty a year and a half later, in October 2018.[33] It initially sought to challenge the size of the penalty, but the judge presiding over the case was unconvinced, and ultimately ordered the tuna company to pay a criminal fine of US$100 million.[34]

Meanwhile, executives alleged to have been involved in the conspiracy have also faced consequences. In December 2016, the DOJ filed several criminal information statements against Bumble Bee executives.[35] The first domino fell in January 2017, when the Senior Vice President of Sales for Bumble Bee pleaded guilty to

29 Wal-Mart Stores, Inc. et al v. Bumble Bee Foods, LLC et al, No. 5:16-cv-05312-TLB (W.D. Ark. filed Oct. 31, 2016).

30 *See* Amended Complaint with Jury Demand, *In re* Packaged Seafood Products Antitrust Litigation, No. 3:15-md-02670-JLS-MDD (S.D. Cal. filed May 8, 2017), ECF No. 337.

31 Brief for Plaintiff, *Lischewski*, *supra* note 11.

32 Press Release, Dep't of Justice, Bumble Bee Agrees to Plead Guilty to Price Fixing (May 8, 2017), https://www.justice.gov/opa/pr/bumble-bee-agrees-plead-guilty-price-fixing; *see also* Plea Agreement, United States v. Bumble Bee Foods, LLC, No. 3:17-cr-00249-EMC (N.D. Cal. Aug. 2, 2017), ECF No. 32.

33 Press Release, Dep't of Justice, Starkist Co. Agrees to Plead Guilty for Price Fixing (Oct. 18, 2019), https://www.justice.gov/opa/pr/starkist-co-agrees-plead-guilty-price-fixing; *see also* Plea Agreement, *Starkist*, *supra* note 11.

34 Press Release, Dep't of Justice, First Charges Brought in Investigation of Collusion in the Packaged Seafood Industry (Dec. 7, 2016), https://www.justice.gov/opa/pr/first-charges-brought-investigation-collusion-packaged-seafood-industry.

35 DOJ, *supra* note 25.

conspiring to fix prices for packaged seafood in the United States.[36] Soon after, additional executives at both Bumble Bee and StarKist pleaded guilty to their roles in their conspiracy.

As for Chicken of the Sea, in October 2015 press reports suggested that Chicken of the Sea had sought leniency from criminal prosecution by the Division for the tuna company's role in cartel conduct.[37] Pursuant to the Division's Corporate Leniency Policy, immunity from prosecution is available to the first-reporting company to confess its role in the conspiracy and cooperate in the Division's investigation into the cartel participants (here, Chicken of the Sea, Bumble Bee, and StarKist). As a result, Chicken of the Sea and its executives have thus far avoided prosecution as a result of that company's leniency application, but that shield has been conditioned upon the continued and indefinite – and costly – cooperation of the company (and its employees) in the Division's investigation and prosecution of other participants.

All three companies continue to be embroiled in civil litigation in the Spring of 2020.

The foregoing saga aptly illustrates all of the challenges that a company can face as it navigates the labyrinth of US laws regulating competition, as the companies – and in some cases their corporate parents – have found themselves mired in criminal and civil enforcement actions as well as class action lawsuits.

II. Perspectives For Transacting Parties

1. Competition Regulation in the US: An Overview[38]

In the United States, competition is primarily overseen by the Division and the Federal Trade Commission (FTC), two agencies that have significantly overlapping authority to preserve competition, including through the review of planned mergers. By interagency agreement, planned business combinations in certain industries are subject to review by a single agency: for example, the Division reviews deals in industries such as telecommunications, banks, railroads, and airlines, while the FTC typically reviews others industries, such as pharmaceuticals. For industries not covered by this interagency agreement, whether the Division or the FTC has oversight depends on the clearance process. On paper, the two agencies aim to complement each other and work together to analyze the deals. But in practice, the negotiated division of oversight responsibilities between the agencies has led to some high-profile turf wars, especially for industries that are perceived as being "hot" in the market or that are priorities

---

36 United States v. Cameron, No. 3:16-cr-00501-EMC (N.D. Cal. Jan. 25, 2017).

37 *See* Part II, section 3 C, Leniency.

38 Fed. Trade Comm'n, Guide to Antitrust Laws, https://www.ftc.gov/tips-advice/competition-guidance/guide-antitrust-laws/antitrust-laws.

for the US government.[39] One important difference between the two agencies, however, is that while both agencies can challenge a planned merger, only the Division can pursue criminal penalties for anticompetitive conduct. If the FTC uncovers evidence of anticompetitive practices that are potentially criminal in nature, they refer the matter to the Division for prosecution.

The Division and the FTC oversee competition primarily under the authority of three federal statutes: the Sherman Antitrust Act, the Clayton Act, and the Federal Trade Commission Act (the FTC Act). Both agencies enforce the Sherman Act, which forbids "every contract, combination, or conspiracy in restraint of trade," as well as any actual or attempted monopolization. The FTC enforces the FTC Act, which prohibits "unfair methods of competition" and "unfair or deceptive acts or practices." US courts have interpreted the FTC Act to include all violations of the Sherman Act, so although the two agencies derive their authority from different laws, in practice they oversee similar types of conduct. Both agencies also have authority under the Clayton Act, which prohibits more nuanced forms of anticompetitive conduct such as price discrimination, as well as mergers or acquisitions that substantially lessen competition or that could create a monopoly.

2. US Merger Control

Under the Clayton Act, companies planning a merger or acquisition may find themselves under an obligation to file a notification with the federal antitrust agencies pursuant to the Hart-Scott-Rodino Act (HSR Act), depending on the size of the transaction as well as the parties participating in the deal.[40] The formation of a joint venture or a licensing agreement might also trigger an HSR filing obligation. Most transactions involving domestic companies and meeting the filing threshold are caught by the HSR Act's requirements. Generally, a filing is required if the target in an acquisition is a non-US company, assets or sales in or into the United States meet the HSR filing threshold,[41] or other filing thresholds are met. Although an HSR notification filing obligation is triggered by the value of the transaction, there are numerous legislative exemptions, including for foreign companies. While acquisitions of US companies are obviously under the jurisdiction of US antitrust regulators, foreign companies looking to acquire a non-US company might be surprised to find that the acquisition does not qualify for a foreign company exemption and could be subject to an HSR notification obligation.

---

39 The turf wars regarding enforcement actions against technology platforms such as Google, Amazon and Facebook have reached headline status.

40 The overall filing threshold is indexed to US GDP and adjusted yearly. Originally set at US$50 million, the threshold for 2019 adjusted for GDP was US$90 million. FTC, *HSR threshold adjustments and reportability for 2019*, Competition Matters Blog (Mar. 7, 2019), https://www.ftc.gov/news-events/blogs/competition-matters/2019/03/hsr-threshold-adjustments-reportability-2019.

41 Adjusted on an annual basis, indexed to US GDP.

HSR notifications are submitted to both the FTC and the Division, and are reviewed by one of the agencies depending on the industry of the acquired company (as set out above). Along with the HSR notification form, companies need to submit documents prepared in connection with the transaction that discuss the market, competition, or similar topics. If there are no substantive issues with a transaction, then it is cleared by one of the agencies within a statutory 30-day waiting period or once the waiting period expires.

If, however, a transaction raises the appearance of substantive antitrust issues, the agency reviewing the filing may issue a voluntary request letter and/or a Request for Additional Information (Second Request). Both the FTC and the Division will consider a deal to be problematic if they believe it creates, enhances, or facilitates the exercise of market power in a defined market (i.e., a company's ability to raise and maintain prices above competitive levels).[42]

Typically, the agencies' voluntary request letters will seek information about topics such as strategic or marketing plans over a recent period (e.g. for the past three years); lists of products manufactured, sold, or in development; lists of competitors and top ten customers for overlap products; and market share information for overlap products. As the name implies, a voluntary request letter is voluntary and there are no statutory penalties for not responding to a request. In practice, however, a voluntary request letter is a signal to the company that receives it that the reviewing agency has concerns about the deal, and responding will be in the company's best interest in order to try to address the agency's concerns before the deal is blocked. Responding may also help the company avoid a Second Request.

A Second Request, on the other hand, is a compulsory demand for information. It requires companies to engage in collecting, reviewing, and producing significant amounts of internal documents and relevant market data, including market shares, competitor and customer information, strategic plans, and similar documents – a process that often takes months. In the course of a Second Request investigation, the reviewing agency may take depositions of key management as well as third parties, such as customers, suppliers, and even competitors. A Second Request is a formal process that pauses the HSR waiting period until both parties have certified "substantial compliance" with the request, at which point a new 30-day waiting period begins (in practice the waiting period is often further extended through negotiation with the US agencies).

The Bumble Bee transaction met the HSR thresholds, and thus required a filing. The deal was valued at approximately US$1.5 billion, and even though Chicken of the Sea's parent, Thai Union, was a foreign company, its acquisition target, Bumble Bee Foods, was a US company with substantial sales in the US.

---

42 US Dept. of Justice & Fed. Trade Comm'n, Horizontal Merger Guidelines 1 (2010), https://www.justice.gov/atr/horizontal-merger-guidelines-08192010.

Accordingly, the parties submitted an HSR filing in anticipation of the acquisition. Some industry experts were skeptical that the deal would be approved without significant concessions.[43] Indeed, the track record was not good: in 1996, the Division had blocked StarKist from acquiring Bumble Bee, citing competitive concerns.[44] Thai Union stock prices actually closed 3.5% *down* after the deal was announced, potentially reflecting investor concern over the prospect of approval.[45] And while HSR reviews are not public, it is clear that the skeptics' concerns were well founded, based on the fact that nearly a year passed between the announcement of the deal and the Division's announcement that the parties had agreed to abandon their plans to merge, after the Division informed them it had "serious concerns" the transaction would harm competition.[46]

3. Division Criminal Antitrust Enforcement

As noted above, the Division is the only US agency that has the authority to pursue criminal penalties for antitrust violations. This authority is derived from section 1 of the Sherman Act, which provides for criminal penalties of up to US$1 million and/or 10 years in jail for individuals, and up to US$100 million in fines for corporations (or up to twice the amount gained by conspirators or lost by victims of the criminal conduct, if either amounts exceed US$100 million).[47]

A. Individual Liability

One somewhat unique, but well-publicized, aspect of US criminal enforcement against corporate misconduct is the focus on executive responsibility. Casual observers may be surprised to learn that the focus on individuals is a comparatively recent development, contrary to the impression given off by the scores of high-profile prosecutions that have dominated headlines in recent years. US law has long allowed prosecutors to target culpable executives of companies charged with criminal misconduct. In practice, however, such prosecutions were comparatively rare, as companies sought to protect their executives from liability, blaming lone rogue employees or agreeing to higher penalties in return for non-prosecution of individuals.

---

43 Nopparat Chaichalearmmongkol & Josh Beckerman, *Bumble Bee to Merge with Chicken of the Sea*, The Wall Street Journal (Dec. 19, 2014), https://www.wsj.com/articles/thai-union-seafood-company-to-buy-bumble-bee-1418958046.

44 Dep't of Justice, *Merger Challenges, Antitrust Division*, https://www.justice.gov/atr/merger-challenges-antitrust-division.

45 Khettiya Jittapong & Manunphattr Dhananphorn, *Thai Union Frozen to buy U.S. tuna firm Bumble Bee for $1.5 billion*, Reuters (Dec. 18, 2014), https://www.reuters.com/article/us-bumble-bee-thai-uno-frozen-acquisitio/thai-union-frozen-to-buy-u-s-tuna-firm-bumble-bee-for-1-5-billion-idUSKBN0JX05G20141219.

46 DOJ, *supra* note 25.

47 Sherman Antitrust Act of 1890, 15 U.S.C. §§ 1–38.

That dynamic changed in September 2015 with the issuance of the DOJ's "Yates memo," which instructed DOJ prosecutors to prioritize the prosecution of culpable individuals.[48] The memo explained that, moving forward, any company seeking cooperation credit in a DOJ investigation would be required to identify all individual employees responsible for misconduct. As for the Division itself, the memo instructed prosecutors to focus on individuals from the very beginning of any corporate investigation, encouraging them to resolve cases against individuals even before cases are resolved against their employers. The memo also discontinued the practice of allowing companies to agree to larger corporate fines or other concessions in order to immunize individual officers or employees.

The impact of the Yates memo appears to have been felt strongly in the tuna investigation. The first individual executive to plead guilty was Bumble Bee's Senior Vice President of Sales, in January 2017 – months before Bumble Bee itself pleaded guilty to price-fixing charges in August of that year. That plea was shortly followed by the pleas of four more executives at Bumble Bee and StarKist. Each individual guilty plea has included an acknowledgment that the pleading executive participated in criminal price-fixing, and required the pleading executive to cooperate with the government in its ongoing investigation, in return for more lenient sentences.

Not all of the executives under scrutiny chose to cooperate with the Division's investigation. In May 2018, a federal grand jury indicted Lischewski, then the sitting CEO of Bumble Bee, for his alleged role in the price-fixing.[49] It was a rare move for the Division to criminally indict a sitting CEO, even after the Yates memo and accompanying Division policy shift. Lischewski temporarily stepped down as CEO after charges were announced and spent the next year and a half fighting criminal charges against him.

The trial was delayed for over a year, but, on December 3, 2019, a California jury found Lischewski guilty of conspiring to fix prices of canned tuna, in a verdict delivered after just five hours of deliberation.[50] That verdict followed a month of trial that included the testimony of two of Lischewski's former lieutenants, both of whom had pleaded guilty to criminal price-fixing, and who testified against Lischewski in hopes of receiving a more lenient sentence.[51] The

48 Memorandum from Sally Q. Yates, Deputy Att'y Gen., Dep't of Justice, Individual Accountability for Corporate Wrongdoing (Sep. 9, 2015), https://www.justice.gov/archives/dag/file/769036/download.

49 Press Release, Dep't of Justice, Bumble Bee CEO Indicted for Price Fixing (May 16, 2018), https://www.justice.gov/opa/pr/bumble-bee-ceo-indicted-price-fixing. See also: Benjamin Craven, Eric P. Enson, John M. Majoras, Julia McEvoy, *The US DoJ indicts the CEO of a seafood company on price fixing charges (Bumble Bee Foods)*, 16 May 2018, *e-Competitions* May 2018, Art. N° 89969.

50 Press Release, Dep't of Justice, Former CEO Convicted of Fixing Prices for Canned Tuna (Dec. 3, 2019), https://www.justice.gov/opa/pr/former-ceo-convicted-fixing-prices-canned-tuna.

51 *Former Bumble Bee CEO's jurors relied on documents, not witnesses, to convict*, MLEX MARKET INSIGHT (Dec. 3, 2019).

testifying executives described their former boss as the mastermind of a "truce" among the three canned tuna producers in order to manufacture profits. According to the government's witnesses, immediately following Bumble Bee's acquisition by Lion Capital, the industry encountered a spike in fish prices amidst an aggressive price war among the three canned tuna producers. The cooperators testified that Lischewski ordered them to fix prices with their counterparts at Chicken of the Sea and StarKist, in response to pressure he was facing to increase profits to facilitate a future sale. The former CEO of Chicken of the Sea also testified at trial, a requirement of his former company's leniency agreement. Somewhat unusually for a criminal trial of this nature, Lischewski himself took the stand in his own defense, a risky move that opened him up to hours of questioning by government attorneys on cross-examination. Ultimately, the jurors reported to the press that emails Lischewski sent to his competitors complaining of low prices had convinced the jury he was guilty of criminal price-fixing.[52]

Lischewski's sentencing is scheduled for April 2020.[53] When he is sentenced, the former executive will face the prospect of up to 10 years in prison and a US$1 million fine, in addition to individual civil liability. As for his former deputies, they face more lenient sentences, including potentially no jail time at all, as a result of their cooperation. This leniency comes at a cost, however, as they spent months cooperating with government attorneys and had to endure withering cross-examination in open court, where they were forced to testify under oath and acknowledge their complicity in the crimes.[54]

B. Corporate Criminal Consequences

Even though the Division recently shifted its focus towards executives (in line with the rest of the DOJ), it continues to vigorously pursue criminal (and civil) antitrust charges against corporations accused of anticompetitive conduct. Indeed, the Division has been one of the world's most active antitrust enforcers for decades, imposing significant criminal penalties on companies in a diverse array of industries including air transportation, vitamins, and LCD panels. The Division made perhaps its biggest splash when it levied billions of dollars in fines against a number of major banks for their participation in the global LIBOR and FX price-fixing conspiracies.

In recent years, the Division has increasingly turned its attention towards international anticompetitive activity, reflective of the fact that the Sherman Act is not limited to US companies, but rather reaches anticompetitive conduct

---

52 *Id.*

53 DOJ, *supra* note 51.

54 *Ex-Bumble Bee sales head testifies to competition during price-fixing period in former CEO's trial*, MLex Market Insight (Dec. 3, 2019).

– including foreign conduct – that has a "direct, substantial, and reasonably foreseeable effect" on US commerce. The extraterritorial scope of the Sherman Act means that not only are foreign companies subject to US antitrust laws and enforcement, but foreign activities of US companies are also subject to antitrust scrutiny (if those activities impact US commerce). This scope can significantly impact the calculation of criminal penalties, since the Sherman Act provides for fines of up to US$100 million or twice the amount gained by conspirators or lost by victims, an amount that may be significantly increased by sales not in the US that nevertheless have an effect on US markets.

The expansive reach – and severity – of US criminal antitrust laws is evident in the tuna companies' guilty pleas. Indeed, Bumble Bee's US$25 million penalty was actually far *lower* than it might have been: according to the Division's charging documents, Bumble Bee's involvement in the conspiracy affected US$567 million in commerce, and the company faced a fine as high as US$272.4 million.[55] But the Division agreed to several reductions of that amount. First, prosecutors agreed to use the low end of the amounts provided under US sentencing guidelines (US$136.2 million) as the starting point for the fine, due to the liability that Bumble Bee also faced in civil suits and because Bumble Bee's conduct had not resulted in any *non*-economic harm. Second, the Division also credited the company's cooperation in the agency's ongoing investigation, meriting a downward departure from the low end of the guidelines range, and further reducing the fine to US$81.5 million. Third, the Division further lowered Bumble Bee's penalty to US$25 million because the Division recognized that payment of a higher amount might lead the company to suffer "adverse consequences" (e.g. bankruptcy).[56] This penalty ultimately contributed to Bumble Bee's bankruptcy in November 2019: in documents supporting its filing, the company cited the fine as well as civil litigation and "tens of millions of dollars in defense costs" as one of the reasons the company was forced into bankruptcy.[57]

StarKist pleaded guilty to price-fixing in November 2018, though it took almost a year afterward for its penalty amount to be set. According to the Division, StarKist's conduct affected at least US$600 million in sales. Unlike Bumble Bee's plea agreement, StarKist's plea agreement specified only a range for the penalty the company was to pay, to be determined by a US district judge. This determination resulted in months of heated litigation. The Division requested the judge impose the top end of the range provided for by US sentencing guidelines: US$100 million. In response, StarKist argued that such a fine would devastate the company, and claimed it could afford to pay only US$50 million – the low

55 Sentencing Memorandum, United States v. Bumble Bee Foods, LLC, No. 3:17-cr-00249-EMC (N.D. Cal. filed July 31, 2017), ECF No. 25.

56 *Id.*

57 Declaration of Chief Financial Officer Kent McNeil, *In re* Bumble Bee Parent, Inc., No. 19-12502-LSS (Bankr. D. Del. Nov. 21, 2019), ECF No. 17.

end of the penalty range recommended by the US sentencing guidelines.[58] The amount of StarKist's fine hinged on whether the company would be able to sell its subsidiary, TechPack Solutions, which was valued at approximately US$155 million. In September 2019, the federal district court judge presiding over StarKist's guilty plea ordered StarKist to pay the full US$100 million penalty, finding that StarKist did not prove that its financial circumstances justified the lower fine as the company had argued.[59]

Both companies have been subjected to criminal penalties at levels they assert they cannot pay, along with penalty provisions that seem almost specifically designed to impact the companies' foreign parents. For Bumble Bee, its guilty plea specified that in the event of a "qualifying transaction" (e.g. the company was acquired), Bumble Bee's fine would revert to the US$81.5 million figure. In essence, this provision added US$56.5 million to the cost to any buyer of acquiring Bumble Bee from Lion Capital, to be paid to the Division in the form of a criminal penalty. As for StarKist, its parent, Dongwon Industries of South Korea, vigorously opposed any resolution requiring StarKist to dispose of assets to pay the criminal penalty. Both outcomes perhaps indicate that the Division holds the corporate parents of the conspiring companies at least partially responsible for the misconduct.

C. Leniency[60]

The Division's leniency program allows individuals and corporations to self-report their role in antitrust crimes and thereby avoid criminal convictions and penalties. The Division's aggressive pursuit of criminal convictions for companies and executives implicated in cartel conduct has had the effect of encouraging companies to self-report such antitrust conduct to pursue leniency. To be eligible for leniency, an individual or a corporation must meet all of the conditions set forth in the Division's corporate or individual leniency policies, including confessing to the antitrust violation and fully cooperating with the agency's investigation and prosecution of co-conspirators. The Division will award leniency only to the first company to come forward and successfully self-report its role in a conspiracy and satisfactorily cooperate with the Division's investigation, however, so prompt action is important if conduct is uncovered during a merger review.[61]

---

58 Hannah Albarazi, *StarKist Says $100M Fine for Tuna Price-Fixing Is Too High*, Law360 (June 12, 2019), https://www.law360.com/articles/1168592/starkist-says-100m-fine-for-tuna-price-fixing-is-too-high.

59 Press Release, Dep't of Justice, StarKist Ordered to Pay $100 Million Criminal Fine for Antitrust Violation (Sept. 11, 2019), https://www.justice.gov/opa/pr/starkist-ordered-pay-100-million-criminal-fine-antitrust-violation.

60 Dep't of Justice, *Frequently Asked Questions about the Antitrust Division's Leniency Program and Model Leniency Letters*, Dep't of Justice (Jan. 26, 2017), https://www.justice.gov/atr/page/file/926521/download.

61 A corporation reporting such conduct does not preclude its employees involved from eligibility for leniency under the first to report rule.

There are two types of leniency available under the Division's Corporate Leniency Policy: "Type A" and "Type B". Type A leniency is available where a company approaches the Division for leniency *before* the agency has opened any investigation into the cartel conduct at issue. Type B leniency is available to the first company that agrees to cooperate with the Division *after* the Division has already launched an investigation into the conduct at issue, but before the Division has sufficient detail to convict any conspirator. There are two significant disadvantages to Type B leniency. First, the Division has more discretion over whether to grant leniency to a Type B applicant. Under the policy, the Division will only grant Type B leniency if it determines that doing so would "not be unfair" to other conspirators. Second (and more significant), the Division has greater discretion over whether to grant immunity to officers, directors, and employees of a Type B leniency applicant. Personnel of Type A leniency applicants who satisfy the requirements for cooperation and admission of guilt automatically receive immunity when their employer receives immunity. Employees of Type B applicants, on the other hand, must separately earn their immunity in return for cooperation. The protections afforded to a Type A leniency applicant are intended to encourage companies to promptly self-report their role in a criminal antitrust conspiracy, rather than waiting to do so once they have received an inquiry from the Division.

When news broke in July 2015 that the Division was investigating potential antitrust violations in the packaged seafood industry, the immediate speculation was that the agency had uncovered evidence of cartel conduct between the parties in the course of its review of the Chicken of the Sea/Bumble Bee deal. As a result, press reports speculated that Thai Union had sought Type B leniency, given that the Division had already begun investigating the industry.[62] Normally, leniency applications are closely guarded secrets; in fact, Division policy is to treat leniency applications as strictly confidential. Indeed, Chicken of the Sea's leniency application was not confirmed until September 2017 when its parent, Thai Union, filed a notice with the Stock Exchange of Thailand stating that the company had received conditional leniency from the Division.[63] Such corporate disclosures to shareholders are typical means by which a company discloses its status as a leniency recipient.

Chicken of the Sea's leniency application illustrates the lengthy and substantial cooperation requirements of leniency applicants. The Division had launched its investigation at least by July 2015, when news of the investigation broke. Chicken of the Sea likely pursued leniency for over two years before the Division finally awarded leniency in 2017. Notably, in Thai Union's Stock Exchange notice, the

---

62 Tom Seaman, *US tuna price fixing lawsuits: Chicken of the Sea is whistleblower, Tri Marine subpoenaed*, Undercurrent News (Nov. 11, 2015), https://www.undercurrentnews.com/2015/11/11/us-tuna-price-fixing-lawsuits-chicken-of-the-sea-is-whistleblower-tri-marine-subpoenaed/.

63 Eric Kroh, *Tri-Union Admits to Blowing Whistle in DOJ Tuna Probe*, Law360 (Sep. 11, 2017), https://www.law360.com/articles/962648/tri-union-admits-to-blowing-whistle-in-doj-tuna-probe.

company was careful to specify that the leniency was *conditional*, which means that the company's cooperation obligations continue indefinitely. This is part of Division policy, pursuant to which the receipt of leniency becomes final only after the Division closes its investigation and prosecution of all co-conspirators related to the conduct that is the subject of the application. As a result, Chicken of the Sea is required to continue to provide significant – and costly – cooperation in the Division's ongoing investigation. Chicken of the Sea's leniency protections will not be final until the Division concludes its investigation of Chicken of the Sea's co-conspirators and their executives, which may take years. In the meantime, Chicken of the Sea is at the mercy of the Division – as the agency has made clear, conditional leniency can and will be revoked if the Division determines that the company's cooperation has not been satisfactory. As long as the company continues to cooperate, however, Chicken of the Sea and its employees will avoid prosecution and the resultant fines and jail time.

Leniency provides some protections for civil penalties as well, although that protection is not complete, as evident from Chicken of the Sea's involvement in the multitude of civil lawsuits that have been brought by consumers in the past few years. Those protections are discussed further below.

4. Civil Liability

In addition to empowering the Division to police antitrust violations, federal antitrust law also permits damages suits by private parties who claim to have been injured by such violations. To compensate for the fact that not all violations are capable of being uncovered or remediated by the agencies themselves, and to increase deterrence, federal law permits plaintiffs to proceed on an "opt-out" class basis (described below), and provides for treble damages for successful plaintiffs. Indeed, civil liability can sometimes be even more costly than criminal liability for a company embroiled in an antitrust scandal, especially given the length of time such proceedings take to conclude, as well as the multitude of different classes of plaintiffs that alleged violators can face in court. This heightened risk of civil liability derives from the prevalence of class actions in antitrust litigation.

A. Class Actions

US law permits plaintiffs to proceed as a "class action," aggregating individual claims into a single suit that can (a) encourage parties to aggregate individual small claims that would otherwise not be asserted; and (b) facilitate the pursuit of these claims more efficiently. To proceed, a purported class of plaintiffs must meet certain criteria to be "certified" as a class by the court: there must be so many class members that litigating individual suits would be impractical; the underlying claims must share common facts and laws; and the class representative must accurately reflect the rest of the class and be capable of fairly protecting and pursuing the entire class's interests.

Would-be plaintiffs are incentivized to lead a purported class. The class representative often gets to control certain aspects of the case, such as litigation strategy and whether to consider a proposed settlement. In addition, lead plaintiffs and their counsel receive an increased amount of any award or settlement. These benefits, coupled with comparatively permissive threshold pleading standards in US courts, often result in a race to the courthouse by numerous would-be plaintiffs suing in parallel on behalf of similarly-defined classes relying on bare-bones allegations that largely parrot news reports and allegations of Division investigations. As a result, a corporation that is the target of a Division antitrust investigation can expect to promptly face a multitude of civil lawsuits if news of the investigation leaks to the press.

The Division's packaged seafood investigation is instructive of this. The first civil plaintiff, Olean Wholesale Grocery, stormed into court with an antitrust class action complaint less than two weeks after news broke of the Division's prepackaged tuna investigation.[64] Olean sought to sue on behalf of itself and all similarly situated wholesale purchasers. Olean's complaint was followed quickly afterwards with class actions filed by other wholesalers, such as PITCO Foods[65] and Affiliated Foods,[66] both of whom sought to represent the same class as Olean. These wholesaler class actions were followed shortly thereafter by individual consumers of prepackaged tuna suing on behalf of purported classes of plaintiffs claiming to have purchased tuna indirectly from the conspirators, leaving the tuna companies facing liability on many different fronts.[67]

B. Opt-out Individual Suits

A judicial decision resolving a class action, or a class resolution approved by the court, is binding on all similarly situated class members unless a would-be class member opts out and reserves their right to pursue an individual suit. There are many reasons why individual plaintiffs may choose to opt out of a class action. Some may do so because they believe they have suffered damages in excess of (or different from) those suffered by the class. Others may simply disagree with the strategy of the lawsuit itself.

The tuna civil antitrust litigation features several large opt-out plaintiffs. Perhaps the most noteworthy opt-out plaintiff was Wal-Mart, which likely decided to opt out of the class action due to the size of the impact it believed it felt as a

---

64 Olean Wholesale Grocery Cooperative, Inc. v. Bumble Bee Foods LLC, Tri-Union Seafoods LLC, and Starkist Company, No. 3:15-cv-01714-JLS-MDD (S.D. Cal. filed Aug. 3, 2015).

65 Pacific Groservice Inc. v. Bumble Bee Foods, LLC, No. 3:15-cv-01791-WQH-JMA (S.D. Cal. filed Aug. 13, 2015).

66 Affiliated Foods, Inc. v. Tri-Union Seafoods, LLC, No. 3:15-cv-03815-DMR (N.D. Cal. filed Aug. 20, 2015).

67 *See* Amended Complaint with Jury Demand, *supra* note 31.

result of the price-fixing conspiracy. According to its complaint, Wal-Mart purchased approximately US$400 million of packaged tuna products per year during the price-fixing conspiracy, constituting approximately a quarter of all packaged tuna products sold in the United States. Chicken of the Sea was the first to settle with Wal-Mart for an undisclosed amount in May 2018,[68] followed by StarKist, which settled with the retailer in January 2019 for a combination of cash and favorable commercial terms valued at approximately US$20.5 million.[69] Bumble Bee settled Wal-Mart's civil suit in June 2019.[70]

Several other opt-out suits continue, involving claims by large grocery store chains. These cases will continue in parallel to the class actions until the tuna companies resolve those claims in court or settle them.

C. Indirect Purchasers[71]

While direct purchasers are able to sue under federal law, the so-called *Illinois Brick* rule disallows indirect purchasers from doing the same. Named after the Supreme Court case setting forth the principle, the rule limits federal antitrust claims to those who purchase price-fixed goods directly from alleged co-conspirators. The rule aims to protect defendants from duplicative damage awards claimed by purchasers at different levels of the market, and to spare courts from the complicated task of apportioning settlements and awards among participants at different levels of a purchasing chain, in which direct purchasers may have "passed on" some or all of an anticompetitive overcharge to downstream consumers.

Most US states have enacted so-called "*Illinois Brick* repealer statutes" that seek to undo the Supreme Court's decision, by allowing indirect purchasers to sue under *state* antitrust and consumer protection laws. These state rules can result in defendants' being forced to defend lawsuits under the laws of multiple jurisdictions, each with different standards, precedents, and remedies, and potentially resulting in some of the inefficiencies in litigation that *Illinois Brick* was intended to foreclose.[72]

---

68 Madelyn Kearns, *Walmart resolves anti-trust lawsuit against Chicken of the Sea*, SeafoodSource (May 23, 2018), https://www.seafoodsource.com/news/supply-trade/walmart-settles-anti-trust-lawsuit-against-chicken-of-the-sea.

69 Mike LaSusa, *StarKist Settles Walmart's Tuna Price-Fixing Claims for $20M*, Law360 (Jan. 25, 2019), https://www.law360.com/articles/1122536/starkist-settles-walmart-s-tuna-price-fixing-claims-for-20m.

70 Jason Smith, *Walmart drops tuna price-fixing lawsuit against Bumble Bee, Lion Capital*, Undercurrent News (June 10, 2019), https://www.undercurrentnews.com/2019/06/10/walmart-drops-tuna-price-fixing-lawsuit-against-bumble-bee-lion-capital/.

71 Clifford Chance US LLP, *Antitrust Litigation*, Chambers and Partners ¶ 2.5, 7.2 (Sep. 18, 2019), https://practiceguides.chambers.com/practice-guides/antitrust-litigation-2019/usa.

72 For example, some states mirror the federal statute in allowing for treble damages, but others limit recovery to actual or double damages.

In the tuna case, at least two sets of indirect purchaser class actions have been filed by plaintiffs who claim to have been downstream purchasers of price-fixed goods from defendants: a class of individual consumers and another class of commercial food preparation businesses (e.g. restaurants). These would-be classes included plaintiffs from at least 32 states and two US territories (Washington, D.C. and Guam) and involved claims under local antitrust and unfair competition laws for each of these states and territories, demonstrative of the headaches that antitrust litigation can present to defendants.[73]

D. ACPERA[74]

Even though Chicken of the Sea has been protected from criminal penalties as a result of its cooperation with the Division's investigation, the company remains subject to claims from private litigants. However, a leniency recipient is not completely out of luck when it comes to civil suits: a leniency recipient that satisfactorily cooperates with the plaintiff's suit may be able to avoid treble damages under the Antitrust Criminal Penalty Enhancement & Reform Act (ACPERA). However, the courts have not spoken clearly on what level of cooperation is sufficiently "satisfactory" to merit ACPERA credit. In addition, a leniency applicant is not eligible for ACPERA credit until civil litigation reaches the damages phase. In the tuna case, it remains an open question whether Chicken of the Sea will ultimately receive ACPERA credit.

III. Tuna Tales: What's Next?

As at the date of publication, the saga of the tuna cartel continues. StarKist faces a US$100 million criminal penalty, the size of which may cause the company's bankruptcy. Chicken of the Sea was able to avoid criminal prosecution for itself and its executives as a result of its leniency application, but its costly cooperation obligations remain ongoing and may continue for years. It also faces the threat of hundreds of millions of dollars in civil liability along with its co-conspirators.

For private equity firm Lion Capital, what started as a promising acquisition when it purchased a majority stake in Bumble Bee has instead turned into years of litigation and reputational harm. On November 21, 2019, Bumble Bee filed for bankruptcy, blaming among other reasons, the US$25 million criminal penalty imposed by the Division in connection with the tuna cartel, as well as the threat of civil litigation damages and "tens of millions of dollars in defense costs" that the company has reportedly been forced to pay to defend itself.[75] Lion Capital

73 Hannah Albarazi, *Tuna Buyers Win Cert. in Sprawling Price-Fixing MDL*, LAW360 (July 31, 2019), https://www.law360.com/articles/1183705/tuna-buyers-win-cert-in-sprawling-price-fixing-mdl.

74 Clifford Chance, *supra* note 72, ¶ 5.3, 7.1.

75 Declaration of Chief Financial Officer Kent McNeil, *supra* note 58.

now indicates it has no choice but to liquidate Bumble Bee's assets in bankruptcy – certainly not the result it envisioned when it purchased the company in 2010 for almost US$1 billion. And this is to say nothing about the liability the parent company faces itself – in early 2018, certain of the private civil plaintiffs added Lion Capital as a co-defendant in the ongoing litigation.[76]

IV. Epilogue

The saga of the tuna cartel illustrates how a planned private equity transaction can morph into a full-blown criminal antitrust investigation when a private equity firm is unaware of conduct at the portfolio company level. Companies need to exercise care starting with due diligence during a merger or acquisition. Although time is often of the essence in acquisitions, parties need to be on the lookout for questionable conduct by their own employees or those of the target company, that could be caught by competition authorities reviewing the proposed transaction. When a planned transaction would take place in a concentrated market, it is all the more important to ask the right questions, both internally and of the counterparty. In such deals, it is important to determine whether there are areas of potential antitrust risk, such as communications between competitors, and whether the parties participate in industry organizations (including trade associations or standard-setting organizations). If the deal is in a concentrated market – especially if there is any history of antitrust violations in the industry – companies might consider asking antitrust counsel to engage in a more thorough investigation to look for issues such as these. Private equity companies are not immune from scrutiny involving the conduct of their portfolio companies: for example, private litigants have made much of accusations that before buying Bumble Bee, Lion Capital executives met with executives of a Bumble Bee competitor.

When there could be a potential antitrust issue in a new portfolio company, it is important for the company to conduct adequate diligence prior to acquisition. It is also important that, after the acquisition, the acquirer properly integrates the new portfolio company, including implementing compliance policies and procedures. Pursuant to newly released guidance from the Division, it is important that the company's compliance policy and procedures are tailored to the risks facing the company.[77] Key components of an effective antitrust compliance program include regular antitrust audits and employee training.

---

76 Lion Capital sought dismissal from the suit, but a judge has refused to dismiss the US arm of the private equity firm from the case, which alleges that Lion Capital helped maintain the artificially inflated prices caused by the price-fixing conspiracy to increase Bumble Bee's market value in support of the company's sale. Christopher Cole, *UK Equity Firm Partly Escapes Tuna Price-Fix Claims*, Law360 (Sept. 7, 2018), https://www.law360.com/articles/1080228/uk-equity-firm-partly-escapes-tuna-price-fix-claims.

77 Press Release, Dep't of Justice, Antitrust Division Announces New Policy to Incentivize Corporate Compliance (July 11, 2019), https://www.justice.gov/opa/pr/antitrust-division-announces-new-policy-incentivize-corporate-compliance. See also: Robert E. Connolly, *The Antitrust Division of the U.S. Department of Justice announces*

If a party to a planned transaction *does* find itself the recipient of a Second Request from antitrust authorities, there are steps it can take to reduce the burden and handle potential issues. Due to the incredibly broad nature of a standard Second Request, a company should often work with antitrust agencies to narrow the request's scope, even though doing so takes time. Further, though a company may be tempted to produce documents in response to the Second Request as quickly as possible, it is generally important to conduct a thorough review of the documents prior to production. A party that is aware of what is in its documents can address issues proactively. If antitrust issues are found at the company, whether during an antitrust audit or during a Second Request, a company should consider what remediation measures are available.

---

new policy aimed at incentivizing corporate compliance, 11 July 2019, *e-Competitions* July 2019, Art. N° 91547.

Criminal Cartel Prosecution: Considerations on Attempts to Compensate Victims

ROXANN E. HENRY*

Abstract

In the United States, criminal cartel prosecutions are frequently followed by private, treble damages class-action litigation. This enforcement model has increasingly faced scrutiny as jurisdictions around the world contemplate systems for victim recompense. This article explores some of the tensions that arise from parallel criminal and civil actions, and questions whether private follow-on litigation in cartel cases results in a decrease in social welfare. Moreover, this article considers alternatives to private follow-on litigation and proposes consideration of replacing certain private antitrust litigation with restitution and other relief in the context of sentencing for conspiracy claims that have been the subject of a conviction obtained by the Antitrust Division of the US Department of Justice. The proposed process could avoid many burdens and costs, eliminate tensions between public and private enforcement, shorten the time to resolution, incentivize corporations to implement effective compliance programs, provide effective deterrence, and better accomplish victim redress.

---

* Roxann E. Henry has handled all aspects of competition law in her over 35 years of antitrust practice, including criminal defense, treble damage litigation, compliance advice, and merger and other civil investigations. As lead counsel, she won a rare corporate criminal antitrust jury acquittal, and clients, domestic and foreign, individuals and corporations, entrust her with the defense of national and international investigations. She regularly appears before enforcers in the US and abroad and has participated an invited non-government advisor to the International Competition Network. Ms. Henry has been recognized repeatedly by *Chambers*, *Global Competition Review* (Leading Attorney and Thought Leader), *National Law Journal* (M&A Antitrust Trailblazer Awards), *Legal 500*, and Best Lawyers in America (including Washington DC's Top 50 Women Lawyers). She is the past Chair of the Antitrust Section of the American Bar Association and has repeatedly co-chaired its International Cartel Workshop and served as its International Officer, Program Officer, and co-chair of the Spring Meeting. Currently she focuses her practice on consulting, second opinions, compliance programs and monitoring, and representing individuals.

The United States has a long history of following criminal cartel prosecutions with private, civil, treble damages, and class actions. Around the world this model is under the microscope as various jurisdictions step up public enforcement and look at how best to provide redress to victims. Few, if any, see the US system as the paragon of efficient redress. Also, it is important to recognize that serious tensions arise between parallel private actions and public enforcement. This article notes some of the concerns that flow from the current system in the United States and looks at potential alternatives to private enforcement in cases where the government has already devoted resources to prosecute. The time has come to consider the merits of handling victim claims for restitution as part of the US criminal process and blocking private litigation purporting to accomplish victim redress in relation to violations that are the subject of public enforcement.

I propose considering the replacement of private antitrust litigation with restitution and other relief in the context of sentencing for any conspiracy claims that have been the subject of a conviction obtained by the Antitrust Division of the US Department of Justice (Antitrust Division). The proposed process would avoid the excessive costs and burdens of compensating victims through the current treble damages litigation process; eliminate potential private litigation interference with government investigations; permit more appropriate calibration of deterrence measures and consolidate that assessment with the Antitrust Division; incentivize corporations to implement effective compliance programs; enable better targeting and quicker payment of compensation; and accomplish these objectives without adding undue burdens on government resources.

I. US Antitrust: Civil Treble Damages Class Actions

The situation in follow-on cartel class-action litigation is very different from typical litigation involving dispute resolution between parties or when a party seeks the protection of legal rights.[1] A follow-on case is when the government does the work to establish a violation of law. The key definitional point is that the civil case uses a government prosecution that results in a sentence. Plaintiffs rely heavily on the existence of the government investigation to try to avoid dismissal and rely on the pressure of the government action to induce settlements. Follow-on cases can be defined to include private litigation commenced only upon the basis of the report of a government investigation. In all of these civil cases, plaintiffs' class-action lawyers fight to take control over the litigation

1 This paper is limited to the antitrust context and does not extend to litigation apart from criminal cartel prosecutions, such as civil rights or employment litigation where government enforcement operates under an entirely different regime. Moreover, this paper does not address the circumstances of litigation, even in the cartel area, that are not based upon government proceedings. Other considerations apply to both of these circumstances.

to garner a lucrative one-third of a damages fund.[2] The lawyers for the class, not the alleged victims, control the litigation process. The cases virtually never go to trial, and the purported victims typically have no emotional, pecuniary, or other investment in the litigation. As an inducement to be the named plaintiffs in the representative action, the plaintiffs' lawyers typically ask the court for a bonus payment to the named plaintiffs. Not infrequently, named individual plaintiffs are related to the lawyers either through a familial or work connection.

The court process takes a long time and cases typically drag on for years until settled. Scores of virtually identical cases filed across the country are consolidated before one court for pretrial proceedings. Then, the burden and expense of antitrust discovery starts in earnest, which even the US Supreme Court has recognized as extraordinary.[3] Many months, or more often years, and many millions of dollars are spent in the civil litigation process.

Yet, none of that money spent on the litigation process goes to the victims. The money goes to lawyers, experts, and supporting services. Electronic database support alone can cost well over a million dollars for a modest case.[4] High-priced experts digest and disgorge massive amounts of data to support class certification and arrive at a calculation of the amount of damages. The experts hired by the defendants then offer their own massive amounts of data to rebut the findings of the expert or experts hired by the plaintiffs. All of these expensive experts will undergo rigorous cross-examination at depositions and often at hearings. And, judges must review whether the experts are basing their conclusions on accepted scientific principles applied according to accepted scientific methods.[5] Case management orders routinely recognize the need for well over a hundred depositions and, not infrequently, depositions take place around the world, including through the time-consuming and intricate Hague Convention process. Dozens of lawyers orchestrate this pretrial process with numerous judicial hearings.

These costs do not encompass the judicial resources used and the time and burden on business executives that distracts from a focus on business. Similarly, there are real foregone business impairment and opportunity costs to operating when a business is known to be facing the type of unquantified substantial potential

---

2 *See* Ryan Kriger, *Clash Of The Class Action Law Firms*, LAW360 (Oct. 3, 2011), http://www.law360.com/articles/275328/clash-of-the-class-action-law-firms.

3 Bell Atlantic Corp. v. Twombly, 550 U.S. 544, 558–60 (2007); Kevin Logue, Barry Sher, Asa R. Danes, *The US Supreme Court holds that an allegation of parallel conduct and a bare assertion of an agreement do not suffice to state a claim of conspiracy under the Sherman Act (Bell Atlantic / Twombly)*, 21 May 2007, *e-Competitions* May 2007, Art. N° 74789.

4 In May 2016, the ABA Journal reported that the market for e-discovery services was forecast to reach $14.7 billion by 2019. *Opening Statements*, ABA JOURNAL 14 (May 2016) (citing International Data Corp. (Jan. 4, 2016)).

5 Daubert v. Merrell Dow Pharm., Inc., 509 U.S. 579, 597 (1993).

liability that weighs on any defendant in the midst of treble damages antitrust class-action litigation. These soft costs should not be underestimated but, because of the difficulty of quantification, are largely ignored.

II. Tensions Between Parallel Criminal and Civil Actions

The government, plaintiffs, and defendants can lose important rights and protections when criminal and civil actions proceed in parallel. Similarly, some parties can seek to procure advantages from the dual proceedings to which they otherwise would not be entitled.

One area where this tension has long been recognized is that the broad discovery rules in civil litigation can interfere with the criminal investigation. Thus, it has not been uncommon for prosecutors to request a stay of some or all discovery in parallel civil proceedings. Sometimes plaintiffs do not object as they would like the government to secure convictions that create a prima facie case in the civil litigation. But sometimes the plaintiffs, especially after some convictions, would prefer the pressure of a faster time schedule to push along settlement negotiations. In general, courts grant government requests for a stay. Sometimes, however, the government seems compelled to limit its request perhaps more narrowly than might be optimal, and stay requests have been denied.[6]

Rarer, but highly intrusive to the governmental investigative process, is when private plaintiffs seek to force the government to share investigative results. In one matter, a judge in pretrial civil redress litigation proceedings involving allegations of price-fixing by three principal players in the packaged ice industry granted the direct purchaser class plaintiffs' motion to compel the Antitrust Division to produce to them certain tape recordings made by the government during its investigation.[7] The government had enlisted the cooperation of certain individuals who agreed to participate in and tape-record conversations with persons of interest, and the government had sole possession of the recordings. The government objected to the plaintiffs' subpoena to the government to procure the recordings, arguing sovereign immunity and various privileges, including federal law enforcement privilege. The court rejected these arguments and forced the government disclosure.

From the perspective of the defendants, this case highlights a perplexing dilemma that may negatively alter the balance against enforcement initiatives. Discoverability of government submissions presents a huge risk for a criminal defendant or leniency applicant cooperating with the government. In balancing the risks and rewards

---

6 *See, e.g.*, *In re* Optical Disk Drive Prods. Antitrust Litig., 3: 10-MD-02143-RS (N.D. Cal. June 24, 2010) (denying the government's motion to stay discovery but indicating a willingness to reconsider the issue on a case-by-case basis.).

7 *In re* Packaged Ice Antitrust Litig., No. 08-MD-01952, 2011 U.S. Dist. LEXIS 51116 (E.D. Mich. May 10, 2011), ECF No. 363.

of cooperation, the detrimental use of the submissions in the US civil litigation weighs heavily against the most comprehensive cooperation with the government. As a minimum, the risk likely creates extra burdens as oral submissions become less risky than written submissions. But, in at least one case, oral proffers appear to have created an even worse disclosure problem. One court found that when a defendant's attorney orally summarized internal work product about interviews to provide facts to the government in the context of cooperation, privilege was waived and the interview memorandums were ordered to be disclosed to the plaintiffs.[8] Essentially, targets of multijurisdictional investigations face a dilemma: cooperate with governmental authorities or protect rights and defenses in US civil litigation.

III. Social Welfare Allocation Issues

A number of factors lead to questions about whether the process and damages assessed through private cartel follow-on litigation result in a decrease or increase in social welfare. Are these actions helping or harming consumers? A strong case can be made that private cartel follow-on litigation merely penalizes the consumer once again.

In the United States, the rules in federal court provide that only the direct purchaser can recover damages. These corporate direct purchasers calculate their injury without regard to whether they passed any overcharge through to subsequent purchasers. Numerous states then reject the federal rule and allow indirect purchasers to sue for damages. While indirect purchasers are often corporations in the supply chain, the possibility also exists for consumer class-action litigation as well. In some cases, this can result in a variety of classes seeking damages – direct purchasers, indirect purchasers for resale, and indirect end-use purchasers. The injured parties seeking damages under the first two classes are typically corporations. The latter category generally consists of individual consumer class-action plaintiffs. Thus, with no allocation of any damages among affected purchasers, the potential for duplicate or triplicate damage payments arises.[9]

With regard to consumers, there is little basis to argue that today's antitrust class actions are the best way to provide redress. This point has been recognized repeatedly.[10] In fact, the difficulties involved in the prosecution of indirect

---

8 SEC v. Herrera, No. 17-20301 (S.D. Fl. Dec. 5, 2017) (order on defendants' motion to compel production from non-party law firm).

9 *See* ANTITRUST MODERNIZATION COMM'N, REPORT AND RECOMMENDATIONS, Ch. III.B, (Apr. 2007), for an excellent discussion of the issues raised by indirect purchaser litigation and a recommendation that Congress should enact a comprehensive statute to consolidate all direct and indirect purchaser action in a single federal forum.

10 *See, e.g.*, Albert A. Foer, *Enhancing Competition Through the Cy Pres Remedy: Suggested Best Practices*, 24 ANTITRUST 86 (2010). A *cy pres* remedy is when assessed damages are given to someone other than the victims as a "next best" substitute.

purchaser claims, especially problems with ascertaining damages, are a key reason for the federal rule that restricts claims to direct purchasers.[11] As consumers generally do not retain receipts or other proof of purchase, determining which consumers should receive recompense and how much is virtually impossible, even before taking into account other difficulties.[12] Indeed, class members often fail to make claims against settlement funds that have been established, and *cy pres* remedies may be employed because of recognition of the implausibility of putting compensation in the hands of victims.[13]

With regard to the corporate plaintiffs and the corporate defendants, there are numerous reasons why these damages actions are neutral at best for social welfare and, more typically, affirmatively adverse. Judge Douglas Ginsburg has cogently explained that the punishment of shareholders, who likely are innocent of any conceivable wrongdoing and who may well have suffered as victims of wrongdoing themselves, does not further social welfare.[14] Similarly, and equally importantly, the author knows of no empirical research to support the assertion that corporate recipients of these windfall damages use such monies in furtherance of consumer benefits. The settlement amounts from the treble damages follow-on cases appear as windfalls on the corporate balance sheet.

The temporal disparity between when the wrongful activity occurred and when the costs and damages settlements are paid creates fundamental impediments to any deterrent value flowing from the imposition of these corporate expenses. This is especially true for cartels that operated over a lengthy period. The injured direct purchasers likely passed on any overcharges long ago, and the shareholders on either side are not the same as, respectively, the ones who benefited or were harmed. The wealth transfer goes from one hapless group of shareholders to a different, much happier, group, who suddenly find themselves enriched.

Moreover, if most industry participants find themselves caught up in a cartel investigation, who truly bears the litigation and settlement costs? What happens when the cost of doing business goes up? Ultimately, it is hard to imagine that consumers do not pay the price or at least bear a major part of the cost.

---

11 Illinois Brick Co. v. Illinois, 431 U.S. 720 (1977).

12 Foer, *supra* note 12, at 86.

13 *See* Mayer Brown LLP, *Do Class Actions Benefit Class Members? An Empirical Analysis of Class Actions* 10–11, Institute for Legal Reform (2013), http://www.instituteforlegalreform.com/uploads/sites/1/Class_Action_Study.pdf (finding that, in a study of six cases with data regarding the distribution of settlement proceeds, five delivered funds to only minuscule percentages of the class: 0.000006%, 0.33%, 1.5%, 9.66%, and 12%).

14 *See, e.g.*, Douglas H. Ginsburg & Joshua D. Wright, *Antitrust Sanctions*, 6 Competition Policy Int'l 2, 18 (Autumn 2010).

Perhaps the largest concern is whether the civil litigation affects the willingness of defendants to cooperate with government. The highest price that consumers could pay for the purported benefit of private follow-on litigation is that fewer cartels are disclosed and prosecuted. While that would not be a result sought by the government, plaintiffs' lawyers, or victims, the potential to kill the goose laying the golden eggs is real. No one today disputes the effectiveness of leniency programs and cooperation in robust government antitrust enforcement.

IV. Alternative Methods for Compensation and Deterrence

1. Fraud Claims

Virtually every jurisdiction already permits victims of fraud to sue for redress. The laws are clear, require specific causation, and focus on the specific relations between the parties to the claim. In a cartel situation, a buyer who knows of the cartel and accepts the price, knowing it to be one that has been agreed among competitors, cannot fairly be viewed as a "victim" when that buyer had had the opportunity to reject the collusive price. The ability to seek fraud damages, with the attendant focus on causation, provides a safety net for instances where compensation should be provided, even if the treble damages system were eliminated. Admittedly, the recovery may not be an easy pile of money for lawyers, but a remedy exists.[15]

2. Fines Geared Toward Deterrence

While deterrence is often cited as a reason to promote private civil damages actions, measuring the appropriate pecuniary amount to provide deterrence has never been a goal of private litigation, nor a by-product. Moreover, the notion of a need for private attorneys general simply does not apply in the context of today's follow-on cartel litigation. Years ago, when this structure and concept were conceived, criminal fines were minimal and the offense was only a misdemeanor. In that circumstance, an argument could be made that supplemental civil damages would further deterrence. Now, the government does the work to expose a violation, imposes huge fines, and sends culpable individuals to jail (on average for two+ years). Moreover, when the action is brought merely on the basis of the report of a government investigation, it may well fall into the category of extortionate litigation that parties settle simply to avoid litigation costs.

---

15 There seems no reason to incentivize the bringing of cases under the current system given the alacrity of plaintiffs' lawyers to leap forward to bring them. And when the government has established a violation, the notion of any need for treble damages to compensate for exceptional risks seems absurd. The government has already provided the prima facie case, and there is little risk for the follow-on case, as it will be the rare case when a corporation chooses to go to a jury and claim that the company engaged in criminal conduct without it having any benefit for the company.

Meanwhile, the government has a range of options that provide it with the ability to review all relevant circumstances and create an appropriate monetary penalty to meet the goals of deterrence, both individual and social.[16]

3. Compliance Programs

The government may also insist upon the institution of compliance programs if specific deterrence is necessary. In the distant past, it was common for the US government to enter into consent decrees along with plea agreements, requiring a defendant company to maintain a robust compliance program for a period of years. More recently, the Antitrust Division has incorporated directly into the sentencing process a compulsion for companies to adopt and maintain compliance programs and reevaluated to take into consideration existing compliance programs.

Two sentencing initiatives of the Antitrust Division demonstrate its new carrot and stick approach. On the "carrot" side, the Antitrust Division has begun to give a discount in computing the fine for companies pleading guilty that have instituted programs that change the corporate culture to one of antitrust compliance.[17] And in July 2019 the Division reversed long-standing practice to state that an existing, robust compliance program will be given credit in determining whether and to what extent to prosecute, even if the program failed to deter the conduct.[18] On the "stick" side, the Antitrust Division has begun to request the institution of compliance programs as a condition of probation in plea agreements. In sentencing on the pleas of Hitachi Chemical Co. and Hoegh Autoliners, and with the conviction of AU Optronics Corp., the courts, at the request of the

---

16 In addition to imposing penalties and fines, the US Department of Justice (DOJ) has the equitable remedy of disgorgement in its arsenal of options to use in fashioning appropriate monetary remedies for Sherman Act violations. In United States v. KeySpan Corp., No. 10-cv-1415 (S.D.N.Y. Feb. 2, 2011), the court approved a DOJ settlement agreement under the terms of which the defendant, KeySpan Corporation, was required to disgorge profits resulting from anticompetitive activities. The DOJ complaint alleged that KeySpan entered into an agreement to restrain competition in the New York City electricity market. The court's holding was significant in that it was the first time the DOJ sought disgorgement in a civil suit for a Sherman Act violation. When making its decision, the court noted that the defendant's anticompetitive conduct had ceased, the derivative instrument used to manipulate the market had expired, no restitution to New York City consumers was available, and there were no assets that could be divested. Accordingly, the court recognized that failure to impose a disgorgement remedy would have "incentivized other generators to manipulate electricity markets using derivative instruments that expire in the short term, with the understanding that they will be permitted to retain their earnings because restitution to consumers is unavailable." See, Jeffrey May, *The U.S. Federal District court rules that the Department of Justice was entitled to seek disgorgement as a remedy for an alleged Sherman Act violation (KeySpan)*, 2 February 2011, *e-Competitions* February 2011, Art. N° 35889. Investment bank Morgan Stanley also agreed to disgorgement of profits for its participation in an electricity market manipulation agreement. United States v. Morgan Stanley, No. 11-civ-6875 (S.D.N.Y. Sep. 30, 2011).

17 Brent Snyder, Deputy Assistant Attorney General, Antitrust Division, Remarks at the Sixth Annual Chicago Forum on International Antitrust (June 8, 2015), *available at* https://www.justice.gov/opa/speech/deputy-assistant-attorney-general-brent-snyder-delivers-remarks-sixth-annual-chicago.

18 US DEP'T OF JUSTICE, ANTITRUST DIVISION, EVALUATION OF CORPORATE COMPLIANCE PROGRAMS IN CRIMINAL ANTITRUST INVESTIGATIONS, July 2019, *available at* https://www.justice.gov/atr/page/file/1182001.

Antitrust Division, imposed probation and required each company to hire a compliance monitor to develop and implement an effective compliance program.[19] In the AU Optronics case, the government justified its requests by reference to the statutory mandate "to protect the public from further crimes of the defendant" and "to provide the defendant with needed education or... other correctional treatment in the most effective manner."[20]

4. Criminal Restitution

The concept of handling victim recompense as part of the criminal sentencing process is not new. "The principle of restitution is an integral part of virtually every formal system of criminal justice, of every culture and every time."[21] Yet, the relationship between civil antitrust treble damages litigation and criminal antitrust restitution still needs further examination to fully understand the interaction of the two.

Today, the practice of combining redress and criminal punishment is still employed in the context of cartels affecting public procurement, albeit often through the use of a supplemental settlement agreement rather than through court-ordered restitution.[22] Most importantly, the concept is embedded into statutory sentencing requirements for federal crimes. Courts are required to impose a sentence mandating restitution unless the case falls into a specific statutory exception.[23]

Most criminal antitrust cases invoke the exception. Plea agreements with the Antitrust Division generally contain language similar to the following: "In light

---

19 Plea Agreement, United States v. Hoegh Autoliners AS, No. 1:17-cr-00505-GLR, 8–9 (D. Md. Dec. 8, 2017), ECF No. 18; United States v. Hitachi Chem. Co., Ltd., No. 4:16-cr-00180-JD, 7 (N.D. Cal. June 10, 2016), ECF No. 22; United States v. AU Optronics Corp., 3:09-cr-00110-SI, 43–44 (N.D. Cal. Sept. 20, 2012), ECF No. 948 (US Sentencing Memorandum); Jeffrey May, *The US District Court for the Northern District of California imposes $500 M fine on a Taiwan-based liquid crystal display (LCD) producer for its participation in a five-year conspiracy to fix the prices of thin-film transistor LCD panels (AU Optronics)*, 20 September 2012, *e-Competitions* September 2012, Art. N° 48812.

20 United States' Sentencing Memorandum, AU Optronics, No. 3:09-cr-00110-SI at 43-44 (quoting 18 U.S.C. §§ 3553(a)(2)(C) & A(D)).

21 United States v. Webb, 30 F.3d 687, 689 (6th Cir. 1994) (citing legislative history of S. Rep. No. 97-532, 1 at 30 (1982)).

22 In one instance, five South Korean companies that paid a total of over USD150 million in criminal fines entered into a separate agreement to resolve parallel civil and False Claims Act violations with civil settlements of USD 200 million in damages. The Antitrust Division of US DOJ has asserted that may seek treble damages for criminal antitrust violations affecting public procurement.

23 18 U.S.C. §§ 3663A(c) provides for mandatory restitution to victims for certain crimes; for example, "in which an identifiable victim or victims has suffered a physical injury or pecuniary loss." *Id.* §§ 3663A(c)(l)(B). There is a statutory exception to mandatory restitution for Title 18 property offenses where "(A) the number of identifiable victims is so large as to make restitution impracticable; or (B) determining complex issues of fact related to the cause or amount of the victim's losses would complicate or prolong the sentencing process to a degree that the need to provide restitution to any victim is outweighed by the burden on the sentencing process." *Id* §§ 3663A(c)(3).

of the civil class action cases filed against the defendant, which potentially provide for a recovery of a multiple of actual damages, the United States agrees that it will not seek a restitution order for the offense charged in the Information."[24]

Because of the invocation of this exception, little discussion or examination of handling antitrust victim claims as restitution has occurred. Yet, the issue has come to the forefront in various criminal cases. In one instance, noted below, the prospect of restitution was simply raised by the court as a possibility. In another, however, restitution was included in the settlement agreement between defendants and various government authorities, throwing a wrench squarely into the civil plaintiffs' pursuit of a follow-on class action. In an older case, restitution was imposed, but the court refused any offset for the settlement of civil claims based on a broader conspiracy.

A. Samsung

The court challenged whether restitution should be part of the sentence when Samsung SDI (Samsung) agreed to plead guilty to a price-fixing conspiracy related to color display tubes (CDTs).[25] The charging information alleged that Samsung participated in a conspiracy from at least January 1997 until at least March 2006 "to suppress and eliminate competition by fixing prices, reducing output and allocating market shares of [CDTs] to be sold in the United States and elsewhere."[26] Pursuant to the agreement, Samsung agreed to pay a fine of $32 million.

Not surprisingly, various private civil plaintiffs also had named Samsung as a defendant in case proceedings seeking treble damages for price-fixing of CDTs. At the initial hearing on the criminal case, when the government and Samsung requested the court to impose the sentence in accordance with the plea agreement, the judge balked and raised the question whether he should impose a restitution requirement. He allowed the parties to reconsider the plea terms in light of his comments, and ultimately restitution was not required.[27] Nonetheless, the negative reaction of seemingly all parties, except the judge, to the prospect of handling redress for private antitrust victims as restitutionary relief in the context of criminal sentencing bears further attention.

---

24 *E.g.*, Plea Agreement, United States v. Akzo Nobel Chem. Int'l B.V., No. CR 06-0160 MMC (N.D. Cal. May 17, 2006), *available at* https://www.justice.gov/atr/case/us-v-akzo-nobel-chemicals-international-bv.

25 *See* Press Release, Dep't of Justice, Samsung SDI Agrees to Plead Guilty in Color Display to Price-Fixing Conspiracy (Mar. 18, 2011), *available at* http://www.justice.gov/opa/pr/2011/March/11-at-350.html; *see also* United States v. Samsung SDI Co., Ltd., No. 11-cr-00162-WHA-1 (N.D. Cal. Mar. 18, 2011), ECF No. 1 (indictment) (Samsung Indictment).

26 Samsung Indictment, *supra* note 25, ¶ 2.

27 The court imposed its sentence on August 17, 2011, accepting the $32 million plea agreement with no restitution apparently based on in camera materials related to the defendant's substantial cooperation. *See* Pamela MacLean & Karen Gullo, *Samsung SDI's Plea Deal in Price Fixing Case Blocked*, Bloomberg (Apr. 20, 2011), http://www.bloomberg.com/news/2011-04-20/samsung-sdi-s-32-million-plea-deal-with-u-s-in-price-fixing-blocked.html. For the judgment, see U.S. v. Samsung SDI Co., Ltd, 3:11-cr-00162-WHA (N.D. Cal. Aug. 19, 2011).

B. Bank of America

The second matter pertains to the US government's investigation into anticompetitive conduct in the municipal bond market. In 2006, the government began an investigation into the competitive practices of providers and brokers of municipal bonds.[28] Soon thereafter, multiple cities, states, and other entities filed suits alleging price-fixing and bid-rigging in the municipal derivatives industry, seeking treble damages under the Clayton Act. The cases were consolidated into a single multidistrict litigation (MDL) lawsuit.[29]

In December 2010, the government entered into an agreement with Bank of America, the amnesty applicant, under which Bank of America agreed to pay "restitution to federal and state agencies for its participation in a conspiracy to rig bids in the municipal bond derivatives market."[30] The government has since entered into similar settlement agreements with UBS, JPMorgan Chase, Wachovia, and GE Funding, requiring, among other conditions, that the parties pay restitution to persons or entities injured by their anticompetitive conduct in return for the government's agreement not to prosecute.[31] Concurrently with these agreements, the banks entered into agreements with a number of governmental agencies and representatives, including a coalition of state attorneys general. The agreement with the latter specifically sets aside funds for restitution to municipalities harmed by the anticompetitive conduct.[32] Under the terms of

---

28 See William Selway & Martin Z. Braun, *U.S. subpoenas muni firms, seizes papers in probe*, BLOOMBERG (Nov. 16, 2006).

29 *In re* Municipal Derivatives Antitrust Litigation, MDL No. 1950, Master Docket No. 08-2516 (VM) (GWG) (S.D.N.Y).

30 *See* Press Release, Dep't of Justice, Bank of America Agrees to Pay $137.3 Million in Restitution to Federal and State Agencies as a Condition of the Justice Department's Antitrust Corporate Leniency Program (Dec. 7, 2010), *available at* http://www.justice.gov/opa/pr/2010/December/10-at-1400.html.

31 Press Release, Dep't of Justice, UBS AG Admits to Anticompetitive Conduct by Former Employees in the Municipal Bond Investments Market and Agrees to Pay $160 Million to Federal and State Agencies (May 4, 2011), *available at* https://www.justice.gov/opa/pr/ubs-ag-admits-anticompetitive-conduct-former-employees-municipal-bond-investments-market-and; Press Release, Dep't of Justice, JPMorgan Chase Admits to Anticompetitive Conduct by Former Employees in the Municipal Bond Investments Market and Agrees to Pay $228 Million to Federal and State Agencies (July 7, 2011), *available at* https://www.justice.gov/opa/pr/jpmorgan-chase-admits-anticompetitive-conduct-former-employees-municipal-bond-investments; Press Release, Dep't of Justice, Wachovia Bank N.A. Admits to Anticompetitive Conduct by Former Employees in the Municipal Bond Investments Market and Agrees to Pay $148 Million to Federal and State Agencies (Dec. 8, 2011), *available at* https://www.justice.gov/opa/pr/jpmorgan-chase-admits-anticompetitive-conduct-former-employees-municipal-bond-investments; Press Release, Dep't of Justice, GE Funding Capital Market Services Inc. Admits to Anticompetitive Conduct by Former Traders in the Municipal Bond Investments Market and Agrees to Pay $70 Million to Federal and State Agencies (Dec. 23, 2011), *available at* https://www.justice.gov/opa/pr/ge-funding-capital-market-services-inc-admits-anticompetitive-conduct-former-traders.

32 Agreement Among the Attorneys General of the States and Commonwealths of Alabama, California, Connecticut, Florida, Illinois, Kansas, Maryland, Massachusetts, Michigan, Missouri, Montana, Nevada, New Jersey, New York, North Carolina, Ohio, Oregon, Pennsylvania, South Carolina and Texas and

the agreement, persons and entities who seek compensation through the restitution fund cannot participate in the civil class action.

Immediately after the government and Bank of America signed the agreement, plaintiffs' counsel in the civil class action complained to the court that the restitution agreement with the government, which awarded compensation directly to the purported victims, effectively circumvented the class action.[33] Unmentioned was the fact that the agreement also cuts plaintiffs' lawyers – and their compensation – out of the settlement.[34]

Following the filing of various motions, the court ordered that before any notice of settlement was issued by the state attorneys general, the court would have to review and approve the notice, and that such notice must let claimants know that they may have rights under the class action.[35] Subsequent settlements have drawn similar criticism from plaintiffs' counsel and similar court orders.[36] The content of the notice was contentious, with state attorneys general indicating that class counsels' proposed language discouraged potential claimants from participating in the settlement, while class counsel argued that the proposed notice did not sufficiently advise potential claimants of alternatives. After a few months of court filings and arguments, the final notice letter for the Bank of America settlement was issued.

C. All Star Industries

Sentencing after a conviction for price-fixing in violation of section 1 of the Sherman Act, the court ordered restitution to the victims of the conspiracy. One defendant claimed that the amount of restitution should have been reduced by the amount paid to settle a related civil class action and that it was unfair to make restitution a joint and several obligation.[37] The Fifth Circuit upheld

---

Bank of America Corporation (Dec. 7, 2010), *available at* https://oag.ca.gov/system/files/attachments/press_releases/n2012_boa_settlement_agreement_12-7-10.pdf.

33 Letter from Interim Co-Lead Class Counsel Michael D. Hausfeld of Hausfeld LLP to the Hon. Victor Marrero, *In re* Municipal Derivatives Antitrust Litigation, MDL No. 1950, Master Docket No. 08-2516 (VM) (GWG) (S.D.N.Y. Dec. 14, 2010), ECF No. 1192.

34 If the Antitrust Division reaches settlements with companies that include restitution, it erodes the class action plaintiffs' lawyers' ability to recover large fees in these lawsuits.

35 Order, *In re* Municipal Derivatives Antitrust Litigation, MDL No. 1950, Master Docket No. 08-2516 (VM) (GWG) (S.D.N.Y. Mar. 1, 2011), ECF No. 1253.

36 Letter from Seth Ard of Susman Godfrey LLP to the Hon. Victor Marrero, *In re* Municipal Derivatives Antitrust Litigation, MDL No. 1950, Master Docket No. 08-2516 (VM) (GWG) (S.D.N.Y. May 9, 2011), ECF No. 1329 (complaining regarding the UBS settlement); Letter from Elinor R. Hoffman, Assistant Att'y Gen., State of New York, to the Hon. Victor Marrero, *In re* Municipal Derivatives Antitrust Litigation, MDL No. 1950, Master Docket No. 08-2516 (VM) (GWG) (S.D.N.Y. July 12, 2011), ECF No. 1553 (responding to Interim Class Counsel's complaint regarding the JPMorgan settlement). The final notice letter issued in mid-November 2011.

37 United States v. All Star Industries, 962 F.2d 465, 477 (5th Cir. 1992).

the restitution order. While noting that an offset should be made in an appropriate case, the court pointed to the law that the civil claims settled needed to involve the same acts of the defendant as those that were the predicates for the criminal conviction.[38] The civil case had alleged a 20-year conspiracy to fix prices "affecting hundreds of projects, fabricators, engineering companies, and end users."[39] But the criminal case concerned "a four-year bid-rigging conspiracy involving sales made through a single fabricator," and "only two of the 28 defendants in the civil case were involved in the criminal conspiracy."[40] The court also placed heavy emphasis on the failure of the defendant to offer any accounting to show how the victims of the criminal conspiracy received restitution through the civil settlement. Arguably, a different result could result from a different set of facts, and it is noteworthy that the case does not examine any argument that both the criminal and civil conspiracies were one, single overarching conspiracy. With regard to joint and several liability, the court of appeals noted that, as a participant in a conspiracy, the defendant was legally liable for all the acts of its co-conspirators in furtherance of the conspiracy and upheld the condition as not an abuse of discretion, even given that the challenging defendant may not have been directly involved in several projects for which restitution was awarded.[41]

5. Standing/Civil Payment Reduction for Restitution

Arguably, if the court provided for restitution to victims as part of the criminal process, having no longer sustained injury to their business or property as a result of the violation, the victims might be precluded from continuing to seek treble damages as a matter of standing rules.[42] It could be argued that the victims no longer had standing to seek treble damages under the Clayton Act.[43] In this manner, the use of treble damages class actions could be cut off in cases of follow-on cartel litigation, while not affecting other types of civil litigation.[44] On the other hand, it might also be argued that such an approach contravenes the statutory scheme

---

38 *Id.*

39 *Id.*

40 *Id.*

41 *Id.* at 478.

42 *See* Brunswick Corp. v. Pueblo Bowl-O-Mat, 429 U.S. 447 (1977).

43 15 U.S.C. § 16; *see also* Nat'l Soc'y of Prof'l Eng'rs v. United States, 435 U.S. 679 (1978) ("The legislative history makes it perfectly clear that [Congress] expected the courts to give shape to the [Sherman Act's] broad mandate by drawing on common-law tradition.")

44 There has been widespread concern that the excesses of the civil class-action claims process may adversely affect overall antitrust enforcement. William E. Kovacic, Chairman, Fed. Trade Comm'n, Competition Policy in the European Union and the United States: Convergence or Divergence? Address at the Bates White Fifth Annual Antitrust Conference 14 (June 2, 2008), *available at* https://www.ftc.gov/sites/default/files/documents/public_statements/competition-policy-european-union-and-united-states-convergence-or-divergence/080602bateswhite.pdf.

enabling restitution as part of sentencing, which requires a restitution offset for compensatory damages for the same loss.[45] As a practical matter, given the long timescale of civil proceedings, this provision would likely create additional complications in the use of restitution in addition to civil proceedings.

V. The Proposal

This background suggests the need to consider potential means for more effective and efficient victim compensation through the sentencing process. It also indicates that there may well be obstacles and some reluctance to creative approaches to employing restitution in antitrust sentencing. Yet, when sentencing can offer significant advantages in terms of speed and the ability to create a cohesive and comprehensive formula for deterrence, and to foster overall consumer welfare, the avenues that could make that happen deserve exploration. Some of these approaches would require legislation, and a comprehensive use of restitution to supplant civil cases would benefit from a legislative mandate.[46] The following provides a rough outline of some potential ways forward:

- In private civil antitrust litigation, upon a motion of defendants demonstrating a current government investigation related to the civil claims, the defendants could receive an automatic stay of all proceedings.
- Then, if the government closes the investigation without convictions, the stay could be lifted but the court would make no inferences from the conduct of the investigation.
- In the event of any conviction related to the civil claims, the civil case(s) could be dismissed with prejudice when restitution had been ordered.
- As one method of determining restitution, as a condition of probation, the court may appoint a monitor to construct and supervise a plan to review whether victim compensation was appropriate and to effect any compensation found appropriate. In this instance:
  - the Antitrust Division could provide guidance to the monitor;
  - third parties could provide the monitor with guidance regarding claims;
  - the monitor could hire an expert and others to assist as needed;
  - the pleading party would compensate the monitor.

---

45 *See* 18 U.S.C. § 3664(j)(2) ("Any amount paid to a victim under an order of restitution shall be reduced by any amount later recovered as compensatory damages for the same loss by the victim in – (A) any Federal civil proceeding; and (B) and State civil proceeding, to the extent provided by the law of the State.")

46 As noted earlier, the current scheme of federal claims by direct purchasers and state claims by indirect purchasers alone raises issues that likely could be resolved only with legislation. *See supra* note 11 and accompanying text.

  - In some instances, the Antitrust Division could recommend restitution without need of a monitor:[47]
  - this would be particularly appropriate with government contracting or other times when the issues related to victim redress have already been explored as part of the substantive criminal investigation;
  - the Antitrust Division can require the defendant to respond to set questions as part of cooperation with a plea agreement and use that to determine restitution requirements;
  - the rules for restitution require notice to all identified victims before the restitution plan is presented to the court as part of the presentencing report, but the notice could be made not only to individually identified victims but also more broadly, in a manner similar to class-action notices.[48]
- In cases where the agreement was complete, thus establishing a violation, but the agreement had no effect on any victim, the Antitrust Division would recommend against imposition of restitution.
- In all instances, the Antitrust Division would set its fine level recommendation to provide adequate deterrence under guidance from the Sentencing Guidelines and in light of the restitution and other relevant factors. In some instances, this could involve some or all of the fine to be "suspended" in favor of the defendant's financial resources going to restitution payments, but in other instances, the fine level might be higher to take into account the restitution payments or to consider the substantial fine, which goes to overall criminal victim compensation, as the best *cy pres* approach to restitution.
- For those with leniency, the Antitrust Division already includes a requirement for the provision of restitution.[49] But instead of leaving restitution for effectuation through civil claims, the Division could evaluate the requirement and construct and execute a plan to meet it, or require the leniency applicant to agree to a monitor or agreed approach for restitution before bestowing leniency.[50]

---

47 For example, in seeking fines above the Sherman Act statutory maximum, the Antitrust Division may feel comfortable with its assessment of the "loss" from the conduct. *See* 18 U.S.C. § 3571(d).

48 *See* 18 U.S.C. § 3664(d)(2).

49 Dep't of Justice, Corporate Leniency Policy 2–3 (Aug. 10, 1993), *available at* https://www.justice.gov/atr/file/810281/download.

50 The current Antitrust Criminal Penalty Enhancement and Reform Act (ACPERA) statutory response to the Antitrust Division's leniency program, which expressly provides that a successful leniency applicant is subject only to single damages without joint and several liability for the conduct subject to the amnesty agreement, would not necessarily need to be changed. By definition, an amnesty applicant avoids sentencing and restitution. And while the Division expressly requires that restitution is required for

- In some instances, putting together the restitution proposal for the leniency candidate or for a defendant would be simple when the defendant or leniency candidate can affirm the existence of settlement agreements with the victims.
- In all instances of restitution, the court acts as the final arbiter. Thus, due-process rights are respected and all with an interest would have the ability to raise concerns if the procedure were not appropriate.

VI. Conclusion

Handling victim compensation for prosecuted criminal cartels as part of the criminal sentencing process could provide a great increase in social welfare over the current method of private follow-on treble damages class-action litigation. It would avoid many costs, streamline and shorten the time involved, eliminate tensions between public and private enforcement, and provide effective deterrence. In any event, as jurisdictions around the world contemplate systems for victim compensation, they would be well advised to scrutinize closely how well the US system should be measured in terms of overall social welfare, and to consider alternatives.

---

leniency and then largely left the implementation to the civil courts, it could more actively look at whether the applicant has made restitution. *See* ACPERA, Pub. L. No. 108-237 § 213, 118 Stat. 661, 666–668, 15 U.S.C.A. § 1 note (2004).

Foreword by Joshua Wright

An Antitrust Professor on the Bench
Liber Amicorum - Volume I

The first volume of Douglas H. Ginsburg Liber Amicorum gathers original essays that pay tribute to the exceptional career of Judge Ginsburg. Known in the legal community as a "giant in antitrust law," Judge Ginsburg has heard appeals in several of the US landmark antitrust cases of our times. This volume looks at Judge Ginsburg's career, offering a unique showcase of antitrust issues acutely analyzed by prominent lawyers, enforcers, academics and economists from the US, Europe and abroad.

Why is Judge Douglas Ginsburg the most respected and beloved member of the international antitrust community? What makes everyone, in every portion of the political spectrum, admire him so much? Why is he revered both for his intellectual brilliance and his personality? This volume was written as a modest tribute to modern competition law's wisest and kindest statesman. These essays, by people fortunate enough to have interacted with him in a wide variety of settings, provide insights into the reasons for the affection we all have for him. Mere words will never be able to fully convey these feelings or the reasons for his influence all over the world. But these essays at least make a valiant attempt to honor and pay respect to a giant. And these aren't just words of praise. They should inspire the rest of us to become a little bit more like him in so many ways.

Robert Lande, Professor of Law, University of Baltimore

DETAILS

Pages: 495
Price: 240€ - 285$ - 214£
ISBN: 978-1939007-62-9

Send your order to

Institut de droit de la concurrence
19 avenue Jean Aicard
75011 - Paris

Institute of Competition Law
61 - 63 Rochester Place
NW1 9JU - London

Institute of Competition Law
106 W 32nd St - Suite 144
10001 - New York

ORDER

Full Name:
e-mail:
Institution:
Street:
City:
Zip Code:
Country:

www.concurrences.com
orders@concurrences.com

Concurrences
Antitrust Publications & Events

Concurrences Review

Concurrences is a print and online quarterly peer reviewed journal dedicated to EU and national competitions laws. It has been launched in 2004 as the flagship of the Institute of Competition Law in order to provide a forum for academics, practitioners and enforcers. Concurrences'influence and expertise has garnered interviews with such figures as Christine Lagarde, Bill Kovacic, Emmanuel Macron and Margarethe Vestager.

Contents

More than 12,000 articles, print and/or online. Quarterly issues provide current coverage with contributions from the EU or national or foreign countries thanks to more than 1,500 authors in Europe and abroad. Approximately 35 % of the contributions are published in English, 65 % in French, as the official language of the General Court of justice of the EU; all contributions have English abstracts.

Format

In order to balance academic contributions with opinions or legal practice notes, Concurrences provides its insight and analysis in a number of formats:

- Forewords: Opinions by leading academics or enforcers
- Interviews: Interviews of antitrust experts
- On-Topics: 4 to 6 short papers on hot issues
- Law & Economics: Short papers written by economists for a legal audience
- Articles: Long academic papers
- Case Summaries: Case commentary on EU and French case law
- Legal Practice: Short papers for in-house counsels
- International: Medium size papers on international policies
- Books Review: Summaries of recent antitrust books
- Articles Review: Summaries of leading articles published in 45 antitrust journals

Boards

The Scientific Committee is headed by Laurence Idot, Professor at Panthéon Assas University. The International Committee is headed by Frederic Jenny, OECD Competition Comitteee Chairman. Boards members include Bruno Lasserre, Mario Monti, Howard Shelanski, Richard Whish, Wouter Wils, etc.

Online version

Concurrences website provides all articles published since its inception, in addition to selected articles published online only in the electronic supplement.

Write for Concurrences

Concurrences welcome spontaneous contributions. Except in rare circumstances, the journal accepts only unpublished articles, whatever the form and nature of the contribution. The Editorial Board checks the form of the proposals, and then submits these to the Scientific Committee. Selection of the papers is conditional to a peer review by at least two members of the Committee. Within a month, the Committee assesses whether the draft article can be published and notifies the author.

The Institute of Competition Law

The Institute of Competition Law is a publishing company, founded in 2004 by Dr. Nicolas Charbit, based in Paris, London and NewYork. The Institute cultivates scholarship and discussion about antitrust issues though publications and conferences. Each publication and event is supervised by editorial boards and scientific or steering committees to ensure independence, objectivity, and academic rigor. Thanks to this management, the Institute has become one of the few think tanks in Europe to have significant influence on antitrust policies.

Aim

The Institute focuses government, business and academic attention on a broad range of subjects which concern competition laws, regulations and related economics.

Boards

To maintain its unique focus, the Institute relies upon highly distinguished editors, all leading experts in national or international antitrust: Bill Kovacic, Mario Monti, Eleanor Fox, Laurence Idot, Fred Jenny, Ioannis Lianos, Richard Whish, etc.

Authors

3,800 authors, from 55 jurisdictions.

Partners

- Universities: University College London, King's College London, Queen Mary University, Paris Sorbonne Panthéon-Assas, etc.
- Law firms: Allen & Overy, Cleary Gottlieb Steen & Hamilton, Baker McKenzie, Hogan Lovells, Jones Day, Norton Rose Fulbright, Skadden Arps, White & Case, etc.

Events

Brussels, Hong Kong, London, New York, Paris, Singapore and Washington, DC.

Online version

Concurrences website provides all articles published since its inception.

Publications

The Institute publishes Concurrences Review, a print and online quarterly peer-reviewed journal dedicated to EU and national competitions laws. e-Competitions is a bi-monthly antitrust news bulletin covering 85 countries. The e-Competitions database contains over 15,000 case summaries from 3,000 authors.

www.ingramcontent.com/pod-product-compliance
Lightning Source LLC
LaVergne TN
LVHW020734300926
849161LV00017B/3077/J